JERUSALEM

JERUSALEM

CITY OF THE BOOK

Merav Mack and Benjamin Balint

With Photography by Frédéric Brenner

Yale
UNIVERSITY PRESS

New Haven & London

Color plates courtesy of Frédéric Brenner / Howard Greenberg Gallery.

Yale University Press books may be purchased in quantity for educational, business, or promotional use. For information, please e-mail sales.press@yale.edu (U.S. office) or sales@yaleup.co.uk (U.K. office).

Set in Baskerville type by IDS Infotech Ltd.
Printed in the United States of America.

Library of Congress Control Number: 2018959044
ISBN 978-0-300-22285-2 (hardcover : alk. paper)

A catalogue record for this book is available from the British Library.

This paper meets the requirements of ANSI/NISO Z39.48-1992 (Permanence of Paper).

10 9 8 7 6 5 4 3 2 1

CONTENTS

CONTENTS

Color plates follow page 88

JERUSALEM

PROLOGUE

I have always imagined that Paradise will be a kind of library.
—*Jorge Luis Borges*

The people of Jerusalem have since antiquity shared a passion for the written word. Yet to this day much of the city's written heritage conceals itself in libraries and archives to which only a few are granted access. What might it mean to see Jerusalem, with its daily encounters between people of diverse faiths and cultures, as a city of the book? Is it possible to use libraries and texts to capture the city's tragedy and its magnificence, to tell the story of a place where some of the world's most far-reaching ideas were put into words, translated into poetry and prophecy?

For all their impermanence and portability, books serve as transmitters of culture; they often outlive many owners. The medieval Hebrew poet Moshe Ibn Ezra called them "briefcases of wisdom." Jerusalem's diverse communities have been bound by a shared reverence for the written word, and each one put down an anchor in the soil of the earthly Jerusalem. Each of these "peoples of the book" curated its memory through the written word and used texts in the search for origins and authenticity. And they each, in their way, suffused Jerusalem with their collective dreams, deposited in libraries, thrown into boxes as scraps, hidden between the covers of worm-eaten tomes, brought back from exile, or secreted by librarians, forgers, and thieves. If we listen carefully the city's texts (and their custodians) can tune us in to Jerusalem's resonances—ancient and modern, lofty and lowly—and to the relationship between the actual city of Jerusalem and the fateful fantasies it continues to inspire.

This is the story we set out to tell in this book; it is not a systematic history of Jerusalem as such, much less a political history, but an essay into how Jerusalem has been imagined, made legible, and shelved in libraries. Rather than attempt to survey, catalogue, or discover unknown manuscripts in the dozens of archives and libraries we visited, we use the history of the collections themselves to excavate the richly layered history of the city and its cultural exchanges and to tell the untold history of how the peoples of the book have populated the city with books.

Like a city, a library is a form of sometimes uneasy cohabitation. We came to see a library, however ordered or disordered, from the humblest to the most venerable, not as simply a collection of books but as an invitation to imagine, a summons toward people, places, and possibilities that we can see only in the mind's eye. A place that both encompasses and mirrors us, a library allows us to bridge the distance between what we see and what we *want* to see.

As the product of collective imagination Jerusalem has inspired its own wishful literary mode. To make it legible we look both at its books as physical objects and at what is written in those books—as well as at the connections between the two. We consider the category of the library to encompass not just a collection of books but a corpus of shared texts. We wonder at how the imagined city has inspired texts—prayers, apocalyptic fantasies, guidebooks, architectural plans—that have flowed outward and then ebbed back to wash over the earthly city. The battles of those who have laid claim to Jerusalem since its inception can be seen through the battles over and within their books, and so can the many forms of reconciliation. We examine how the city rescued its wisdom despite the flames that consumed its libraries and memories in numerous wars fought over more than three millennia. Finally, we ask how Jerusalem can shed light on the transformations in the technology and meaning of the written word—as momentous as the move to print, and perhaps even more so. Above all, we inquire into not only what kinds of texts Jerusalem has produced but also what kinds of Jerusalem its texts have created.

In looking for material traces of the written word, we glimpse Jerusalem's profound antinomies, within a city perched between East and West, antiquity and modernity, violence and piety. Awash with memory, Jerusalem is a place both real and imagined. The earthly city, a mundane metropolis of decadence and decay, is tethered in the imagination to the symbols of timeless Jerusalem: a city of liturgy and song, an omphalos—a place touched by the divine where heaven and earth are said to meet that has "no need of the sun or of the moon to shine in it, for the glory of God illuminated it" (Revelation 21:23). How can viewing Jerusalem through its libraries, past and present, shed light on the gap between the abidingly real and the fancifully imagined, or on the ways that gap has been bridged?

Jerusalem has given birth to some of the world's greatest literature, yet the writers of Jerusalem, though renowned the world over, are not usually thought of as a distinct school; their story as Jerusalemites has never been woven into a single narrative. In some cases, their fame has grown so great that their connection to the city has receded into oblivion: David, Solomon, and Isaiah of the Bible; Josephus, Jerome, and Empress Eudocia of late antiquity; al-Ghazali and Ibn 'Arabi of the Sufi tradition; the historians al-Muqaddasi and Mujir al-Din. Their writings emanated from Jerusalem to the four corners of the known world.

The kings and queens of Jerusalem entered into our memory not only because of their valor in battle or the monuments they commissioned but also because of the texts they composed and inspired. Some of their words ignited wars; others prompted reflections on compassion and peace. In both cases, the celestial city has left indelible traces in the earthly—even provincial—city, all too often turning it into a screen onto which millennial fantasies were projected.

King Solomon, son of David, purportedly both set and set down his erotic poem the Song of Songs in Jerusalem, and beautiful copies of the Song can be found in many of Jerusalem's libraries, though none as richly decorated as the ones kept in the library next door to Saint Philippos Ethiopian church. The Song of Songs tells of a Lover and her elusive Beloved who seek each other: "I adjure you, O daughters of Jerusalem, if you find my beloved, what will you tell him? That I am love-sick" (5:8). Who are the lovers of Jerusalem, within the city and from afar, and in what ways do they seek to possess it? How jealous and possessive is their love, how ennobling or full of folly, and how far are they willing to go to consummate it? In this book we tell the stories of Jerusalem's poet-librarians and through them the story of Jerusalem afresh. The true lovers of Jerusalem, we came to see, are the custodians of its written words.

And not of written words alone. Our time in the city's archives encouraged us to take a broad understanding of archival material to include photographs, artefacts, and models. In part, then, the story of this metropolis of monotheisms takes visual form. Ancient manuscripts bear the traces of a tumultuous past—two-dimensional pages that under the press of our imagination open up into three. They are often torn, brittle, even blood-stained. Some have crossed continents or survived genocides. Their visual testimony tells a story far beyond the content of the texts themselves. It is no coincidence that among the first objects photographed by Henry Fox Talbot, one of the inventors of the medium, were library books. In that spirit, Frédéric Brenner's photographs are intended not as mere illustrations, however beautiful, but as statements in their own right that act as counterpoints to our text.

Brenner's photograph of the Armenian manuscript library, for example, captures its sacredness as well as its mysterious austerity (plate 1). The room emerges as a temple of reverence for the volumes it keeps locked away from human eyes. An image on a single open page suddenly breaks this spell (plate 2). An archway is painted in a ray of brilliant Armenian blue (*kapoyt*). A peacock stands guard over the page, and a tree of life penetrates through the torn folio. (Depictions of portals to heaven have featured on frontispieces since the early Middle Ages.)

Another example: Brenner's portrait of Jerusalem's Greek Orthodox Patriarch Theophilos with Archbishop Aristarchos, director of the Greek Orthodox manuscript library. Brenner affords us an intimate glimpse of the two men bending over a page, deciphering together thousand-year-old Greek letters (plate 3). They stand in a shrine-like manuscript library which is almost never used: it contains neither readers' desks nor room for additional manuscripts. In this image, too, a photograph of a single page has the momentary power of lifting a text out of obscurity.

In still another sense, this book is a kind of flânerie, a form of getting lost in the city in order better to know it. "Walk about Zion and go around her," says the Psalmist (48:13). The artist Paul Klee once said that he saw drawing as a way of taking a line for a walk. This book takes an idea about cultural memory for a stroll through a city of contention and consolation. As pedestrians we experienced Jerusalem not chronologically but with all the jumble of juxtapositions and incongruities a walker in the city would encounter. In fact, we take these very juxtapositions as the eloquent grammar of Jerusalem's many languages. Every city follows its own logic of walking, but Jerusalem invented the idea of walking as a pilgrimage along symbolic "stations." In this journey our stations were libraries and archives, some still vibrant and others seldom consulted.

While our story follows a chronological line, we do not pretend to historical comprehensiveness. Reading Jerusalem is like deciphering a palimpsest, a text in which one layer has been written over an older layer without erasing the text beneath. A palimpsest does not eradicate memory so much as it appropriates and recycles earlier memories. We attempt to read Jerusalem as a conversation among languages, in which writers reached for each other across the centuries.

More than any other place, Jerusalem has always existed by the power of words. As the poet Paul Celan writes, "Say that Jerusalem *is*." Perhaps Jerusalem can be read as a poem that has been written and rewritten, constructed and fractured through language. Jerusalem reveals itself through language, and has served as a homeland for both the death and the resurrection of languages.

INTRODUCTION
THE HIDDEN

Over the past several years, we have had occasion to chant with Sufis, sit at a Hasidic court alongside dozens of followers waiting to meet their master, and hold audiences with patriarchs and sheikhs. We have gained unprecedented access to the shrines, sacristies, and elusive archives where Jerusalem's literary heritage is kept under lock and key. We have come to admire the custodians' dedication to safeguarding Jerusalem's literary legacies. In the realization that our story is as much about them as it is about the treasures entrusted to them, we set out in search of Jerusalem's keys—to the libraries and to the hearts of their keepers.

Often these gatekeepers and guardians greeted us at first with suspicion. Time and again they turned us away. In order to see Jerusalem's greatest collection of Islamic manuscripts at the al-Aqsa Mosque, for instance, we had to obtain the permission of Sheikh 'Azzam al-Khatib. As director general of the Islamic Waqf (Department of Religious Endowments), the sheikh was in charge of Jerusalem's Islamic sites and treasures. Most of his time was spent dealing with protests against the Israeli police limiting access to prayer, but months of petition finally led to a meeting with him. Among other collections, we wished to visit a library known as al-Khataniyya. It is housed beneath the al-Aqsa Mosque, where Muslims identify the spot at which, long before the monumental Islamic shrines were built, Muhammad prayed humbly at the ancient passage that once led to the temple. This vast underground space is now considered too holy to allow access by non-Muslims. Sheikh ʿAzzam let us understand that even making a scholarly visit to libraries situated in arguably the most politically sensitive place on earth was a risky matter. Nor did the Israeli police officers who guarded the site welcome our visits. They forbade us to bring our laptops in with us, and perused our notebooks.

Each community erects its own scaffolding of hierarchies and protocols. To visit the Ethiopian Orthodox library, for instance, we discovered that even an audience with Jerusalem's archbishop and repeated meetings with his monks would not suffice. We had to travel to Addis Ababa to obtain the patriarch's written permission in person. Only after two years of persistent and patient negotiations, and numerous meetings with Greek scholars and clergy, were we granted access to the Greek Orthodox library. And the keeper of Jerusalem's most extensive Hasidic library told us that no one steps foot into it other than the rebbe himself. Since each of its manuscripts is digitized before being handed over to the rebbe there was no need to see the library itself, he insisted.

Often, Jerusalem librarians regard the visitor, as Umberto Eco put it, as "an enemy, a layabout (otherwise he'd be out working), and a potential thief." Some libraries, he added, aimed "*not* to encourage reading but to hide, to conceal books."[1] To peel back the layered modes and motives of the city's concealment, we began with a simple question: Why were some of the greatest libraries of Jerusalem so forbidding and unwelcoming by design? What manner of secrets did the librarian-gatekeepers attempt to conceal—from others and perhaps from themselves?

Today, swept up in the most far-reaching technological revolution since the invention of writing in the fourth millennium BCE, our tech gurus like to speak of "knowledge sharing" and universal access to information. In the age of Wikipedia, we create digital libraries written by everyone, containing everything and belonging to no one.

With our quest to render everything intelligible and our skepticism of the sacred, many inhabitants of modernity feel the temptation to unlock secrets, if not to explain them away. The Enlightenment, committed to openness, endeavored to render esotericism obsolete. Ever since, concealment has rubbed us the wrong way.

In this spirit, the modern library aims to be a democratic space, one of the few institutions, writes the photographer Diane Asséo Griliches, "where any soul may walk through its doors free, and depart enriched."[2] Such a library is staffed not by priestly gatekeepers guarding an intimidating temple from philistines but by welcoming facilitators of a collaborative cultural exchange.

Not so in Jerusalem. Like families, Jerusalem's libraries are riddled with secrets and concealments. Secrecy sometimes cloaks deception or conspiratorial silence. By taking up these secrets, we explore how the city's libraries teach something else: secrecy can take the form of intimacy. In this city, with its affinities for the esoteric, the library acts as an enclosed realm that often hides more than it reveals. For that reason it offers the ideal lens through which to see the city's forms of concealment.

Here can be found both mundane secrets and sacred secrets. Some of Jerusalem's finest libraries are closed for more arcane reasons than impoverishment, perhaps, but ones that are no less psychologically charged. Their shelves hold the kind of esoteric knowledge that has to be kept secret and transmitted by and to a close circle of initiates if it is to retain its power. Many gatekeepers of Jerusalem's libraries dedicate themselves to preserving mystery, not to dispelling it. To earn their trust is to recognize the difference between loving knowledge and giving unfettered and uncensored access to it.

In Jerusalem's libraries, we learned that knowledge is far from equally accessible to all its seekers. A different epistemology is at work. The transmission of knowledge is a form of intimacy. In Jerusalem and elsewhere, the highest knowledge could be transmitted orally and privately only from a teacher to a student who had earned the privilege of acquiring it. Both eros and knowledge were predicated on such intimacy.

Jerusalem's communities have more than one reason for hiding books, for making them inaccessible: not just fear of loss or theft but a reluctance to reveal too much.

Probing the winding alleyways of the Christian Quarter, we arrived one afternoon at the Church of Saint Mark, home to one of Jerusalem's smallest but oldest Christian communities and to the oldest surviving liturgy in Christendom. The Syriac Christians who live around the church—by tradition built over the home of Mary, mother of Mark the Evangelist—regard their presence in Jerusalem as unbroken. On the church's far wall hung an icon of the Virgin Mary said to have been painted by Saint Luke himself. Inside the door, a seven-line sixth-century inscription carved in stone in Syriac read, "This is the house of Mary, mother of John, called Mark. Proclaimed a church by the holy apostles under the name of the Virgin Mary, mother of God, after the ascension of our Lord Jesus Christ into heaven. Renewed after the destruction of Jerusalem by Titus in the year A.D. 73 [sic]."

Unlike the Armenians, the Syriacs do not have a quarter of their own in Jerusalem's Old City. In the Middle Ages they were centered around Saint Mary Magdalene Church in the vicinity of today's Flowers Gate (also called Herod's Gate) on the northern edge of the Old City. When the city surrendered to Saladin in 1187 and the church was converted to a mosque, the small community moved to the citadel area. The Syriac community purchased Saint Mark's from the Copts only in the 1470s.[3] Today the monastery is home to a handful of monks and a hostel for pilgrims. A few dozen families live nearby, and the club next to it serves the small Syriac scout group. Several hundred Syriac families live in Bethlehem. Despite their recent numerical decline, Syriacs in both Jerusalem and Bethlehem have preserved their Aramaic language with remarkable persistence— remarkable, too, in the face of more recent obstacles such as the Israeli security fence that separates Jerusalem from Bethlehem.

A less visible fence has rendered Saint Mark's precious library inaccessible for many decades, even to renowned researchers who wish to consult its substantial collection of manuscripts. A century ago, the German Orientalist Carl Anton Baumstark and the French scholar Frédéric Macler were allowed to see a small portion of the collection. Since then few outsiders have gained entry. "The access to St. Mark's manuscripts became more difficult, if not impossible," a Dominican scholar named Jacques Marie Vosté reported in 1937. In the early 1990s, the Syriac scholar Andrew Palmer complained that in three months of research he was allowed to examine only a handful of books, and the bishop selected which ones he would see.[4]

We approached the present keeper of the library, a hard-of-hearing monk named Abuna Shimon Can (the surname means "spirit" in Turkish), not with a request to catalogue or publish or purchase, but with an offer to put him in touch with experts in conserving and digitizing books. Abuna Shimon came to Jerusalem in 1980. His family—mother, four brothers, and a sister—now lived in the German town of Leimen, near Heidelberg. They spoke Syriac among themselves, he explained. He agreed to meet with us after a service one afternoon.

Before the service began, we were greeted by Justina, a familiar presence at the Syriac church. She was a volunteer from Nineveh, in the heart of Mesopotamia. Today most people know the city on the banks of the Tigris as Mosul, but for her it remained the city of the prophet Jonah. The Syriac liturgical calendar has a three-day fast, called Ba'uta d-Ninwe, "Nineveh's Wish," to commemorate Jonah's prayers for a city that now more than ever, she said, could use them. Justina was mourning the end of Christian presence in her homeland, thousand-year-old communities exiled by a wave of murders and threats in 2008 and by the Sunni extremists of ISIS in the summer of 2014. That July, ISIS militants had destroyed the mosque built over the tomb of Jonah, and in February they ransacked Mosul's central museum, destroying statues and artefacts, regarded as idolatrous, that dated from the Assyrian Empire.

At the start of the service the church, walled by unhewn stone, was nearly empty. Halogen bulbs in the chandeliers cast a stark light on the white embroidery of twelve crosses on Abuna Shimon's black hood as he prostrated himself three times, touching his forehead to the marble floor, and then swung an incense censer before Saint Luke's icon. In mid-chant, he penned in a sentence in the margins of the large book of liturgy on the lectern, a stencil copy of a beautifully scripted manuscript brought to Jerusalem from Turkey. Afterward, as he covered the open book with a dark velvet cloth, we were reminded that many of Jerusalem's books are not on display as relics but remain in daily use.

When the service concluded, Abuna Shimon led us upstairs through a grille gate and told us with evident pride that Syriac was his mother tongue. He was born in 1951 and grew up in Tur Abdin, "the mountain of the servants," in southeastern Anatolia, the historical center of Syriac monasticism and cultural life until the genocide of 1915. A century before

Abuna Shimon Can, Saint Mark's Convent, with a fifteenth-century manuscript in Syriac (SMMJ 290-Old). (Photo by Frédéric Brenner, 2016; courtesy of the photographer / Howard Greenberg Gallery.)

the present-day ethnic cleansing from which Justina had fled, three hundred thousand to five hundred thousand Syriac Christians were slaughtered. The Syriacs refer to this massacre as the Syriac genocide, or in Syriac as *Sayfo,* "The Sword." Many families in the community today descend from refugees of those Turkish massacres during World War I.

To come into possession of valuable treasure can be intimidating. In his short story "The Book of Sand," Jorge Luis Borges describes a book lover who comes to own the most valuable book in the world, an eternal book with no beginning or end, like sand. The euphoria of owning it and leafing through its ever-changing pages is soon replaced by fear of responsibility. "Against the joy of possessing the book grew the fear that it would be stolen, and later the suspicion that it was not truly infinite. . . . Prisoner of the Book, I almost never left the house."[5]

The Syriac library points toward a surprising reason for the secrecy that enshrouds some of Jerusalem's libraries: shame. The Syriac collection, we could not help but notice, was in a poor state: it suffered from bookworms, mold, disintegration of pages. Brittle paper crumbled between our fingers. Several manuscripts showed signs of being hastily bound and lined with older volumes that had fallen apart. (These linings sometimes yielded up hitherto lost manuscripts.)

Abuna Shimon was embarrassed by the condition of the collection. Although he did not treat the library as a holy shrine, he did venerate some of the books in his care, especially those by the Desert Fathers—so much so that he would kneel in reverence as he read them. Yet maintaining that collection of fewer than four hundred manuscripts required resources and expertise that the impoverished monks did not have. On a subsequent visit, he apologized for not being able to show us the library. A pilgrim was lodging there. "I told the bishop, the library is not a hotel. But no one respects the library."

His efforts to save the library persisted throughout the years we knew him. He once showed us a handwritten catalogue of 289 volumes compiled in 1926–1930 by Johanan Dolabani. The most beautiful of these were already missing when the Library of Congress selected 31 for its microfilm project in 1987–1988. The community itself sent them for safeguarding to Damascus in 1948 and never managed to get them back. Finally, beginning in 2011 the entire collection was digitized by the

Minnesota-based Benedictine Hill Museum and Manuscript Library. Abuna Shimon is pleased that his community's treasures were made available for scholars, but he is still concerned about the decaying volumes that require the professional care of a conservator.

It is often the value of Jerusalem's manuscripts that endangers them and makes guardianship so burdensome. The threat comes not only in the form of theft but also in the guise of offers one cannot refuse from wealthy collectors, museums, or states. If a literary treasure becomes too well known, its keepers face the risk of losing it not only to thieves and buyers who cannot resist the thrill of acquisition but also to authorities who may wish to confiscate what they perceive as national heritage "for its own protection."

The first manuscript in Dolbani's catalogue is a Syro-Hexapla with parts of the book of Isaiah, possibly from the eighth century.[6] It lists other considerable treasure, including a seventh- or eighth-century manuscript containing the *Book of Steps* (an anonymous Syriac treatise of spiritual instruction known in Latin as *Liber Graduum*, SMMJ 180), a fifteenth-century copy of Antony of Tagrit's *Rhetoric* (SMMJ 230), and perhaps the only copy in the world in Garsuni script of Daud al-Antaki's sixteenth-century medical work *The Reminder for Those with Understanding, and the Collector of Prodigious Wonders* (SMMJ 235). This last manuscript is dated 1757. In the margin of the penultimate page someone has penned a note in Arabic script: "Property of the monastery of the Syrians in honorable Jerusalem. Anyone who steals or removes [it] from its place of donation will be cursed from the mouth of God! God (may He be exalted) will be angry with him! Amen."[7]

Another wonderful colophon can be seen at the end of a manuscript of the library's copy of the early-sixth-century theologian Jacob of Serug's poetic homily *Memra on Love*: "Pray for the sinner who has written [it], a fool, lazy, slothful, deceitful, a liar, wretched, stupid, blind of understanding, with no knowledge of these things, [or] more than these things, but pray for me for our Lord's sake!"[8]

Saint Mark's bears another kind of shame, too: the undervaluing or loss of a precious heritage. The Syriacs of Jerusalem must have experienced that shame when their former archbishop Mar Athanasius Samuel sold off the Dead Sea Scrolls in 1954 for $250,000. The most momentous historical discovery of the twentieth century, including a scroll in Aramaic, had slipped through their fingers, leaving them without enough money to care for their small community and its remaining library.

On our last visit, Abuna Shimon held up a worm-eaten manuscript dated 1474. It was written by a Jewish-born thirteenth-century bishop of Aleppo ("Halab" in Arabic), Gregorius Abu al-Faraj Bar Hebraeus, a convert renowned for his erudition, his poetry, and his grasp of matters both human and divine. Abuna Shimon deciphered the title for us: *Ktaba d-awsar raze*, "Storehouse of Mysteries" (SMMJ 41). The margins brimmed with notes in the hand of Mar Samuel. The library also holds a manuscript of Bar Hebraeus's work *Ethicon* (SMMJ 188). Copied in two sturdy columns of handsome Serto script in 1724, the volume concludes with the following colophon: "The precious book is titled *Ethicon*, that is, book of good morals; it gathers together the corporeal and spiritual antidotes in regard to virtues and kinds of actions, following the opinion of the Fathers who were guides composed by . . . Mar Gregorius, Mafrian of the East, the mother of luminaries, who is Abu al-Faraj, son of Aaron the Physician, who is known as the Hebrew." The ways in which Abuna Shimon initiated us into the mysteries of Saint Mark's set the tone for our subsequent forays into Jerusalem's libraries—both those that yielded up their secrets and those that remained gated.

CHAPTER ONE

CREATING A CANON

Antiquity

We have come back from Jerusalem where we found not
what we sought.
—*Richard Siken, "Litany in Which Certain Things Are Crossed Out"*

In October 2016, Israeli Prime Minister Benjamin Netanyahu announced an astonishing discovery: a fragment of papyrus from the
seventh century BCE which features the name "Jerusalem" in ancient
Hebrew script. Responding to a UNESCO resolution that had recently
referred to Jerusalem as an occupied city, Netanyahu pointed to the fragment as proof of the antiquity of Hebrew in Jerusalem and the historical
connection between the city and the Jewish people.

The papyrus is kept in a climate-controlled lab in the basement of the
Israel Museum, and we went there to examine it. Pnina Shor, the conser-
vationist who headed the Dead Sea Scrolls Project at the Israel
Antiquities Authority, and the antiquities dealer Lenny Wolfe led us
through labyrinthine hallways to where Shor's team—Yana Frumkin,
Asia Vexler, Tanya Bitler, Tanya Treiger, Lena Libman, and Beatriz
Riestra—were gathered around a broad table. They, too, seemed aware

of the special significance of this fragment, a receipt for the delivery of two wineskins from the Jordan valley to the king of "Jerusalem."

Paleographical evidence suggests that the fragment is from the seventh century BCE. A carbon-14 analysis of the papyrus led to the same conclusion, but the team could not authenticate the ink. "You can't test the ink without destroying part of the text," Shor explained. Yet because of the text's exceptional political significance, her lab might decide to carry out this test too.

Lenny Wolfe told us that when he was offered the fragment by a dealer from Bethlehem (who had since died), he called Amir Ganor, head of the Robbery Prevention Unit of the Israel Antiquities Authority. "If I don't buy it," Wolfe warned, "this priceless piece will no doubt be smuggled out of the country." Ganor consulted his superiors and called Wolfe back minutes later to give the green light. According to Wolfe, the National Library of Israel was not interested in buying the fragment. As of this writing, he has yet to find a purchaser.

Rulers both ancient and modern make political use of texts and archives. Some of the decisive moments in the history of Jerusalem, in fact, turned on real or alleged discoveries of scrolls and archives.

In the second book of Kings, God sends the prophet Isaiah to instruct the frail King Hezekiah: "Set your house in order, for you shall die." The eighth-century BCE king, who had saved Jerusalem from destruction at the hands of the Assyrians, obediently set up a treasury (*beit nekhot* in Hebrew, from *bit nakamti* in Assyrian) for the kingdom's gold, silver, spices—and scrolls. Nearly a century later, a high priest of Jerusalem named Hilkiah discovered an ancient scroll referred to as the Book of the Covenant—possibly an early version of Deuteronomy—in the Temple treasury (2 Kings 20). He brought it to a royal scribe named Shaphan, who in turn read it to King Josiah. Upon hearing the scroll read, Josiah tore his clothes in mourning, sent emissaries to consult the prophetess Huldah about its meaning, and finally launched a large-scale reform of Jewish practices, establishing the "religion of the book."[1]

In excavations of the city of David, beneath the slopes of today's Silwan neighborhood, Israeli archaeologists discovered inscriptions bearing the names of the sons of these protagonists: "Hanan son of Hilkiah the priest"; "belonging to Gemaryahu ben Shaphan." Their names were

Lenny Wolfe, Jerusalem's leading antiquities dealer. (Photo by Frédéric Brenner, 2015; courtesy of the photographer / Howard Greenberg Gallery.)

inscribed on bullae, clay impressions used to seal documents. These bullae would probably not have survived were it not for the great fire that ravaged Jerusalem during the Babylonian conquest. The clay, baked in the intense heat, endured among the ruins of the city until it was discovered in our own day.

What is the relation between libraries and archives and political power? In the ancient world, collections of written records chiefly served kings and rulers rather than scholars. The Greek word *arkhion* gives us *archive*, a word related to *archon* (ruler) but also to *arkhaios* (ancient) and *arkhe* (beginning). Yet the close association of archives with political rule extends even farther back than the Greeks. In the 1970s, Italian archaeologists excavating the ancient city of Ebla (south of present-day Aleppo, Syria) unearthed an archive containing parts of some twenty thousand tablets inscribed in Sumerian and Eblaite. These included administrative, legal, and commercial texts; correspondence about contracts, wages, and taxes; bills and receipts; dictionaries and grammars; lists of kings; and royal edicts. Some made reference to biblical figures such as Ab-ra-mu (Abraham) and Da-u-dum (David). Although the wooden shelves had burned down when Ebla was sacked by invaders around 2300 BCE, the tablets, or fragments of them, survived. The discovery, noted the historian of libraries Hans Wellisch, was "a sensational event second in importance, perhaps, only to the discovery of the Dead Sea Scrolls."[2]

Nor was this an isolated case. In 1985–1986, Iraqi archaeologists discovered the approximately eight hundred tablets of the Sippar library, the oldest library found intact on its original shelves. The royal library of the seventh-century BCE king Ashurbanipal at Nineveh, discovered in the 1850s on the outskirts of the present-day city of Mosul, preserved some thirty thousand cuneiform tablets, including the Epic of Gilgamesh. Far from Nineveh, in a region subject to Babylon, archaeologists found two copies of a letter sent by Ashurbanipal to his agent Šadûnu instructing him to gather scholars and collect from their homes books and tablets for his newly built imperial library: "Search out for me . . . tablets concerning the amulets of the king [followed by a long list of other compositions] and any texts that might be needed in the palace [lit., "good for my kingship"], as many as there are, and also rare tablets that are known to you but do not exist in Assyria, and send them to me."[3] Given how significant a role writing on stone, clay, parchment, and papyrus played in the ancient Near East (the Swedish Assyriologist Olof Pedersén counts 253 archives and libraries in 51 cities),[4] the hope of unearthing texts from Jerusalem of the first millennium BCE seemed not entirely far-fetched.

Singing the Psalms

The Psalms teach us the way back to Paradise.
—*Thomas Merton*

On our visits to Jerusalem's libraries we could hardly have failed to en-counter editions of the book of Psalms, illuminated or unadorned, in all the city's languages. At the Ethiopian Tewahedo Church at the archbish-op's residence in the Old City, for example, we came across an illuminated Psalms in the ancient Ethiopian Semitic language Ge'ez housed in a leather box (*Mazmura Dawit,* JE133E). Not far away, the Saint Mark's mon-astery library treasured a manuscript of the Psalms in Syriac, with com-mentaries in red and black ink (MS 290). Among the rich collection of Greek psalters in the Greek Orthodox manuscript library we found two of the most gloriously decorated manuscripts in Jerusalem: Taphos 55 from the twelfth century (a 266-folio manuscript) and Taphos 51 from the thir-teenth (a 356-folio manuscript featuring a full-page miniature of David kneeling in penitence before the prophet Nathan; plate 4).[5]

The earliest mention of a library in Jerusalem comes in the second book of Maccabees, a volume written in Greek by diasporic Jews in the second century BCE.[6] The book recounts the history of Jerusalem during a short period of about twenty years (175–161 BCE). But in the back-ground it also tells the story of the return of the Jews to Jerusalem and Judea from the Babylonian exile at the time of the prophets Ezra and Nehemiah (first half of the fifth century BCE). It records that Nehemiah established a library (*bibliotheke* in the original Greek) and collected the writings of David, letters of the kings concerning offerings, and books about the kings and prophets. According to the book of Maccabees the legendary Jewish general and king Judas Maccabeus had followed the ex-ample of Nehemiah (who went in the footsteps of none other than King Solomon) and established a library in Jerusalem. He "collected books that had been scattered because of the war, and we still have them." In a letter to the Jews of Egypt the anonymous Jerusalemites wrote, "If you ever need any of these books, let us know, and we will send them" (2 Maccabees 2:13–15).

In their material forms, libraries and books—available today in hitherto unimaginable formats—have seen dramatic changes since Nehemiah's library. Yet in Jerusalem the pulse of ancient texts still palpably beats today. There is no better example than the masterpiece of "the writings of David," the book of Psalms: one of the city's defining and most widely shared texts, the anthology of poems that the literary critic James Wood calls "the great oasis in which a desert people gathers to pour out its complaints, fears, hopes."[7]

Jerusalem's royal libraries of antiquity held Psalms at the core of their collections. In medieval times, some of the most magnificent illuminated manuscripts in and from Jerusalem were psalters commissioned by royalty. Psalters also offered children an introduction to the Bible and a means of learning the alphabet. "There was hardly a text more widely used and better known to medieval audiences, be they religious or lay, learned or barely literate," writes Stella Panayotova of the Fitzwilliam Museum, Cambridge.[8]

Even today, the book of Psalms ascribed to David, one of Jerusalem's oldest poetical texts, is also the most pervasively read. Jerusalemite Jews mutter the Psalms under their breath on buses and recite them at funerals. Ethiopian Christians carry handwritten psalters wrapped in leather boxes, and recite from them daily. We have seen the Psalms—presumably written in Jerusalem—raised from illegibility in the infrared spectrums of the Dead Sea Scrolls imaging lab. We have heard them sung in Arabic, Syriac, Armenian, Greek, Ge'ez, and even Gregorian chant. Father Pakrad Berjikian, who came to Jerusalem from his native Lebanon at age eleven, recited psalm 121 to us by heart in a beautiful lilting Armenian: "I will lift up mine eyes unto the hills, from whence cometh my help." "Sixty percent of our liturgy is taken from the Psalms," he noted.

If every translation is an interpretation, it is no surprise that modern translators of the Psalms into Arabic have permitted themselves certain liberties. In the 1970s, the Lutheran Church in Jerusalem published a revised Arabic prayer book in which politically charged terms were rendered neutral. In the section devoted to the Psalms, the name "Israel" was replaced with "God's people" (*Sha'ab Allah*), and "Zion" with "sacred hill." Martin Luther in his *Open Letter on Translating* (1530) explained that in order for a translation to be "clear and vigorous" it needed to convey "the sense of the text." To avoid mistakes, Luther added, the translator "must let the literal words go."[9] The modern translators of Psalms to Arabic let the literal words go, but some of the older members of the congregation felt that the new translation represented a censor's meddling with the sacred text.

David, often called the founder of Jerusalem, is also indentified as the poet of the Psalms, the "sweet singer of Israel" who achieves some of the Bible's highest poetry. He is the irresistible lover whose very name means "beloved." He is also the inventor of the idea of the Temple—the man who danced the Holy Ark to Jerusalem.

It comes as no surprise, then, that many of his psalms sing the praises of Jerusalem. In psalm 46, for example, Zion (as Jerusalem is called) is both the navel of the world and the fount of blessing, the mountain-city from which the waters flow out to water the earth (see also Genesis 2:10–14 and Ezekiel 28). In psalm 65, the city is the source of the world's fertility. Psalm 48 depicts Zion as the meeting place of heaven and earth, as "the joy of all the earth"; psalm 50 as the place where God reveals himself (Jerusalem as the new Sinai). Zion is the center of pilgrimage (psalms 84, 122), the center of peace (psalms 87, 122), a place toward which exiles direct their memories ("By the rivers of Babylon, there we sat down, yea, we wept, when we remembered Zion," in the 1611 King James translation of psalm 137), and, significantly, the place God chose to anoint kings (psalm 2).

The Christian readings of David's Psalms begin with Jesus on the cross quoting the opening verse of psalm 22: "My God, my God, why have You forsaken me?" Jerusalem—as a symbol of the living church in its pilgrimage of "return" toward God—permeates both Jerome's homilies on Psalms and Augustine's commentary on the Psalms in the late fourth and early fifth centuries. Fourth-century scholars like Jerome and his student and colleague Paula (a Roman aristocrat who gave up her wealth to live as an ascetic in Bethlehem) studied Hebrew to be able to read the Bible in the original. In a letter to Paula's daughter, Jerome remarked that Paula sang Psalms in Hebrew without a foreign accent (that is, a trace of the Latin pronunciation).[10] Another fourth-century author, Saint Hilary, compared the book of Psalms to a jumble of keys that could open every door in a great city; but it is left to us, he said, to discover which key opens which lock.

The seven penitential psalms made an especially deep impression on early Christian readers. Psalm 51 (50 in the Greek Septuagint)—known as *Kyrie eleison* in Greek, *Miserere mei* in Latin, or "God Have Merry"— established the mythical image of David not just as a warrior-poet or the shepherd-king but as the prodigal penitent begging for forgiveness. Augustine's hagiographer recounted that on his deathbed Augustine asked that "the Davidic Psalms, the few that were written about penitence," be transcribed and placed on the wall opposite him so that he could gaze upon them and weep "copiously and continually."[11]

Variations on Psalms and previously unknown copies discovered in Qumran aroused interest even in ancient times. In the third century, Origen used one such manuscript and compared it to known versions. In the early ninth century, Timothy I, patriarch of the Eastern Syrian Church (the Nestorian Church of the East), noted that Jews in Jerusalem had recently discovered books in a cave near Jericho including "a David"—a psalter—"containing more than two hundred psalms."[12] In Jerusalem's libraries we found editions with 151 psalms.

Even in antiquity, students and translators of the Psalms (including Jerome, Eusebius, and Origen) noticed the different styles and authorial hands. "They err who deem all the psalms are David's and not the work of those whose names are superscribed," wrote Jerome.[13]

If, as we suggest in this book, it is nearly impossible to understand or experience Jerusalem without recourse to textual tradition, we can do no better than to begin with the Psalms of David, the biblical book largely written in Jerusalem and more intimately connected to the city than any other. Jerusalem libraries of antiquity had copies of Psalms in numerous languages, and psalters continue to be used and treasured in the city today.

Secrets of the Scrolls

The concealed libraries of the desert surrounding Jerusalem fared better than their counterparts in Jerusalem proper; their rediscovery would touch the very sources of Judaism and Christianity. For thousands of years, scrolls preserved in the desert have kept the literary heritage of the city: its prophecies, histories, and eschatologies.

Is it possible that the desert was purposefully used to store and safeguard the library of Jerusalem's Temple? If so, this hypothesis would make the collection of scrolls the earliest remains of a Jerusalemite library.

Even in antiquity, stories of scrolls in the caves and crevices of the desert east of Jerusalem were elaborated from one generation to the next. Shortly before the Babylonians descended on Jerusalem in the sixth century BCE, God instructed the prophet Jeremiah, author of Lamentations, to write two scrolls and store them inside clay jars "that they may last a long time" (Jeremiah 32:14). In the third century CE, Origen claimed that he consulted a scroll "found in a jar in Jericho in the time of Antoninus, the son of Severus." In the ninth century, a dog led his master to a cache of scrolls: "They say that the dog of an Arab who was hunting game went into a cleft after an animal and did not come out; his owner then went in after him and found a chamber inside the mountain containing many books. The huntsman went to Jerusalem and reported this to some Jews. A lot of people set off and arrived there; they found books of the Old Testament, and, apart from that, other books in Hebrew script."[14]

In the middle of the twentieth century, a shepherd from the Bedouin Ta'amara tribe nicknamed al-Dib (the Wolf) chased an errant goat into the desert cliffs of Qumran, overlooking the Dead Sea east of Jerusalem. There he chanced across the hidden entrance to a cave, in which he found the first scrolls of the "Qumran library"—seven ancient manuscripts, six in Hebrew and one in Aramaic. Scholars who examined this first group of Qumran scrolls immediately noticed its homogeneity. It did not include mundane or administrative documents of the type later found in other caves, or any of the great books of antiquity in Greek, Akkadian, or Persian. There were neither fragments of Homer, Plato, Aristotle, and Gilgamesh nor traces of Jewish writers of the diaspora such as Philo.

Could this have been the very library of the Temple in Jerusalem, preserved by the desert from destruction? Some scholars, including Rachel Elior and Norman Golb, argue that the Qumran texts could not have been anything but a library that came from Jerusalem during the Roman siege in 70 CE. Even those who dispute this theory acknowledge that the Qumran collection can shed light on what the Temple's library must have been like.[15]

Few doubt the existence of a such a library. Sidnie White Crawford, an internationally recognized expert on the Dead Sea Scrolls and chair of the board of trustees of the W. F. Albright Institute in Jerusalem, has collected many references to a Temple library by writers of antiquity. The best known among them is the first-century CE Jerusalemite soldier-statesman and historian Flavius Josephus (born Joseph ben Mattathias). Josephus remarked that sacred books had been deposited at the Temple since antiquity. In his work *Against Apion,* he boasts of the superiority of the Jews' record keeping to that of the Babylonians, Egyptians, Phoenicians, and Chaldeans (Assyrians): "Our ancestors took greater care over the records than did those just mentioned, assigning this task to the chief-priests and prophets, and this has been maintained with great precision down to our own time."[16]

As a young man, Josephus lived for three years as an ascetic in the Judean desert. In 66, at age twenty-nine, he was commissioned governor-general of Galilee. In that role, he overcame numerous plots and calumnies as he tried in vain to persuade the Jewish rebels against Rome, bent on war and inflamed by volatile messianic fantasies, to lay down their arms. He endeavored, as he put it, "to restrain the insurgents (agents of sedition)" in order to save his country from political suicide.[17] After a forty-seven-day siege by Roman forces of the Jewish town of Jotapata, Josephus was captured. He saved his skin by switching sides and predicting that Vespasian, the Roman commander, would soon become emperor. Like his biblical namesake, Josephus ventured an oracular prediction, and when it came to pass he was rescued by the ruler whose future he forecast.

Several years later, in 70, Josephus accompanied Titus—Vespasian's son and his successor as Rome's commander in Judea—to the fateful siege of Jerusalem. He faced a difficult position: "I was often in danger of death," he wrote, "both from the Judeans, who were keen to have me at their mercy for the sake of revenge, and from the Romans, who imagined that whenever they suffered defeat, this resulted from my betrayal." Josephus had to hide his anguish as he witnessed thousands of Jews massacred, Jerusalem sacked, the Temple destroyed.[18]

Outside the Temple, libraries could also be found in private hands. Josephus's own library is one example. We know that he had access to volumes of history (like those of Polybius), philosophy (Plato), and literature (Homeric texts). But Titus permitted him to salvage from the ruins of the Temple whatever he wanted: "Having nothing of greater value in the fall of my native place that I might take and cherish as a consolation for my circumstances, I put the request to Titus for the freedom of persons, and for some sacred volumes."[19]

Returning to Rome with Titus and the loot from Jerusalem, Josephus was rewarded with Roman citizenship, the imperial family name (he was now Titus Flavius Josephus), and comfortable lodging in a former palace of Vespasian's. He spent the last three decades of his life surrounded by reminders of Jewish humiliation and sovereignty lost, currying favor with the men who had laid waste to his native land. He also spent those years setting down the four remarkable works that have come down to us: *The Jewish Antiquities,* in which he shows himself an adept exegete of the Bible; *The Jewish War,* in which he chronicled the death throes of his country; *Vita,* the oldest autobiography that survives from antiquity; and *Against Apion,* a stirring polemic against anti-Jewish prejudices that joins a learned knowledge of Greek philosophy with a valiant defense of his people and his faith.

Josephus does not tell us which volumes he salvaged from the Temple. But the core of its collection probably resembled the works that were found at Qumran: the five books of the Torah, Psalms, and writings of the prophets, mainly Isaiah.[20]

One afternoon, Pnina Shor unveiled for us a thin glass case. Inside was a fragment of Deuteronomy from the first century BCE found in August 1952 in Qumran cave 4 (shelf number 4Q41981 and known also by the name All Souls Deuteronomy). The fragment was small—2¾ inches (7 centimeters) high and 17¾ inches (45 centimeters) long—but beautifully preserved. Joining forces with Roland de Vaux of the École Biblique in Jerusalem, Frank Moore Cross of Harvard University, the author of *The Ancient Library of Qumran,* had purchased it in 1958 with funds supplied by the Unitarian All Souls Church in New York City. As we bent down to read it, the clearly legible words took our breath away. It included the Ten Commandments, in a version that differed from the canonical version with which we were familiar. (It harmonized the two different versions of the Fourth Commandment, the Sabbath law, from Exodus and Deuteronomy, for example.)

Next door, the photographer of the scrolls welcomed us into the windowless darkness of Leon Levy Dead Sea Scrolls Digital Library lab. Along with Yair Medina, Shai Halevi was responsible for conducting the imaging process. In partnership with the Google Research and Development Center in Israel, the Israel Antiquities Authority is documenting the entire Dead Sea Scrolls collection online. Halevi turned on the custom-made MegaVision camera developed by Greg Bearman, who was formerly a principal scientist at the Jet Propulsion Laboratory at the California Institute of Technology. It is one of the most sophisticated imaging technologies in the world. Multispectral LED lights, developed at Johns Hopkins University, flash successively in twelve wavelengths, seven visible and five near-infrared, producing twenty-eight exposures of each side of each fragment. In this manner, Halevi can produce one terabyte of data a week. His camera has revealed previously illegible letters and words that had faded, enabling new interpretations of biblical texts. In this small room, modern technology met ancient theology.

The new imaging technology has brought new layers of text to light. In September 2016, researchers in Kentucky and Jerusalem announced that using "virtual unwrapping," a 3-D digital analysis of an X-ray scan, they had managed to decipher a charred two-thousand-year-old scroll that was too brittle to open. It turned out to contain the world's earliest instance of the Masoretic text of the first two chapters of the book of Leviticus. "You can't imagine the joy in the lab," Pnina Shor told us. The technology, funded by Google and the U.S. National Science Foundation, promises to illuminate more layers of the Dead Sea Scrolls.

Consider the papyrus palimpsest known as Midrash Moshe (4Q249is). The upper text, interpretations of the laws of leprosy in Leviticus 14, is written in a code so simple as to be baffling. What is the point in encoding a message badly? The scholars Jonathan Ben Dov and Daniel Stökl Ben Ezra have suggested that encryption, however obvious, lent texts some sort of prestige. Now that imaging techniques allow us to read both layers of text and to determine their age, perhaps Midrash Moshe too will yield up more of its mysteries.

When the scrolls were first carried to Jerusalem in 1947, dirty and darkened and unprovenanced, it was hard to imagine that they could be authentic. The first person to address the question of their authenticity was not a scholar but a priest—Metropolitan Athanasius Yeshue Samuel, archbishop of one of Jerusalem's smallest Christian communities, the Syriac Orthodox. His friends and advisers doubted that these mysterious scrolls were worth the parchment they were written on, but Mar Samuel saw in the seemingly worthless scraps of leather the oldest, most valuable manuscripts in the world. Yet Mar Samuel was also the man who sold them—a decision he would spend the rest of his life trying to justify. As he records in his memoirs, some in his community condemned him as a "smuggler," "traitor," and "conspirator."[21]

The literary critic Edmund Wilson, in his *Scrolls from the Dead Sea*, described Mar Samuel as a "handsome man who would recall an Assyrian bas-relief if his expression were not gentle instead of fierce." Mar Samuel recounts that as a child he was known as Yeshue ("Jesus" in Aramaic). At age seven, during World War I, he and his family fled for their lives from Hilwe, a village not far from the Syrian-Turkish border in Upper Mesopotamia that had been the center of the Syriac people. The murder of an "infidel Christian," Mar Samuel recalled of those days, "was of no greater consequence than the crushing of a flea caught in the folds of a turban." The family escaped and arrived by foot at the Syriac Orthodox Monastery of Saint Malky, a veritable fortress with high, three-foot-thick walls. The monks granted sanctuary to them and many other refugees.[22]

Fearing the destruction of a priceless record of Syriac Christian culture, the monks decided to bury their precious books. One of the monks asked for young Yeshua's help: "Rise up, good boy. It is time that you tasted adventure." In the bitter cold they waited till darkness fell, unbarred the wooden gates, and sneaked out. From inside his ankle-length robe the monk produced a precious manuscript, "the colors of its elaborate lettering faded like old pressed flowers. Then another, and another, until a considerable bundle lay before us on the ground." They used sharpened sticks and stones to dig a hole in the nearly frozen ground, then dropped the books into the hole, sealed it with pitch, and covered it with stones. "Now *let* them raze the monastery. Those who follow after us will have our records and our books of liturgy to guide them. The work of God will prevail."[23]

Days later, the Kurds murdered all the monks. Yeshue escaped before the final assault and fled to Aleppo. From Aleppo he was sent on to

Damascus for his education, and then to Jerusalem. There, at Saint Mark's, he remained and became the leader of the monastery. What remained vivid throughout his life was his boyhood experience of burying old books in the earth in order to preserve the memory of an ancient community.

When Syriac antiquity dealers of his own flock approached Mar Samuel in Jerusalem with a story of a Bedouin discovery of old writings wrapped like mummies in the desert, his curiosity arose: What if millennia-old scrolls still lay buried in the wilderness of Judea? A learned man, Mar Samuel spent his days in the monastery library, where he was able to study the ancient manuscripts, revising the inventory and adding notes in the margins of thousand-year-old volumes written on vellum. He became fascinated by the idea of exploring the desert for buried literary treasures and on several occasions had the opportunity to join scholars searching for ancient Syriac manuscripts in Sinai and Egypt.

During the Holy Week of 1947, he heard of a dealer from Bethlehem, Khalil Iskandar Shahin, nicknamed Kando, from a Syriac Orthodox family that had migrated from southern Turkey to Palestine, who supplied Bedouins with provisions in return for antiquities and other unearthed treasures. Mar Samuel met with Kando, and during the meeting Kando produced an object the size of a wine bottle. Mar Samuel picked up the ancient vellum, dark with age, gingerly unrolled it, and recognized the writing as Hebrew. He later described the scroll as "the most beautiful thing in the world." He bought four scrolls from Kando for 60 dinars, the equivalent of $250, all the money he privately owned. In return, he received the Isaiah Scroll, the Community Rule, a commentary on the book of Habakkuk, and what came to be known as the Genesis Apocryphon. The first three were in Hebrew, which he could not read, and the fourth was in Aramaic, "the very language of Christ himself!" (The Genesis Apocryphon proved to be so badly damaged that it would take years before scholars could fully decipher it.) Kando concluded the deal with the words "much dirty paper for little clean paper!"[24]

The sixty-dinar investment made the Syriac archbishop the owner of the most valuable texts in the world. For the next several months Mar Samuel tried to convince various scholars and archaeologists working in Jerusalem of the scrolls' antiquity; without exception he was met with skepticism. They well remembered the forgeries, including scrolls, that had flooded European museums in the previous century. These, too, were alleged to have been discovered by Bedouins in the hills of Moab across the Jordan River. The consensus was that the scrolls had neither scientific nor market value. Scholars gave Mar Samuel a wide range of dates for the scrolls: from late medieval to the eighteenth century. One theory was that they had been looted from a synagogue during the 1929 Palestine riots, buried in camel dung for a few years to give them the appearance of antiquity, and then peddled to the gullible Mar Samuel. No one thought parchment could survive for two thousand years.

William F. Albright of Johns Hopkins, one of the most acclaimed archaeologists of the time and the man who would later date the scrolls to 200 BCE, dismissed the skeptics; to those who scoffed at the antiquity of the scrolls he pointed out that "the discovery of Pompeii and Herculaneum was in its time relegated to the realm of fiction by outstanding personages." He noted, "In none of the similar episodes of the past two centuries has there been such a wide refusal on the part of scholars to accept clear-cut evidence."[25]

In late summer 1947, Mar Samuel's attempts at finding someone to back up his claims about the scrolls convinced Kando that there must be value in them, and he pressed the Bedouins for more. The men of the Ta'amara tribe obliged, and this time, instead of returning to the impoverished Syriac Metropolitan, Kando thought he could get a better price by turning to the Jews.

He sent an Armenian dealer to contact Professor Eleazar Sukenik, who took a risky trip to Bethlehem to buy the three scrolls. Sukenik's son Yigael Yadin, who would become Israel's first military chief of staff and its leading archaeologist (another example of the tangled relation between ancient history and contemporary power), argued in *The Message of the Scrolls* that the acquisition of the scrolls represented an act of providence:

> I cannot avoid the feeling that there is something symbolic in the discovery of the scrolls and their acquisition at the moment of the creation of the State of Israel. It is as if these manuscripts had been waiting in caves for two thousand years, ever since the destruction of Israel's independence, until the people of Israel had returned to their home and regained their freedom. The symbolism is heightened by the fact that the first three scrolls

were bought by my father for Israel on November 29, 1947, the very day the United Nations voted for the re-creation of a Jewish state in Israel after two thousand years. . . . It was a tremendously exciting experience, difficult to convey in words, to see the original scrolls and to study them, knowing that . . . these very scrolls were read and studied by our forefathers in the period of the Second Temple. They constitute a vital link—long lost and now regained—between those ancient times, so rich in civilized thought, and the present day.[26]

Between them, Sukenik and Mar Samuel owned all seven of the known Dead Sea Scrolls. But in 1948 communication had ceased between the two men. All-out war had broken out after the U.N. partition vote, and Jerusalem was a city divided.

Mar Samuel's confidence in the authenticity of the scrolls grew when an expert on Hebraica took a look at the Isaiah scroll and assured him, "Your Grace, if these came from the time of Christ as you imply, you couldn't begin to measure their value by filling a box the size of this table with pounds sterling." For the first time he began to think of the material value of the treasures. Thousands of Syriac Christians in the Middle East were living in poverty. They needed schoolrooms, books, clothing. Selling the scrolls might help. As the war raged on, Mar Samuel took the scrolls, now touted by William F. Albright as "the greatest manuscript discovery of modern times," to America.[27]

Back in West Jerusalem, Professor Sukenik devoted the remainder of his life to the study of an apocalyptic Qumran text (the Greek word *apokalypsis* literally means "unveiling"), which had not otherwise survived in either the Jewish or Christian canon: "The War of the Sons of Light Against the Sons of Darkness." Yigael Yadin, after resigning his post as chief of staff in 1953 shortly before his father's death, published a critical edition of the text for his doctorate at the Hebrew University. The publication of the previously unknown scroll launched him on a spectacular career of scholarship and discovery. (Inspired by the apocalyptic scrolls, the American architects Armand Phillip Bartos and Frederick John Kiesler constructed in 1965 the Shrine of the Book at the Israel Museum. Its white dome, narrowing as it rises to an open neck, stands against a black basalt wall, an evocation of the imagery from the scroll of the War of the Sons of Light Against the Sons of Darkness.)

Mar Samuel's lectures at Yale, Harvard, and the University of Chicago had meanwhile made the Dead Sea Scrolls a public sensation. Newspapers, Sunday supplements, *Popular Science* magazine, and church bulletins devoted enthusiastic attention to the discovery.

In 1954, Yadin, too, came to the United States on a lecture tour. The Israeli consul-general in New York had alerted him to a classified ad in the *Wall Street Journal:* "Biblical manuscripts, dating back to at least 200 BC, are for sale. This would be an ideal gift to an educational or religious institution by an individual or group."[28]

The Syriac community in Jerusalem was in desperate need of financial help, and Mar Samuel had decided to sell the scrolls. Using a middleman, Yadin at once agreed to Mar Samuel's $250,000 asking price. An American Jewish philanthropist, banker, and paper manufacturer, D. Samuel Gottesman, put up the funds. (A decade later, his children would fund the construction of the Shrine of the Book in his memory.) When the deal was inked at the Waldorf-Astoria Hotel in July 1954, the scrolls were transferred to the Israeli consulate in New York, and from there sent once more to Jerusalem, each on a separate airplane. On February 13, 1955, Israeli Prime Minister Moshe Sharett held a press conference to announce Israel's acquisition of the four scrolls. But Mar Samuel's decision to sell them did not sit well with his own community.

The libraries of antiquity did not just preserve books; they also served as places where scrolls were copied and codices were bound. Archaeologists excavating Qumran assigned to one of the upper rooms—in which they discovered a copper inkpot as well as fragments of inscribed leather and pottery that were probably used for scribal teaching and practice—the anachronistic term "scriptorium."

In the end, eleven Qumran caves yielded a dozen full scrolls written on parchment or papyrus, one embossed on copper, and thousands of fragments (80 percent of them on leather and parchment, and the remainder on papyrus) from 813 original documents. Most are in Hebrew or Aramaic, but a small number are in Greek (including all 19 texts found in cave 7). Apart from Qumran, other ancient Greek texts were found in Wadi Murabba'at, Wadi Nar, the "cave of letters" in Nahal Hever, and Nahal Ze'elim. The Qumran library held not only the book of Isaiah (a thousand years older than the earliest known Hebrew manuscript of that work) but apocryphal works never included in the canon, such as Tobit and the book of Ben Sira/Ecclesiasticus. It also contained apocryphal works unknown until the discoveries at Qumran, such as the Genesis Apocryphon and the Psalms of Joshua.

The Dead Sea Scrolls were not immediately made accessible, either to the public or to scholars. Over a period of more than forty years, first under Jordanian rule and later under Israeli rule, a small team of scholars headed by Roland de Vaux was exclusively entrusted with editing and publishing the scrolls.[29] Until 1991 these scholars kept to a "secrecy rule." Leading scholars of biblical history including Geza Vermes and Morton Smith complained about efforts to withhold the Dead Sea Scrolls and deny access to scholars, efforts that only fueled speculation in the popular press that the scrolls contained subversive secrets, even a secret gospel. Only when photographs taken by a Jerusalem-born Christian Palestinian photographer named Najib Albina were made public by the Huntington Library in San Marino, California, did the scrolls emerge from the shroud of secrecy.

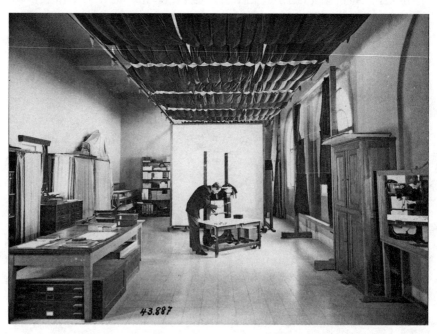

Najib Albina photographing scroll fragments in the 1950s. (Courtesy of the Leon Levy Dead Sea Scrolls Digital Library; Israel Antiquities Authority.)

The story of the Dead Sea Scrolls is not yet over. Kando kept some for himself, including the longest one: the almost twenty-seven-foot-long Temple Scroll, probably written in the second or first century BCE, which takes its name from God's first-person description to Moses of the construction, furnishings, and ritual laws of the Temple in Jerusalem. During the Six-Day War, Yadin, then military adviser to the Israeli prime minister, dispatched intelligence officers to Kando's home in Bethlehem. After an interrogation, they forced him to give up the remarkably well-preserved scroll, hidden in a shoebox under a floor tile in his bedroom. Kando was given $105,000 in compensation. (A British businessman, Baron Wolfson, put up most of the money.) Yadin published the text ten years later.[30]

In 1993, two years after the scholarly monopoly was broken, Khalil Iskandar Shahin died at age eighty-three, bequeathing his secret collection of remainders to his sons, who kept them in a safe-deposit box in UBS Bank in Zurich. The family, now known simply as the Kando family, began selling fragments, some no larger than a postage stamp. In the 1990s, a Norwegian collector, Martin Schøyen, purchased sixty fragments unknown to the scholarly community until they became part of his collection, including fragments of Leviticus, Joshua, Judges, and Daniel. "In those years I joined the scholars chasing numerous 'ghost scrolls': fragments that were rumored to exist, but that no one had ever actually seen, and which never surfaced even in photographs," Schøyen wrote. "They were just ghosts, invented to get attention or to be incorporated into the Dead Sea Scrolls legacy. The most famous of these ghosts was a 1 Enoch scroll. . . . It was first said to be in Jordan, then Kuwait, but it has never surfaced. Another famous example is the 'Angel Scroll' claimed to have been found east of the Dead Sea, and now said to be in a Benedictine monastery on the German-Swiss border. This scroll has never been seen by anybody—not even in photographs."[31] The Kandos sold other fragments to evangelical Christian institutions in the United States. Asuza Pacific University, an evangelical university near Los Angeles, bought five fragments. Southwestern Baptist Theological Seminary in Fort Worth, Texas, acquired eight more.

More recently, Kando's family is said to have offered a butterfly-shaped scrap of the Joseph story from Genesis for $1.2 million to the Israeli diamond billionaire and antiquities collector Shlomo Moussaieff, who was described by the Israeli antiquities dealer and epigraphist Robert Deutsch as "the world's most important private collector of Jewish and biblical-related antiquities." Moussaieff (whose grandfather, a well-known collector of Kabbalistic manuscripts, built the Bukharan Quarter in Jerusalem) thought the asking price was too high. He died in 2015 without having added the ultimate Jewish manuscript to his vast collection. Now Kando's family is said to be asking many times that sum.[32]

We met with William, youngest of Khalil (Kando) Shahin's five sons, at the shop he inherited from his late father near the Albright Institute in East Jerusalem. He greeted us with an impassive expression. He seemed almost mistrustful of us; if we had hoped to find him eager to show off his most prized possessions, we were disappointed. Although his lawyer (a Palestinian patron of the arts) Mazen Qupti had vouched for us, the dealer continued to probe. Reflecting bitterly on the fate of Jerusalem's textual treasures, William insisted that the late archbishop Mar Samuel had kept the profits from the sale of the scrolls to himself instead of supporting the Syriac community of Jerusalem. William at first cagily refused even to acknowledge that he owned fragments of the scrolls. When pressed, he said that he did have some but would disclose nothing of their whereabouts, their contents, or the price he was asking for them. It is astonishing to think that fragments of the Dead Sea Scrolls, unstudied and undeciphered, might still be available to the highest bidder. (Kando's Genesis fragment, the largest Dead Sea Scroll fragment still held in private hands, along with another eleven previously unseen remnants of scrolls, was displayed in an exhibition in Texas in 2012.)

William's fears can be better understood against the backdrop of the fates suffered by others who had the chance to lay hands on previously unknown scrolls. In 2005, after buying a scroll from three West Bank Bedouin, the late Israeli archaeologist Hanan Eshel and his student Roi Porat were taken in for questioning by Israeli police on suspicion of "unlawful possession of antiquities, failure to report the purchase of the scroll to the IAA [Israel Antiquities Authority] within the required 15 days, and . . . unlawful excavation." Reports of the discovery of new fragments of a Leviticus scroll from the Bar Kochba period (132–135 CE) had alarmed the police and the Israel Antiquities Authority. Bar-Ilan University backed its professor: "Professor Eshel has worked tirelessly to study the treasures of Jewish history. He saved a scroll of inestimable value and gave it to the state, and thus prevented antiquities theft and perhaps the destruction of an important find. Bar-Ilan University is convinced at the end of the investigation that it will be clear that Professor Eshel acted innocently and out of purely academic motives." Although no charges were brought against Eshel, the incident soured his relationship with the Israel Antiquities Authority until his death in 2010.[33]

William was well aware that under the 1978 Antiquities Law of the State of Israel no fragments of the scrolls can leave the country. And even though his scrolls had left the region long beforehand he remained very cautious, fearing anger and jealousy. Amir Ganor, of the Israel Antiquities Authority anti-looting squad, was not pleased. "I told Kando many years ago, as far as I'm concerned, he can die with those scrolls," Ganor told the Associated Press. "The scrolls' only address is the State of Israel."[34]

Others dispute that assertion. Hamdan Taha of the Department of Antiquities and Cultural Heritage in the Palestinian Authority claims rights to the material because it was found in the West Bank. As recently as the fall of 2016, UNESCO officials told Eitan Klein, a deputy director of the Israel Antiquities Authority, that at a meeting of the Intergovernmental Committee for Promoting the Return of Cultural Property to Its Countries of Origin or Its Restitution in Case of Illicit Appropriation (ICPRCP) the Palestinians had informally demanded a return of the scrolls and were likely to make an official request.[35]

International interest in the Dead Sea Scrolls has hardly diminished. In 2011, the Israel Museum published online ultra-high-resolution photographs (1,200 mega-pixels each) by Ardon Bar-Hama of five of the scrolls. Within a week, the site had received more than a million hits. Millions of visitors have come to the Shrine of the Book at the Israel Museum to see the eight scrolls on display there. The writer Amos Elon remarked that Israeli guides invariably point out that any ten-year-old schoolchild can easily read the Isaiah Scroll: "Can a ten-year-old in Athens or Rome read ancient Greek or Latin inscriptions? In Greece and Italy, the language is no longer the same. In Jerusalem it is."[36] The hidden past, preserved by the desert, has become public present.

Jerusalem's libraries, private and public, were dispersed in the year 70 when the Roman forces sacked the city. Some books were spirited away to the desert for safekeeping; others began a new journey—copied, translated, and shelved alongside a new corpus of books.

Jerusalem in Translation. From the Septuagint to the Vulgate, with Faint Traces of Georgian and Armenian

According to a midrash (an early rabbinic commentary on the biblical text), Jerusalem has seventy names (Numbers Rabbah 14:12).[37] The Hebrew Bible variously knows Jerusalem as Zion, Neve Tzedek (Oasis of Justice), Ariel, and Kiryat Melekh Rav (City of the Great King, as in Psalms 48:2). Another midrash (Genesis Rabbah 22:14) comments that Noah's son Shem called the place Shalem. Abraham after the binding of Isaac called it Adonai-Yireh (the Lord will see). The midrash concludes that the good Lord, in order to please them both, combined the two into the Hebrew Yerushalayim.

In Arabic the city has been called al-Quds (the Holy), Bayt al-Maqdis (House of the Holy), and al-Balāṭ (from the Latin *palatium*, "palace"). On several sixteenth- and seventeenth-century maps, cartographers note that in Turkish the city is called "Cusembareich," a Latin mispronunciation of the Arabic name al-Quds al-Mubaraq, "Blessed Jerusalem." It is Hierosolyma for the Greeks, Aelia Capitolina for the ancient Romans.

In the Hebrew Bible, the four-letter name YHWH never appears in geographically embedded form. There is no Yahweh-of-Jerusalem. And yet Jerusalem is the site of the divine appellation, the City of the Name. Because the Decalogue warns against taking the name of God in vain, many scribes of the Qumran library, authors of the Dead Sea Scrolls, abstained from writing the Tetragrammaton and other divine names, replacing them in various ways. In Greek manuscripts from the first to the third centuries CE, certain divine names, or *nomina sacra*, including God, Lord, Jesus, Christ, Son, Spirit, Savior, and so on, are likewise abbreviated into shorthand. God (Θεός), for instance, becomes ΘΣ, and Lord (Κύριος) becomes ΚΣ. But one of the nomina sacra is Jerusalem (abbreviated to ΙΛΗΜ). Jerusalem is the only city treated as a divine name.[38]

Many of Jerusalem's libraries can be best described using the Greek word *polyglot* (many-tongued), which refers both to a book containing versions of the same text in several languages and to a multilingual person. The plurality of Jerusalem's languages, especially when they serve as barriers, calls attention to the incompleteness of each. In the book of Genesis, the diversity of languages represents not multi-hued richness but rather humankind's punishment for the hubris of constructing the Tower of Babel. The fragmentation of language into imperfect dialects is associated with the expulsion from Paradise and the fall of Adam and Eve. Here language is the first barrier. And so it remains. It is a common enough experience in Jerusalem to be confronted by something you cannot read. As we are continually reminded, no single person, no matter how linguistically gifted, can master all the languages in which Jerusalem speaks.

And so we depend on translations and encounter their reverberations between languages at almost every turn. Jerusalem reminds us that translation, whether cultural or linguistic, depends on the hospitality of the host. At the Ben-Zvi Institute we found a book in Hebrew and Portuguese published in 1773 by the Spanish Portuguese Jewish community of Hamburg. At the Greek Orthodox library, we found medieval bilingual manuscripts: Greek-Arabic (Stavros 26), Greek-Russian (Nikodemos 3), and Greek-Turkish (Taphos 62 and 530). At the Church of Pater Noster on the Mount of Olives, built over the Constantinian basilica of Eleona (on a site purchased by the princess de la Tour d'Auvergne in 1868), we encountered translations of "Our Father who art in heaven . . ." attached to the walls in 140 languages.

We discovered that the oldest manuscript in the Franciscan library of the Custody of the Holy Land, dated to the second half of the eleventh century, is not in Latin but is a fragment of a Greek text that survived as an endpaper to an Armenian book of hymns (MS Arm. 1). The same library holds a 1905 papal encyclical written in Turkish in the Armenian alphabet (what scholars call Turkish-Armenian heterography). The Franciscans also keep Hebrew manuscripts, such as a 1765 edition of *Sefer Magen Avraham* (a three-part Jewish polemic against Christianity and Islam by the Italian Renaissance scholar and geographer Abraham ben Mordecai Farissol) and a collection of medical recipes (dated 1780–1790) in Judeo-Arabic.

In one small private library in East Jerusalem, named Bayt al-Maqdis after Jerusalem's oldest Arabic name, the owner, Fahmi al-Ansari, showed us a translation of part 3 of the Mishna (Nashim) into Arabic. It was translated by a Jerusalemite scholar, Hamdi Nubani, who was a student of Eleazar Sukenik at the Hebrew University before 1948. Contemporary Palestinian literature often ignores Jerusalem's old Arabic name because it traces its origins to the Hebrew *Beit Hamikdash*, the name of the Temple. But Fahmi al-Ansari, at age eighty-two, had little interest in what he regarded as politics. His sole interest was in making the history of Jerusalem—Muslim, Christian, and Jewish—available to all in his free library.

Jerusalem's linguistic horizons expanded considerably in the Hellenistic period, as its corpus of writings in Greek and Aramaic translations began to be exported. In subsequent centuries, Jerusalem's libraries began to benefit from translated literature imported from elsewhere. How do those translations attune us to the city's syntax and determine the way Jerusalem's communities say "us" and "them"? How might they reveal kinships among those communities and their modes of remembering? What, in other words, can the translated texts in Jerusalem's libraries teach us about the city's polyglot past?

Perhaps the paradigm of all translation, especially in Jerusalem, is translating the word of God, a process that has been ongoing since the Bible was first set down. Among the first translations in the Common Era was that of the Hebrew Bible into Greek. In the ancient world Athens and Jerusalem stood as symbols of opposing worldviews: philosophy and faith. "What has Athens to do with Jerusalem?" the early Christian theologian Tertullian asked.[39] Quite a bit, as it turns out. In a sense, translating the Bible from Hebrew into Greek meant translating Jerusalem into Athens.

We made a visit to the Greek Orthodox manuscript library, where Archbishop Aristarchos offered us the chance to peruse a nearly complete manuscript of the Greek translation of the Old Testament dating to the late ninth century (Taphos 2). This is the first translation of the Hebrew Bible into another language, known as the Septuagint (Latin for "seventy"). As he took the thick volume from the shelves, Aristarchos explained that it was a "decapitated" manuscript, missing the first folio of Genesis. The manuscript opens on the second folio in medias res with the verse "And they heard the voice of the Lord God walking in the garden in the cool of the day" (Gen. 3:8).

Two other pages (27 and 56) went missing. They were replaced in the twelfth or thirteenth century with stitched-in palimpsests, the biblical text written over a faded fifth-century Greek fragment, possibly the Wisdom of Sirach, written in a hand similar to that of the Codex Sinaiticus, the famous early Greek Bible. In these two pages, we could see the transition from the earlier uncial script (written entirely in capital letters) to minuscule (featuring lowercase lettering).

The legend of the seventy has its origins in Jerusalem. As told by Flavius Josephus, Philo, and Talmudic sources, Ptolemy II, the third-century BCE ruler of Egypt and patron of the Library of Alexandria, sent a letter to Elazar, the high priest in Jerusalem: "We have decided to have your laws translated from Hebrew into Greek, so that they may take their place beside the rest of the king's books." A delegation from Alexandria to Jerusalem led by a Jew named Aristeas returned with seventy-two learned Jerusalemites, "six elders of translation" from each of the twelve tribes of Israel, and a master copy of the Torah. Ptolemy greeted them with a banquet that lasted seven days, after which the sages were given lodgings on the island of Pharos, where they are said to have completed their monumental task in seventy-two days. The first-century CE Hellenistic Jewish philosopher Philo recorded the scene from his hometown Alexandria: "Sitting here in seclusion with none save the elements of nature, earth, water, air, heaven, the genesis of which was to be the first theme of their sacred revelation, for the laws begin with the story of the world's creation, they became as it were possessed, and, under inspiration, wrote not each scribe something different but the same word for word, as though dictated to each by an invisible prompter."[40]

The Septuagint produced a perfect—and perfectly unanimous—translation that has since become the authoritative Greek translation of the Bible and remains the primary Bible of Eastern Orthodoxy. In the voyage into the new language, crucial terms gained new connotations: *Torah* becomes *nomos* (law), *chochma* becomes *sophia* (wisdom). Despite its canonical status, however, it had its critics (including Saint Jerome), who pointed out the inadequacies of translation as such. According to a rabbinic teaching, "When the Septuagint was translated, three days of darkness enveloped the world" (Megillat Ta'anit).

In "The Task of the Translator," Walter Benjamin raises the possibility that "no translation, however good it may be, can have any significance as regards the original."[41] One who reads the Bible in translation, the Hebrew poet H. N. Bialik said, is like a groom who kisses his bride through a veil.

For Philo and others, the bride herself remained inaccessible. Some suspect that Philo, a master of Greek style, may not have known Hebrew at all. According to the sixteenth-century Italian Jewish polymath Azariah de' Rossi, Philo "never saw nor knew the actual original text of Torah. . . . The Torah which he studied and wrote about throughout his works was entirely based on his reading of the Septuagint."[42] Philo's admiration for the Bible clearly derived from its Greek translation by the seventy-two divinely inspired Jerusalemites.

In the library of the École Biblique, the heart of Jerusalem's Dominican community, we came across a magnificent Walton polyglot Bible (shelfmark 328.13), printed in London in 1657. Each page features translations into Latin, Aramaic, Syriac, Arabic (by the tenth-century philosopher Saadia Gaon), and Samaritan, followed by each of the translations translated into Latin. The origins of this project go back two thousand years.

Jerusalem by no means ceased to be a city of learning and libraries when Roman legions under the command of Titus razed the Temple in the first century. This was, after all, the heyday of writing and copying throughout the Mediterranean basin. The Christian historian Julius Africanus (ca. 160–ca. 240), a native of Jerusalem, traveled the world in search of manuscripts. He records finding a manuscript of Homer's *Odyssey* in "the archives of the ancient fatherland [*archia patris*] of Colonia Aelia Capitolina of Palestine" (the Roman name for Jerusalem).[43]

At a time when Christians faced persecution and worse in the Roman Empire, Jerusalem was distant from Rome and from the emperor's wrath. Still, the city did not lack for martyrs who "accounted a horrible death more precious than a fleeting life, and won all the garlands of victorious virtue," as Eusebius, the father of church history, noted in his *The Martyrs of Palestine*.[44] One of the martyrs mentioned by Eusebius was Bishop Alexander, founder of the first library of Aelia and leader of the small Christian community living in the area of today's Mount Zion. Building monumental churches was not possible in the pagan city, but copying manuscripts and building a library was. Alexander fled Cappadocia (central Anatolia), where he had been imprisoned for his faith, and came to Jerusalem. There he was nominated as the successor of Bishop Narcissus in 212 and governed the Church of Jerusalem for thirty-eight years until he died a martyr in 251. During this time, he established the first library of Christian theological works in Jerusalem. In the monumental *Ecclesiastical History,* Eusebius mentions the works of "many learned churchmen" whose epistles were preserved "in the library of Ælia, which was equipped by Alexander." Eusebius himself used the library to consult the writings of Beryllus, Hippolytus of Rome, and Caius, as well as texts by local theologians such as Clement of Alexandria, Bishop Alexander, and Origen.[45]

In 231, the Christian theologian Origen escaped persecution in Alexandria, fled to Caesarea, and established his own library there. On the way from Alexandria to Caesarea, Origen passed through Jerusalem, where Bishop Alexander permitted him to teach the Scriptures. Because Origen was a layman, this caused a scandal in the small but hierarchical church of those days. Wherever he traveled, Origen collected manuscripts: copies of the Bible that he used for the purposes of critical comparison; Jewish, Christian, and Gnostic commentaries, which he collected mainly for polemical ends; and philosophical works and histories, such as Flavius Josephus's *Antiquities* (a work he often cited).[46] What we know of his achievements comes mainly from the works of his native Palestinian student, and the man who inherited his library in Caesarea: Eusebius.

Eusebius, born in the late third century, served as bishop of Caesarea. He not only documented the inauguration of the Church of the Holy Sepulchre in 335; he also created one of the great libraries of antiquity from the collections of his predecessors, Origen and Pamphilus. In Origen's Hexapla (Greek for "sixfold"), he joined a column of the Hebrew text of the Bible to a transliteration of Hebrew in Greek letters, the old Septuagint translation into Greek, and three newer translations in Greek. Modern scholars have called the Hexapla "one of the greatest single monuments of Roman scholarship, and the first serious product of the application to Christian culture of the tools of Greek philology." Numerous copies of Origen's writing—produced with the help of seven secretaries and "girls trained in beautiful writing"—have survived.[47] Ironically, Origen's original Hexapla has not. It disappeared after Origen's condemnation by the church

Biblia Sacra Polyglotta, 1657, by Brian Walton, from the École Biblique et Archéologique Française, Jerusalem (6 vols. EBAF 328.13). (Photo by Frédéric Brenner, 2015; courtesy of the photographer / Howard Greenberg Gallery.)

S.S.
BIBLIA
Polyglotta.

Complectentia Textus Originales

HEBRAICOS cum
Pentat. Samarit:
CHALDAICOS
GRÆCOS.

Versionumq; Antiquarum

SAMARIT.   GRÆC. SEPT.
CHALDAIC.   SYRIACÆ.
LAT. VULG.   ARABICÆ.
ÆTHIOPIC.   PERSICÆ.

Quicquid comparari poterat.

MSS. Antiquis, variisq; Consultis opti-
mæ; q; Exemplaribus Impreßis, Summa
fide Collata.

Edidit
Brianus Waltonus S.T.D.
Anno M.DC.LVII.

in the sixth century and with the destruction of the library at Caesarea by Muslim forces in the seventh century. Jerome, in the early fifth century, was the last to mention its presence in Caesarea's library.⁴⁸

In the Biblioteca Terra Sancta, at the heart of Jerusalem's Franciscan monastery, we came across a 1482 copy of a book by the twelfth-century scholastic theologian Peter Lombard, or Petrus Lombardus (INC A24). It caught our attention not so much for its content as for its binding. The book's paper boards were covered with a broad sheet of fourteenth-century parchment, containing a commentary on psalm 30 by Saint Augustine. The rest of Augustine's volume, perhaps because of its large size, fell apart, but the monks found a new use for its pages. The sight reminded us that when Augustine composed his commentary on Psalms in the last decade of the fourth century, he sent it for corrections to Jerome, the translator of the Bible into Latin. And now Augustine's text has come back to Jerusalem in the guise of a book cover.

The book of Samuel depicts King David as a great warrior, valorous in battle but also susceptible to temptation. In pursuit of Bathsheba, he sends her husband to his death in battle. Broken and contrite, David re-pents, and his anguish prompted one of the greatest of the psalms (51/50): "Have mercy on me, O Lord!" By the end of the poem, David turns private anguish into a plea for his city. "Do good in thy good plea-sure unto Zion: build thou the walls of Jerusalem."

Almost fourteen hundred years later, Jerome, overlooking the same Judean hills, translated this cry into Latin: "Miserere mei, Deus!" Accused of improprieties with a wealthy Roman woman, his own Bathsheba, Jerome had fled Rome in 385, and settled in Bethlehem, south of Jerusalem. He wrote a letter to a friend in Rome, addressing these accusations, and eulogizing the love of learning he and the Roman matron shared and the intimacy that resulted from studying together: "It often happened that I found myself surrounded with virgins, and to some of these I expounded the divine books as best I could. Our studies brought about constant intercourse, this soon ripened into intimacy, and this, in turn, produced mutual confidence."⁴⁹ In the Holy Land, Jerome aimed to make the erudition of "the masters of the synagogue" available in Latin. He transformed the original language of the Scriptures into the vernacular of the common people (*vulgus*). He intended his translation of

A page from *Enarrationes in psalmos* by Saint Augustine used
in the binding of Petrus Lombardus, *Sententiarum libri IV*
(Basel: Bernard Richel, ca. 1482), Biblioteca Generale della
Custodia di Terra Santa, INC A24. (Courtesy of Biblioteca
Generale della Custodia di Terra Santa.)

the Bible—known in the sixteenth century as the Vulgate—for all in the
Roman Empire who were not instructed in Greek, let alone Hebrew, including scholars like Augustine, who confessed to a hatred for his Greek
instruction in childhood.

Augustine could not summon up unqualified enthusiasm for Jerome's
masterwork. Jerome had departed from the commonly accepted Greek
as a source of translation and introduced corrections based on the
Hebrew.[50] In a letter sent to Bethlehem in 394, Augustine wrote: "For my
own part, I cannot sufficiently express my wonder that anything should at
this date be found in the Hebrew manuscripts which escaped so many

translators perfectly acquainted with the language." Jerome did not reply. A few years later, Augustine sent another letter complaining bitterly about this lack of response. When Jerome finally replied, he defended his work with passionate conviction: "You seem to me not to understand the matter. . . . I am surprised that you do not read the books of the Seventy translators in the genuine form in which they were originally given to the world, but as they have been corrected, or rather corrupted, by Origen."[51]

Neither man could anticipate that Jerome's translation would become canonical for centuries to come. In 1455, when Johannes Gutenberg of Mainz set the first book in movable type and printed it in multiple copies, he chose Jerome's Vulgate. A century later, after the Council of Trent in 1546, the book became the standard Bible of the Roman Catholic Church.

The fourth and early fifth centuries (until the Huns attacked western Europe and Africa and sacked Rome) saw a great exchange of letters that connected Jerusalem to other centers of learning. Jerome corresponded with Augustine in Hippo (in modern-day Algeria) and with friends in Rome, such as the noblewoman Marcella and his friend Paula's daughter Eustochium. The fourth-century Spanish pilgrim Egeria wrote home about her trip to the Holy Land.[52]

In those same years a widowed Spanish aristocrat known as Melania the Elder gave up her riches, came to settle in Jerusalem (via Rome and Egypt), and enriched the city's textual culture. Renowned as a "desert mother," she founded a convent on the Mount of Olives. There she lived for almost thirty years in a double monastery (with separate sections for monks and nuns) with her spiritual partner, Rufinus Tyrannius, a Roman scholar and translator (from Greek to Latin). One of her biographers reported on the years she spent in Jerusalem: "Being very learned and loving literature, she turned night into day perusing every writing of the ancient commentators, including three million [lines] of Origen and two hundred fifty thousand of Gregory, Stephen, Pierius, Basil and other standard writers. Nor did she read them once only and casually, but she laboriously went through each book seven or eight times."[53]

When Jerome and Paula arrived in Jerusalem in 385 they settled in another double monastery. Rufinus exchanged books with Jerome and instructed monks in his monastery to copy books for Jerome's library. While

Jerome and Paula focused their efforts on translating texts from Hebrew to Latin, Rufinus and Melania focused on translation from Greek to Latin. Rufinus translated Flavius Josephus and Eusebius. Rufinus and Melania followed the rule of Saint Basil (which Rufinus later translated into Latin), with its reverence for the copying of manuscripts.

Melania and Rufinus eventually fell out with Jerome and Paula over their different interpretations of Origen's theology. In one of his more barbed letters, Jerome referred to Melania (whose name means "black" in Greek) as "her, whose name bears witness to the blackness of her perfidy." Back in Rome, Rufinus continued to translate Origen into Latin, to the dismay of the papal curia. Much of Origen's work has survived solely in Rufinus's translation.[54] Each of these figures—Jerome and Rufinus, Paula and Melania—introduced to the Latin-speaking world the great works they encountered in Hebrew and Greek, including texts that were lost in their original and preserved solely in translation.[55]

Consider the apocryphal texts expelled from the rabbinic canon but preserved and adopted by Christians. Though the Hebrew original was lost, these texts survived in Latin as an appendix to the Vulgate (and in translations to Ge'ez, Arabic, and Syriac). Like many other Jerusalem texts, these books survived thanks to their translation to another language and adoption by another faith. *Esdras* was translated back into Hebrew only in 1956.[56]

Many of Jerusalem's languages have all but died out, leaving only faint traces behind. Jebusite, for example, the city's spoken language before its capture by King David, has long since sunk into oblivion. So too with Palestinian-Aramaic, once Jerusalem's lingua franca. Yet in some cases Jerusalem's dead languages merited a renewed lease on life in the form of translations. In Jerusalem as elsewhere, translation is practiced not only as a form of interpretation but as a form of rescue.

The "Jerusalem liturgy" used in the Church of the Holy Sepulchre, for instance, has survived not in its original Greek but in Georgian and Armenian, the languages of two of the earliest nations to adopt Christianity.[57] Jerusalem attracted Christians from throughout the Byzantine Empire. In addition to learned Latin-speaking communities, archaeological finds at Jerusalem churches and monasteries give evidence of other spoken languages. In fact, the world's oldest extant inscriptions in both Armenian and Georgian were discovered in Jerusalem.

The Armenian and Georgian presence in Jerusalem dates to the fourth and fifth centuries, respectively. In 404, two Armenian scribes known as the Holy Translators invented a script for the Armenian language specifically intended for the translation of the Bible. Fifteen Armenian monasteries sprang up between Egypt and Jerusalem. (Each adopted the Jerusalem calendar, which they continue to use to this day.)

The Armenian historian Kevork (George) Hintlian took us one afternoon to an unremarkable nineteenth-century residential building in Musrara, a Jerusalem neighborhood outside of Damascus Gate. He opened the door to the basement, disclosing a stunning mosaic of the Byzantine period, first discovered in 1894 (plate 5). Measuring 21 by 13 feet (6.5 by 4 meters), it depicts a vine entwining flamingoes, ibises, ducks, an eagle, a partridge, and peacocks drinking from an amphora. At the head of this colorful tree of life is one of the oldest Armenian inscriptions in the world: "For the memory and salvation of all those Armenians whose name the Lord knows."[58]

Jerusalem's "bird mosaic" (detail). (Photo by Frédéric Brenner, 2016; courtesy of the photographer / Howard Greenberg Gallery.)

The same week, Father Eugenio Alliata, director of the Franciscan archaeological museum and a professor at the Studium Biblicum Franciscanum, met us on the Via Dolorosa, the path Jesus walked from sentencing to crucifixion. He agreed to show us a fifth-century treasure: the world's oldest-known inscription in Georgian. The mosaic lay in a storage room surrounded by ancient artefacts: Byzantine vessels, sculptured marble fragments from the Church of the Holy Sepulchre, funeral busts from Palmyra (in the Syrian desert), capitals from the basilica in Nazareth, pottery found in the Latin cemeteries on Mount Zion, and Jewish ossuaries of the Roman period discovered on the Mount of Olives. The dedication of the Georgian mosaic reads, "By the help of Christ, and with the intercession of Saint Theodore, have mercy O Lord on the Abbot Anthony and on Josiah the founder of this mosaic and of the father and mother of Josiah. Amen." The inscription was unearthed in the 1950s beneath the Georgian monastery of Bir al-Qutt (today surrounded by a new neighborhood in East Jerusalem known as Homat Shmuel).[59] Another

Georgian inscriptions from the ruins of Saint Theodore Monastery in the Judean desert, dated 430. (Photo by Anna Gawn, 2016; courtesy of the photographer.)

mosaic with a Georgian inscription from the sixth century lay facing the wall; it was too heavy for us to turn around. One of the mosaics will be put on display when the Franciscans complete the renovations of their museum

Unlike the mosaics and stone inscriptions, the books and scrolls from the libraries of the Israelite kings, Bishop Alexander, Jerome, and Melania have left no visible traces in the Jerusalem of our day. Many fell victim to the flames of now-forgotten wars. But Jerusalem's texts, from the Psalms to the Vulgate, still resonate far beyond the city walls.

CHAPTER TWO

THE ARABIC ERA

637 to 1099

At first, Muhammad and his followers faced Jerusalem in prayer. Even after the Prophet changed the direction of prayer, or *qibla*, his followers referred to the city as Ūlā al-qiblatayn, "the first of the two qiblas." More often, they called it al-Quds, "the Holy." In the Muslim tradition, this was the place where the archangel Gabriel accompanied Muhammad, on his winged horse, al-Burāq, on his night journey from Mecca before Muhammad ascended to Paradise. And it is here that people will be judged by God in the end of time. According to one hadith, or prophetic saying, at the end of days the Ka'bah shrine will be transferred (or translated) from Mecca to Jerusalem, which will again be the center of pilgrimage.[1]

Beginning in the late ninth century, Islamic poets rhapsodized Jerusalem in a literary genre called *faḍā'il al-Quds* (the merits of Jerusalem). In volumes with titles like *The Book of Arousing Souls to Visit the Divinely Guarded Jerusalem* (by the fourteenth-century theologian Ibn al-Firkaḥ), they hailed the city's most glorious figures, from Jacob to David and his son Solomon, to Muhammad on his night journey.

Medieval Muslims similarly saw the city through guidebooks that imagined Jerusalem not so much as the stage of biblical episodes but as a location in which prayers were more likely to be pleasing to God. Take, for example, the Persian traveler Nasir-i Khusraw, who arrived in Jerusalem during Ramadan, 1047, and stayed for a year. The city is called "the Holy," he writes in his book *Safarnama* (Book of Travels), because the throngs of believers unable to make the hajj to Mecca come to Jerusalem on Eid al-Adha, the holiday of sacrifice that marks the end of the hajj. In some years, he says, as many as twenty thousand pilgrims come to Jerusalem on the first days of the hajj.

The Islamic conquest and waves of pilgrimage not only introduced a new corpus of books to Jerusalem—the Qur'an, the hadith, poetry, and legal literature—they also shaped the existing collections.

The Manuscripts of Mar Saba

Jerusalem, set among stony hills, is a city of the desert, and its literature bears something of the starkness and timelessness of the expanse that extends from the heights of the Mount of Olives eastward to the Dead Sea. This desert—what the Bible calls "the wilderness"—has long lent its transcendence to poets and its austerity to monks.

This elemental landscape represents not just contemplative stillness but also parched apocalyptic prophecies. Isaiah describes Jerusalem as an arid wasteland: "Thy holy cities are a wilderness, Zion is a wilderness, Jerusalem a desolation" (Isa. 64:10). One of the Dead Sea Scrolls discovered in the canyons and cliffsides of this pallid wilderness, far from Jerusalem's clamor, predicts that in the end of days the Sons of Light will return from exile in the "desert of the nations" to pitch camp in the "desert of Jerusalem."

It is also a place of refuge—for fugitive kings and soldiers, for roaming hermits and Bedouins. To escape Absalom's uprising, David crossed Jerusalem's Kidron valley and fled into the desert (2 Sam. 15) as, in a later revolt, did Judas Maccabeus (2 Macc. 5:2). According to Matthew, John the Baptist preached repentance "in the wilderness of Judea" (Matt. 3:1).

Early Christians, the Benedictine scholar Mark Sheridan explains, "created a powerful icon of the desert." They "associated the desert with spiritual combat, nearness to God, progress in the spiritual life and withdrawal from society understood as the world opposed to God."[2] As a warning, then, or as a place of refuge and a source of serene inspiration, or as the topography of temptation, the desert has served many of the scribes of Jerusalem. With its arid climate and forbidding terrain, this desert also happens to be one of the great manuscript repositories in the world, where many of the volumes now shelved in Jerusalem's libraries originated.

If you follow the Kidron (or Jehoshaphat) Valley southeast from Jerusalem, you will reach Mar Saba (Saint Sabbas) monastery, which has been in continuous use since the fifth century (plate 6). On one of our visits, we met with the Greek Orthodox monk Father Efrem, the monastery's gatekeeper and time-keeper. Once a week he would walk out to the balcony overlooking the cliff to watch for sunset. When the day's last beams touched the holy cave of Saint Sabbas across the wadi he would calibrate his watch to midnight. This desert enclave was a time apart, and a place apart. The Sabaites lived in a time zone of their own—as, in a sense, did their texts.

Father Efrem and his fellow monks adhere to their own rites (known as the Typikon of Saint Sabbas), which at one time influenced large parts of the Christian world. They are committed vegetarians but refrain from eating apples, as the monks of Mar Saba have done since the time of the monastery's founding in the fifth century. Every Sunday, the monks celebrate an all-night vigil. On weekdays, they pray for six or seven hours a day. Their divine worship cycles weekly through David's Psalms, divided into twenty sections (*kathisma*). To this day, no women are admitted into the confines of the monastery, so only Ben was allowed inside, while Merav sat outside with Father Efrem and recorded his stories.

In the fifth and sixth centuries, Christians arrived from across the Roman Empire to live as monks in Jerusalem and its desert. Saint Sabbas, born in Cappadocia, followed thousands who had already settled in monasteries in the Judean desert south of Jerusalem. Pursuing his wish to live in hermetic solitude, he moved to a cave in the Kidron valley—the site where around 483 he founded the monastery named after him. Soon he was joined by a large number of monks, who built their cells into the caves lining the valley—so many, in fact, that Mar Saba became known as "the Great Lavra." (A lavra, or laura, is a cluster of cells or caves, or a monastery.) Saint Sabbas consecrated a church in 502 over a spring. According to tradition, the Virgin Mary appeared to him, promising that the church would remain intact until the Second Coming. After he died in 532, his body was said to be uncorrupted. Five centuries later, in quest of relics of the greatest saints, the Crusaders spirited off his remains, which were returned to Mar Saba only in 1965, when Pope Paul VI visited the Holy Land.

Mar Saba, the largest lavra in the Judean desert, flourished into a great theological center. At its height, as many as five thousand monks—Greek, Georgian, Armenian, and Syriac—lived in and around the cliffside monastery, including the great seventh-to-eighth-century theologian John of Damascus, whose remains are buried there.

A generation after Saint Sabbas, the prolific writer Cyril of Scythopolis settled in the lavra, where he composed the official version of the saint's life. The Sabaite scribes gained fame for copying theological compositions, for translations, and for poetry. The abbot of Saint Catherine's monastery in Sinai, for one, commissioned manuscripts from the skilled scribes of Mar Saba.[3] The library at Mar Saba continued to expand in the eleventh and twelfth centuries until it became the most significant monastic library of the Judean desert. Today, the Mar Saba collection is kept intact in the manuscript library of the Greek Orthodox Patriarchate in Jerusalem. (We describe our visit to it in the Epilogue.)

Having survived numerous Muslim and Christian conquests of the Holy Land, Mar Saba's library bears witness to one of the great cultural transformations in the intellectual history of the region: the Christian adoption of Arabic as a literary and religious language. Home to John of Damascus, a leading Arab Christian poet and thinker, and writers such as the ninth-century Arab Christian monk Anthony David, it soon became a center of manuscript production in Arabic. Starting in the seventh century, when Islamic troops conquered Jerusalem and Islam was ascendant, the earliest translations of Christian texts (including the Gospels) from Greek into Arabic were carried out at the monastery, which acted as a crucial nexus of translation between cultures.[4] In effect, Mar Saba introduced Christian literature to the Arabic-speaking world.

Until the Islamic conquest, Jerusalem's lingua franca was Aramaic. Although Arabic was spoken in small circles of Arab Christians, it gained wide currency as a theological language only with the emergence of Islam. As Arabs flocked to Islam, Christian theologians in the Holy Land realized the time had come to translate Christian theological ideas and texts into Arabic. It fell to the monks of Mar Saba to complete this monumental mission. The Christian answer to Islam began there.[5]

Mar Saba thus served as the center of the thriving Arabophone monasticism that flourished between the Islamic conquest of Jerusalem and the Crusades. The most brilliant of its writers, Yuhanna ibn Mansur ibn Sarjun, is better remembered today as John of Damascus. Mansur was born in Damascus in 675, just two decades after the death of Muhammad. Mansur's father, one of Caliph al-Walid's ministers of finance, instructed him to "learn not only the books of the Saracens [Muslims], but those of the Greeks as well."[6] Damascus under al-Walid was a capital in turmoil. The caliph confiscated the great cathedral of Saint John the Baptist, which had been shared for half a century between Christians and Muslims, and reconsecrated it as a mosque. He purged Christians from his administration and stripped them of their privileges. He published a decree mandating that all official records must be written solely in Arabic.

Mansur left Damascus and joined the Mar Saba monastic community, where he took the name John. He witnessed the monumental achievements of the Umayyads in Jerusalem (the glorious Dome of the Rock and the al-Aqsa Mosque). Their nonfigurative aesthetic stood in stark contrast with the Christian churches of the city. The great Islamic monuments challenged Christianity's own sense of monotheism in the thrice-holy city. Despite the Second Commandment's injunction against the making of graven images, Jerusalem's churches were heavily decorated with icons.

Determined to shield Christianity from the rise of Islam, John wrote the earliest Christian polemic against Islam, a short text of a half-dozen columns called "Heresy of the Ishmaelites." He also wrote a book in defense of the icons and reiterated the mysteries of the Trinity to his fellow Christians.

John stood on the seam between two languages. As the British scholar Cyril Mango notes, "The most active center of Greek culture in the eighth century lay in Palestine, notably in Jerusalem and the neighboring monasteries." At the turn of the eighth century, John still wrote in Greek, but not long afterward the Arab monks of Mar Saba switched from Greek and Syriac (or Palestinian Aramaic) to Arabic.[7]

Numerous copies of the works of John of Damascus—dating between the eleventh century and the eighteenth—can be found in the Greek Orthodox library of Jerusalem. John's homilies and poems are still widely quoted and, as in the following lines, often used as funeral hymns:

> Where is the pleasure in life which is unmixed with sorrow?
> Where is the glory which on earth has stood firm and unchanged?
> All things are weaker than shadow, all more illusive than dreams;
> comes one fell stroke, and Death in turn, prevails over all these vanities.[8]

To this day, John's memory is commemorated alongside Saint Sabbas by an extraordinary all-night vigil on the anniversary of his death at Mar Saba, where he is buried. The caves and crags of the Kidron valley below the monastery are illuminated with hundreds of candles and lanterns, mirroring the star-pierced sky above.

From the eighth century on, Sabaite scribes translated church books into Arabic and composed original works in the language of the Qur'an. To illustrate how completely Arabic eclipsed Greek, the scholar Sidney Griffith cites an account of the twenty martyrs killed by Arab marauders at Mar Saba in 796 or 797. The report concludes with a catalogue of miracles attributed to the intercession of the martyrs. The list describes a Syrian (that is, Arabic-speaking) man who made himself ill with his intense but futile efforts to learn Greek. Then one night one of the martyred monks came to him in a dream and wiped his tongue clean. On awaking, the Syrian could speak Greek with astounding fluency.

A generation after John of Damascus, the Edessa-born theologian Theodore Abu Qurrah (ca. 750–ca. 825) became one of the first monks at Mar Saba to write in Arabic and employ Islamic vocabulary to articulate Christian theology. The manuscripts we saw were the original Arabic (fourteen works) and in Greek (forty-three works, although Griffith contends that these are translations from Arabic). Abu Qurrah also claimed to have written thirty works in his native Syriac, none of which has survived. A copy of his *Treatise on the Veneration of the Holy Icons* made at the monastery of Mar Chariton in the Judean desert by Stephen of Ramlah is now at the British Library (Oriental MS 4950).

We visited the monastic library of Saint Catherine's in Sinai, where we met with the librarian, Father Justin. Father Justin was born in El Paso, Texas, and grew fascinated with Byzantine history and the Orthodox Church as a student at the University of Texas. After serving twenty years at a monastery in Brookline, Massachusetts, he joined the Greek Orthodox community of Saint Catherine's in 1996.

Father Justin showed us an astonishing product of the so-called Jerusalem desert: one of the earliest-known dated Gospels in Arabic (Sinai MS 72).[9] This text was translated from the Greek but influenced by texts in Palestinian Syriac, a dialect used in Jerusalem for non-Greek speakers since the fourth century. It is not just a lectionary but the complete Gospels, in their canonical order, with added marks of readings during the liturgical year.

Of the ninth-century Christian writers of Arabic in Jerusalem and its desert, Anthony David of Baghdad must be ranked among the most important. Two Arabic manuscripts bearing his colophon and signature, both written in 885–886, are extant.[10] In the colophon, Anthony writes:

> Abba Anthony of Baghdad, David the son of Sina, copied this volume in the laura of the holy Mar Saba. Abba Isaac asked him to write it for Mount Sinai. Through the intercession of the honorable mother of the Light, the pure, blessed Lady Mary, the prayers of all his apostles, disciples, prophets and martyrs, and the prayers of our holy father, Mar Saba, and all his holy friends, we ask Christ, our God and Savior, to have mercy and to forgive the sins of the one who has copied, and the one who has asked for a copy. Amen. . . . It was copied in the year 272 of the years of the Arabs.[11]

The Mar Saba monastery attracted the earliest and hungriest Western manuscript hunters. We shall leave Mar Saba with a description by a nineteenth-century British visitor who followed his bibliophile's instincts from Jerusalem to Mar Saba in 1834: the Honourable Robert Curzon, a member of Parliament, a scholar, and an explorer. Curzon's account of the monastery and his manuscript purchases illustrates the fate of many of Jerusalem's lost treasures:

> In one part of the church I observed a rickety ladder leaning against the wall, and leading up to a small door about ten feet from the ground. Scrambling up this ladder, I found myself in the library of which I had

heard so much. It was a small square room, or rather a large closet, in the upper part of one of the enormous buttresses which supported the walls of the monastery. Here I found about a thousand books, almost all manuscripts, but the whole of them were works of divinity.

There were a great many enormous folios of the works of the fathers, and one MS. of the Octoteuch, or first eight books of the Old Testament. It is remarkable how very rarely MSS. of any part of the Old Testament are found in the libraries of Greek monasteries; this was the only MS. of the Octoteuch that I ever met with either before or afterwards in any part of the Levant.

There were about a hundred other MSS. on a shelf in the apsis of the church: I was not allowed to examine them, but was assured that they were liturgies and church-books which were used on the various high days during the year.

I was afterwards taken by some of the monks into the vaulted chambers of the great square tower or keep, which stood near the iron door by which we had been admitted. Here there were about a hundred MSS., but all imperfect; I found the "Iliad" of Homer among them, but it was on paper. Some of these MSS. were beautifully written; they were, however, so imperfect, that in the short time I was there, and pestered as I was by a crowd of gaping Arabs, I was unable to discover what they were.

I was allowed to purchase three MSS., with which the next day I and my companion departed on our way to the Dead Sea.[12]

Curzon walked away that day with a twelfth-century psalter, thirteenth-century parchment copies of the four Gospels, and medieval Greek lectionaries with notes in Arabic.

We tracked down some of the manuscripts he purchased in the Holy Land at the British Library in London. Several bear Curzon's handwritten notes (for example, Add MS 39585, 39586, and 39587–88). One is an illustrated Gospel with portraits of the evangelists (Add MS 39591). Another is a heavy Gospel lectionary from the twelfth to the fourteenth century in Greek with notes in Arabic (Add MS 39604). According to its series of colophons, the manuscript was first in the possession of Saint John the Baptist Church on the Jordan River, then after a stay in Jerusalem was deposited at Mar Saba, where it was purchased by Curzon. Curzon took the liberty of adding his own colophon:

1834.

I bought this manuscript from the monastery of St Sabba, which stands on
the ravine of the brook Kidron, about an hour from the Dead Sea, this was
my first visit to the monastery, when it was garrisoned by the Bedouins. I
gave the superior, or Agomenos, 20 pieces of gold for it about [erased], and
it served me for a pillow during 3 nights, when I was wandering on the
banks of the Jordan. The book was written in the eleventh century, from
the style of the ornaments I should think it came originally from
Constantinople, the first 24 leaves have been added at a later period.[13]

Less respectful book hunters who visited the Mar Saba library tore
out pages for their miniatures and illuminations. In the 1880s, the Greek
Orthodox Patriarch Nicodemus gathered the remaining collection of
priceless manuscripts for safekeeping to the central library at the Jerusalem
Patriarchate. This heavily guarded collection remains one of the most valuable literary treasures of Jerusalem.

Despite innumerable conquests and raids, Mar Saba's great literary
achievements have survived for fifteen hundred years. Copies and translations made there of older manuscripts, and original literature varying
from poems to hagiographies written by the Sabaites, can still be found in
Jerusalem and throughout the world.

The Dome as Text

"In looking at works of architecture," writes the historian of Islamic art
and architecture Oleg Grabar, "we are not accustomed to read, nor even
to notice, the words that have been put in them." We recalled his words
as we stood beneath the tilework inscription bands encircling the exterior
of the Dome of the Rock at the center of Jerusalem's sacred esplanade.
The verses inscribed on this monument can be found in the Qur'an (Sura
of the Night Journey 17:1–20). But the inscriptions on the Dome of the
Rock predate the canonization of the Qur'an. They "precede by over
two centuries," Grabar notes, "any other dated or datable quotation of
any length from the Holy Book."[14] The spectacular Dome of the Rock
was completed in 691, at the center of the sacred esplanade (the Haram
al-Sharif). Because of earthquake damage and for other reasons, it has
been renovated a number of times, including by the Ayyubid and

Mamluk rulers of Jerusalem after they took the city from the Crusaders, and most strikingly in the sixteenth century by Sultan Suleyman, the "second Solomon." In 1998, the dome covering was refurbished following a donation of $8.2 million by King Hussein of Jordan for the 175 pounds of gold plating required. The interior mosaics and decorations were cleaned and restored as recently as 2017. Each layer of restoration amounts to a selective reinterpretation of earlier strata.

Jews' attachment to Jerusalem had tended to express itself through texts, rather than through architecture. "Significant Jewish monumental presence appears only in the nineteenth century," notes Grabar.[15] It was texts, rather, in all their variety and possibility, that gave Jerusalem such an enduring place in the Jewish imagination.

Islam combined text and architecture. Just as the foundational works of Christianity were being translated into Arabic at Mar Saba, the Umayyad caliphs were translating an Islamic response—a polemics of supersession—into Jerusalem's sacred architecture. Jerusalem's Islamic monuments introduced the use of calligraphy as part of the architecture and decoration, inscribing meaning into the ornamentation of the building. Along the inner arcade of the octagonal building, a seventh-century inscription runs for almost 800 feet in beautiful gold-lettered Kufic script against a dark-blue background. The *bismillah* invocation to merciful Allah appears six times, opening each section. In addition to Qur'anic passages relating the story of Muhammad's night journey (al-Isra'), a few other verses have an additional polemical purpose. They make a remarkable proclamation in what in the seventh century was still a predominantly Christian city:

> O ye People of the Book, overstep not bounds in your religion; and of God speak only truth. The Messiah, Jesus, son of Mary, is only an apostle of God, and His Word which he conveyed into Mary, and a Spirit proceeding from Him. Believe therefore in God and His apostles, and say not "Three." It will be better for you. God is only one God. Far be it from His glory that He should have a son. [Sura 4:171]

Sidney Griffith writes that the "import of these repeated Qur'anic phrases is crystal clear: Islam has supplanted Christianity even in Jerusalem."[16] Muslims require neither icons nor God's son to mediate our relationship with the divine. The text itself suffices.

In fact, writers of the genre known as the merits of Jerusalem used to read not just the Dome of the Rock but the entire sacred esplanade as a kind of self-contained biblical narrative: the *mihrab* (prayer niche) of Mary, where angels brought her heavenly fruits (Qur'an 3:37); on the east wall, near the closed Gate of Mercy, the mihrab of the priest Zechariah, where angels relayed the good news of the birth of his son John the Baptist (Luke 1 and Qur'an 3:39, 19:11); the mihrab of Jacob on the north wall; Solomon's Throne; the Minaret of Abraham, who is said to have worshipped there; and the Dome of the Chain just to the east of the Dome of the Rock, on the site where David is said to have judged the Children of Israel by means of a chain suspended between heaven and earth.[17] This legendary cartography of Jerusalem underscored Islam's position as heir to previous Abrahamic monotheistic faiths, while at the same time asserting its supremacy as the last of God's revelations.

Muslims made the Haram al-Sharif a veritable history of God in all his prophetic revelations. A fourteenth-century schematic map by the traveler Ibn al-Sabbah al-Andalusi features sites associated with Moses, David, Solomon, Mary, and Jesus. Mihrab Daud (or in other traditions the Gate of Mercy) marked the place in which David begged God to forgive his sins (see sura 38 of the Qur'an). Sufi pilgrims from as far away as the Maghreb write about visiting the cradle of Jesus as part of their tours of Jerusalem. Contrary to the Gospels, in the eleventh century Al-Musharraf ibn al-Murajja al-Maqdisi (also known as Abul-Ma'ali) fixed the entire life of Jesus in Jerusalem. Mujir al-Din al-Hanbali, chief judge of Jerusalem, wrote a biography of Jesus. "Jesus, peace be upon him, was born and spoke from the cradle in Jerusalem, received the table in Jerusalem, was ascended by God to heaven in Jerusalem, and will descend from heaven to Jerusalem."[18]

Not coincidentally, Caliph 'Abd al-Malik raised the Dome of the Rock on the site of the ruined Jewish Temple atop the hill facing the Holy Sepulchre. In the tenth century, the Jerusalem geographer al-Muqaddasi remarked on the juxtaposition of the two shrines. He recorded a conversation with his uncle, an architect, who explained that the caliph "sought to build for the Muslims a mosque that should be unique and a wonder to the world. And in like manner is it not evident that 'Abd al-Malik, seeing the greatness of the martyrium [*qubbah*] of the Holy Sepulchre and its magnificence, was moved lest it should dazzle the minds of the Muslims, and hence erected above the Rock the Dome which is now seen there."[19]

Jerusalem's rival domes the Dome of the Rock, the cupolas of the Holy Sepulchre, and more recently the Hurva Synagogue—still vie for the skyline, and testify even today to the city's enduring theological polemics and exchanges, and the challenges of translating across them.

The Sultan's Qur'an

Rulers from across the Islamic world, driven by a prayerful reverence for Jerusalem, have endowed the city with layer upon layer of textual treasures. When we visited the al-Aqsa Mosque Islamic Museum in the southeastern corner of the Haram al-Sharif, Ahmed Taha, the curator, removed one of these from its glass case and showed it to us with reverence. The museum, which houses one of the world's most important collections of Islamic heritage, has been closed to the public since 1999. It occupies a building on the southwest corner of the Noble Sanctuary originally constructed by the Knights Templar in the twelfth century and used as a madrassa during the Mamluk era. Sheikh 'Azzam al-Khatib, the director of Jerusalem's Islamic Waqf, had given us rare permission to see its most remarkable manuscripts.

In 1344, Abu al-Hasan al-Marini, Sultan of the Maghrib, copied three manuscripts of the Qur'an on gazelle skin in Maghribi-style kufic script (a calligraphy named after the Iraqi city of Kufa, formerly a capital of the Caliphate). Each volume contains about a hundred folios of five beautifully proportioned lines of calligraphy per page, with ample space for decorations. According to Ibn Khaldun, a young man who lived during the rule of Abu al-Hasan, when the "Black Sultan" (nicknamed for the dark complexion inherited from his Abyssinian mother) finished copying the Qur'an he gathered artists to complete its gilding and illumination, and readers to proofread it.[20] For each set of the Qur'an, he commissioned an exquisite *rab'a* box made of sandalwood, leather, and silver (plate 7). (*Rab'a* is the Arabic term for a multi-volume Qur'an.) Taking great pride in his work, the sultan donated two copies to the mosques in Mecca and Medina. In a letter to the Mamluk sultan of Egypt, Ibn Qalawun, he wrote that he delivered the copy made for the mosque in Medina himself. Qalawun replied that he gave instructions to take special care of it and place it between the Prophet's tomb and the *minbar* (the mosque's pulpit). Despite these precautions, the copies of Mecca and Medina are now lost. The third, and sole surviving, copy, bearing a golden inscription commending it for use for Bayt al-Maqdis, was the one brought out for us to view.

On the other side of the vaulted room, the al-Aqsa Mosque Islamic Museum preserves some of the world's oldest copies of the Qur'an. Several are gifts to the city from patrons. As the eighth-century theologian and mystic al-Hasan al-Basri said, "Whoever gives one dirham in charity in Jerusalem gains his ransom from hellfire, and whoever gives a loaf of bread there is like one who has given [the weight of] the earth's mountains in gold."[21]

One of the manuscripts behind glass was donated by the fourteenth-century princess, patroness, and pilgrim Hajja Ogul Khatun (*Khatun* means "princess" in Turkish), also remembered as the Lady from Baghdad. It is the sole survivor of the multi-volume Qur'an she commissioned. It was placed in a Sufi lodge, or *zāwiyah*, that she built in 1358 near the Iron Gate, on the western side of the Haram al-Sharif. The Khatuniyyah lodge, intended according to its endowment as "a special nurturer of princes and sultans," bears her name and now her grave.

Mystical Languages

Our visits to Jerusalem libraries twice brought us face to face with manuscripts of a masterpiece of Islamic thought called *Ihya' 'Ulum ad-Din* (The Revival of the Sciences of Religion). Its author, Abu Hamid al-Ghazali, a leading eleventh-century theologian of Sunni Islam, wrote part of this magnum opus during his stay in the vaulted rooms above Jerusalem's Gate of Mercy, on the eastern wall of the Old City. Not far from where al-Ghazali wrote it, Radwan Amro showed us a fraying copy of the *Ihya'*. Amro heads the UNESCO-supported manuscript restoration library of the al-Aqsa Mosque, housed in a building of unusual beauty built in 1472 by Sultan Qaitbay along the western edge of the Haram al-Sharif. As he gingerly took the manuscript from its box, a restorer next to him wielded her scalpel on a damaged page resting on a lightbox.[22]

Sura al-Baqara (2:220–21) in the Sultan's handwriting, Rab'a 3, al-Aqsa Mosque
Islamic Museum. (Photo by Frédéric Brenner, 2016; courtesy of the
photographer / Howard Greenberg Gallery.)

A few streets away, just outside the sacred esplanade, we found a sixteenth-century copy of al-Ghazali's book (MS 374/342) in a library belonging to the Budeiri family. This collection of more than eleven
hundred manuscripts, kept in unsightly but fireproof metal cabinets, was
founded more or less at the time of Napoleon's failed invasion of
Palestine in 1799. When its founder, Sheikh Muhammad Budeiri, returned to Jerusalem from three decades of study at al-Azhar University
in Cairo, he used the collection of manuscripts he had amassed as a basis
of a family waqf. It includes six unique manuscripts and eighteen manu-

scripts copied by Sheikh Budeiri himself. The present librarian, Shaima Budeiri, studied manuscript preservation in Dubai. Working with the Hill Museum and Manuscript Library in Minnesota, she has been digitizing the family's manuscripts.

Born in 1058 in Tus, in present-day Iran, al-Ghazali gained renown as a teacher in the Nizamiya College of Baghdad. Yet he began to doubt his own sincerity. In the wake of a profound spiritual crisis, he gave up his wealth, his family, and his prestigious post, and set out on a quest for knowledge. Drawn to Jerusalem, he found lodgings over the Gate of Mercy. Until al-Ghazali's time the lodge was called Naṣiriyyah after the tenth-century Sheikh Nasr al-Tusi; it would henceforth be called

Conservator Samar Nimer, al-Aqsa manuscript restoration lab. (Photo by Frédéric Brenner, 2016; courtesy of the photographer / Howard Greenberg Gallery.)

al-Ghaziliyya in his honor.[23] To free his mind, al-Ghazali would practice ascetic spiritual exercises in solitude. "I busied myself purifying my soul, improving my character and cleansing my heart for the constant recollection of God most high, as I had learnt from my study of mysticism."[24]

During al-Ghazali's stay, Jerusalemites introduced him to an extraordinary practice called the Rajab prayer. Named after the seventh month of the Islamic calendar, this was an all-night ritual of ecstatic repetition: seventy prayers for Muhammad, seventy prostrations, and seventy petitions for forgiveness. More than any other time of the year Rajab is the month of Jerusalem—the month during which the Prophet experienced his night journey and ascension—both events centered in Jerusalem and inscribed on its mosques.[25] It was said that a person who completed the Rajab prayers could save seven hundred relatives from their suffering in the liminal *barzakh*, the Islamic equivalent of purgatory. Rajab also had a personal meaning for al-Ghazali. This was the month of his conversion, in which he abandoned his position and wealth in Baghdad for the contemplative life: "For nearly six months [until] Rajab, 488 (July 1095), I was continuously tossed about between the attractions of worldly desires and the impulses towards eternal life. In that month the matter ceased to be one of choice and became one of compulsion. God caused my tongue to dry up so that I was prevented from lecturing." Inspired perhaps by his stay at the Gate of Mercy, al-Ghazali composed a poetic prayer to the all-merciful God. Its opening lines are:

O Allah, of Grace I ask You its perfection;
and of protection its duration;
and of mercy its completion;
and of health its attainment.[26]

Al-Ghazali's works rapidly spread to Europe in Latin translation; Thomas Aquinas quotes him. But the teacher who was so mesmerized by Jerusalem and its closed gate also retains his hold on Jerusalemites.

In 2013, Mustafa Abu Sway was named the first holder of the al-Ghazali Chair, a joint appointment at al-Aqsa Mosque and al-Quds University in East Jerusalem. The chair is endowed by Jordan's King Abdullah II. Abu Sway, who wrote his dissertation on al-Ghazali at Boston College in 1993, teaches his *Ihya' 'Ulum ad-Din*, which has been continuously taught in Jerusalem since the Middle Ages. He met us at the Ambassador Hotel in East Jerusalem and explained how in this work al-Ghazali reached for something beyond Islamic dogma and law. "In our legally oriented world," he noted, "it is important to reconnect to spirituality." Jerusalem's "Masters of the Heart," as the Sufis are sometimes called, continue to teach al-Ghazali's methods of meditation, repentance, and dreams of mystical union with the divine.

Sura 18 of the Qur'an describes a mysterious encounter between Moses and one of God's servants, a divine messenger often identified with the legendary Khaḍir. Moses has set off on a long journey in search of knowledge when he meets Khaḍir and begs to follow him. Khaḍir warns Moses that he will lose patience: "For how can he have patience about things that his understanding fails to encompass?" (18:67). Yet Moses insists. Along the way, he witnesses Khaḍir drowning a boatful of passengers, slaying an innocent boy who is an unbeliever, and rewarding the inhabitants of a city who had refused them hospitality. Moses challenges Khaḍir about what seems to be his injustice.

Khaḍir reveals to Moses the hidden justifications for each of these apparent injustices. By sinking the boat in the harbor he had saved its passengers from a worse fate. By killing the boy, he had spared his pious parents the grief of his unbelief and would reward them with an affectionate son. What had seemed to be a reward to the city was in fact a means of protecting a treasure from falling into the wrong hands. In this way Khaḍir acquaints Moses with the limits and pretensions of human knowledge.[27]

The celebrated Sufi mystic Ibn 'Arabi, whose travels brought him to Jerusalem in the early thirteenth century, commented on this episode: "For every knowledge there are people suitable for it, and . . . time, circumstances and the various configurations of minds do not allow that knowledge be singled out equally for all."[28] Moses here represents the knowledge of the Law, which is different from divine knowledge. The former is accessible to us, the latter hidden.

In the sura above, Moses tells his servant: "I will not give up until I reach the point where the two rivers meet, though I spend years and years in travel." In one interpretation, the rivers represent the exoteric (*zahir*) and esoteric (*batin*). These may be the only rivers of which the otherwise arid Jerusalem can boast; if so, we might understand the city as situated at the confluence of that which is displayed and that which is hidden, that which is broadcast and that which remains unarticulated.

In mystical literature the elect were those who knew the omnipotent name and could use it to create and demolish. As with the masters of Sufism and Kabbalah, we have here a distinction between the elite and the masses, a distinction that underlies the art of esoteric writing. Truth is reserved for the initiated, for those sufficiently trained to grasp it. Maimonides writes: "I say that it is not fitting for one to stroll in the Orchard [*pardes*] unless his belly is full with bread and meat."[29] Already in the Talmud the Orchard is a symbol of esoteric knowledge. Early medieval Hekhalot literature warns that comprehensive knowledge of the Scriptures and the Law (the revealed knowledge) must precede esoteric knowledge.

Similarly, the Sufi tradition, as we saw earlier, divides knowledge into that which is manifest to human beings (the zahir) and that which is hidden (the batin). The closer a truth's proximity to the inscrutable divine—the more sacred, in other words—the more hidden it is. In both cases, it is not enough to be a devoted and concentrated observer. Spiritual ascent requires *loving* effort. The mystical Hekhalot literature stressed the words of Solomon, the wise king of Jerusalem: "It is the glory of God to conceal a thing" (Prov. 25:2).

One evening we knocked on the imposing gates of the Afghaniyya, a Sufi lodge (*zāwiyah*) just north of the Haram al-Sharif. A four-line inscription in *naskhi* script graced the entrance arch. It included the name of the zāwiyah, the name of the order's founder, and the date of construction, 1633. Members of the order appeared surprised to see us, but they believe that providence brings people to Sufism, and they welcomed us in. The entrance opened onto a broad courtyard flanked with Sufi cells. From the courtyard, we ascended a staircase to reach the mosque, east of the entrance.

A ceremony called *dhikr* (from the Arabic word for "remembrance") was just beginning. A circle of Sufi men, absorbed in trancelike meditation, chanted a liturgical litany, the rhythm quickening until at last they were repeating only the two syllables of God's timeless name, Allah. Sufis are sometimes called wayfarers, after the stations they travel on their spiritual journeys. The ultimate station is union (*ittiḥād*) with the divine, a return to the "Source of Being."

Mystics, like ascetics, naturally attract suspicion. They are often perceived as threats to more conventional authorities. A Sufi sheikh who carries a whole community with him into religious ecstasy represents a sort of leadership that departs from orthodoxies. In some parts of the Islamic world, Sufi practices such as the dhikr are strictly prohibited. Most Salafis view Sufism as plain heresy. Students of the Hanbali school of Islamic jurisprudence were commonly anti-Sufi.[30] But Mujir al-Din, the fifteenth-century Hanbali judge of Jerusalem, makes respectful references to the Sufis of Jerusalem. Visiting the Ashrafiyya madrassa, where sixty Sufi scholars were funded alongside students of law, Mujir al-Din described it as "the third jewel of the Haram."[31]

The esoteric Sufi tradition (*taṣawwuf,* in Arabic) has left its imprint on Jerusalem in the form of lodges, for scholars and pilgrims. Their imaginations seized by the night journey and the ascension, Muhammad's horizontal and vertical journeys, Sufi devotees were passionately drawn to Jerusalem, which they considered the earthly point closest to heaven, and the place that represented the possibility of an unmediated experience of the divine. This was the place where, according to a traditional interpretation of sura 17, the Prophet received his supreme illumination. This was the one place in which Muhammad connected with God without the mediation of the archangel Gabriel. Many believed that the highest form of hajj was one that began from Jerusalem, in accordance with the hadith which says that God forgives the sins of one who begins a hajj from the al-Aqsa Mosque and travels to the Sacred Mosque of Mecca.[32]

Whereas formal prayers would be performed in the Noble Sanctuary, the ceremonial meditations and Sufi rituals would be practiced in the zāwiyah. Many patrician families of Jerusalem established their own zāwiyah, a kind of Sufi salon, which would host the trancelike dhikr. In the thirteenth century, the Monastery of the Cross was converted into a Sufi zāwiyah. During the Ottoman era several zawāyā were founded for non-Arab Muslim pilgrims, including Afghans (al-Qadiriyya), Indians (al-Hindiyya), and Uzbekis and Central Asians (known as al-Naqshabandi-yya). The last, which houses a special collection of books dedicated to

Sufism, was founded by Sheikh Muhammad Baha al-Din al-Bukhari, who settled in Jerusalem in 1616 near the northern edge of the Haram al-Sharif. Today the compound encloses the home and library of the late Sheikh 'Abdul 'Aziz al-Bukhari (until his death in 2010 one of Jerusalem's prominent proponents of nonviolence and interfaith unity), a mosque, and a tiny cemetery.

Around 1200, little more than a decade after the armies of Saladin had vanquished the Crusaders, an Indian Sufi named Bābā Farīd, belonging to the Chisti order, arrived in Jerusalem. There he fasted and wrote poems in his native Punjabi. After his death, a shrine and pilgrim lodge were built, and they stand inside Herod's Gate (Bab al-Zahra, in Arabic) as the Indian Hospice, still graced by an Indian flag.[33]

Over the next three centuries, Sufi groups from across the Islamic world—Morocco, Crimea, Anatolia, Afghanistan, Uzbekistan—put down roots in Jerusalem. In 1670, the Turkish governor of Jerusalem, Jawishzadah Muhammad Pasha, carried out a census. It counted no fewer than seventy Sufi orders represented in the city, including the Kilaniyya, Sa'adiyya, Rifa'iyya, and Mawlawiyya orders.[34] The great seventeenth-century Otto-man traveler Evliya Celebi called Jerusalem the Mecca of the dervishes. Today, several Sufi zawāyā built during the Ottoman period still serve Jerusalem's Sufi communities.[35]

The Sufis have also left a rich textual legacy in this city. The National Library of Israel keeps a manuscript from 1361 called *Qaṣidat al-Burda* (Ode to the Mantle, Yah. Ar. 784). It was composed by the Sufi imam al-Busiri and copied by the Persian calligrapher and lexicographer Muhammad al-Firuzabadi, who lived in Jerusalem from 1358 to 1368. Al-Busiri, half paralyzed by a stroke, had lain in bed one night weeping and praying to God until he fell asleep. Muhammad appeared to him in a dream, wiped his face with his palm, and covered him with his mantle. On waking up miraculously recovered, al-Busiri composed this poem. So rapidly did the poem gain fame that its lines were inscribed on the walls of the mosque in Medina. The library's manuscript of this poem cele-brating a return to life is adorned with flowers and peacocks.

To learn more about the profound ways Jerusalem has seized a place in the Sufi imagination, we consulted Ali Qleibo, an anthropologist at al-Quds University and the author of *Jerusalem in the Heart*. He is descended from an aristocratic Jerusalem family with Sufi roots and occasionally guides tours of Sufi shrines and zawaya. In 1714 his ancestors built the first house outside of the Old City (today on the grounds of the Rockefeller Museum). He claims descent from Tamim al-Dāri, a Christian priest from Palestine who converted to Islam in Medina.

Qleibo, true to his Sufi roots, was one of those Jerusalemites who identified themselves with the city almost to the point of unio mystica: "When I take a walk and stroll downtown, I am aware that I am opening myself up to the archetypal spiritual energy of the Holy City, which rises up and completely fills me, transforming my own energy, so that I at some point incarnate and actually become Jerusalem, overflowing my body boundaries and becoming one with the universal spirituality it exudes."[36] Perhaps the real Jerusalem syndrome does not befall visitors who imagine themselves as Jesus or King David but comes upon longtime lovers of the city who dream of becoming one with it.

In the 1830s, a German Jewish geographer, Joseph Schwartz, described an unusual Jerusalem tomb: "Men and women and children climb to the top of the mountain to prostrate there." By consensus it is the burial place of a female saint, but there is argument over who she is. Since the fifth century, some attribute the grave to the penitent Saint Pelagia, a reformed prostitute and actress who left Antioch in the late fourth century and lived as a hermit in a cave at the Mount of Olives, concealing from the Jerusalemites her identity as a woman. Others since at least the early twelfth century have identified the site as the resting place of the admired eighth-century Sufi teacher Rabi'a al-'Adawiyya. In fact, Rabi'a is buried in Basra, and the renowned fourteenth-century Muslim traveler Ibn Battuta commented on this mistake, which seems to remain firm nonetheless.[37] A Jewish tradition from the fourteenth century ascribed the same tomb to the biblical prophet Hulda (a set of now blocked gates in the southern wall of the Temple Mount bears her name). The tomb, owned by the al-'Alami family, which claims direct descent from Hasan, a grandson of the Prophet Muhammad, continues to attract women worshippers of three faiths.

Rabi'a left Jerusalem a great literary legacy. "It was a woman, Rabi'a al-'Adawiyya . . . , who first expressed the relationship with the divine in a language we have come to recognize as specifically Sufic by referring to God as the Beloved," writes Camille Adams Helminski. "Rabi'a was the first human being to speak of the realities of Sufism with a language that anyone could understand."[38]

Those who walk in the footsteps of the three female saints who share (or do not share) a tomb on the Mount of Olives seem to seek a similar timeless transcendence that extends across the city's barriers of language and faith.

Judeo-Arabic and the Karaites

In the wake of the Arab conquests of the seventh century, a number of schismatic Jewish movements—loosely united by a rejection of the rabbinic monopoly of interpreting the biblical law—consolidated by increments into what became known as the Karaite sect. The Karaites called themselves Ba'alei Ha-Mikra (People of the Scripture); they rejected the rabbinic oral traditions and mystical revelations as a source of legislation.[39] "Nothing outside the Torah itself," they insisted. Long before Martin Luther, they proclaimed *sola scriptura:* the unmediated text more than sufficed—unmediated in that everyone has the right to interpret the Torah without relying on rabbinic authority. Although their own interpretive traditions have much evolved since the Middle Ages, they do not forbid the eating of meat and milk together, do not wear tefillin, and do not require a quorum (minyan) of ten men for prayer. Unlike their rabbinic sisters, Karaite women can serve as witnesses in court, sign marriage contracts, and initiate divorces.

The sage Daniel al-Qumisi, from present-day Iran, led a large Karaite community to Jerusalem in the ninth century. In his *Epistle to the Diaspora,* he urged his fellow Karaites to return to the Holy Land. A fragment of this letter, now at the Bodleian Library (MS. Heb. d. 36/5), urges Karaites in the diaspora to send at least five men from each town to form a nucleus "of the new congregation of Karaites in the Holy City." He criticizes the "fools in Israel that say to each other, 'We need not go to Jerusalem till God will gather us as He has exiled us.'" Besides, he adds, the Muslims of Jerusalem "constantly help the Karaites to keep the Torah of Moses."[40] Under al-Qumisi's leadership the Karaite community further dissociated itself from the mainstream Rabbanites. He strongly opposed astrology and amulets and other "heathenish ways of some Jews," especially the practices of taking vows and making pilgrimages to sages' tombs.[41]

In the second half of the tenth century, a Karaite polemicist living in Jerusalem named Sahl ben Mashah (Arabic names, such as Sahl, were common among the Karaites) described the Karaite settlers in the city. In mourning for Zion and praying for its restoration, he said, "they have abandoned their merchandise and forgotten their families, they have forsaken their native lands and left palaces in order to live in reed huts." He expresses the wish that God would fulfill his promise "to turn the ashes covering the heads of Zion's mourners into an ornament of splendor."[42]

Between the ninth and eleventh centuries, the golden age of Karaism, Karaites belonged to Jerusalem's wealthy strata—prolific theologians and grammarians who left to posterity an entire literature, much of it written in Judeo-Arabic. Foremost among Jerusalem's tenth-century intellectual elite, for example, was a Karaite named Yefet ben 'Ali (or 'Eli, known in Arabic as Abū 'Alī al-Ḥasan ibn 'Alī al-Lāwī al-Baṣrī), who translated the Hebrew Bible into Arabic (accompanied by extended exegesis).[43] The Karaites of Jerusalem rejected the earlier translation of the Bible into Arabic by the Babylonian rabbinic sage Saadia Gaon; they regarded it as too poetic and not literal enough. They preferred Arabic or Hebrew in Arabic letters. Most manuscripts of Yefet's translation have made their way to Saint Petersburg, and of these most can be accessed digitally at the National Library of Israel.

The Karaites in tenth-century Jerusalem considered the psalter their prayer book. In 1861, the Parisian scholar Jean-Joseph Léandre Bargès translated Yefet ben 'Ali's Arabic translation of Psalms into Latin and published it in an Arabic-Latin edition under the title *Kitab al-Zabur, Libri Psalmorum David Regis et Prophetae.* (We came across a copy at Jerusalem's École Biblique, and versions of it are available on the internet.)

Jerusalem's Karaite synagogue, built in the ninth or tenth century, is the city's oldest. Named after the Karaite leader Anan ben David, the synagogue was destroyed in 1099 by the Crusaders, who seized both people and books. From their base in Fustat (Old Cairo) the Karaites sent emissaries to negotiate with King Baldwin I for the ransoming of their holy books and Torah codices. But their synagogue was not rebuilt until after Saladin's conquest in 1187. It was refurbished in the 1860s by Abraham

אַשְׁרֵי הָאִישׁ אֲשֶׁר לֹא

הָלַךְ בַּעֲצַת רְשָׁעִים וּבְדֶרֶךְ חַטָּאִים לֹא

עָמָד וּבְמוֹשַׁב לֵצִים לֹא יָשָׁב׃

טובא אלאנסאן אלדי לם יסלך פי

תדביר אלפסאק ופי טריק אלכטיין

לם יקף וכי מגלס אלסטנזון

לם יגלס

Psalm 1 in Hebrew followed by Yefet ben 'Ali's translation into Judeo-Arabic: "Blessed is the man who walks not in the counsel of the ungodly, nor stands in the path of sinners, nor sits in the seat of the scornful." (Cod. Sim. Jud.-Arab 3, vol. 1, fol. 17, 1855; courtesy of the Royal Danish Library.)

Firkovich, who also bought up most of the Karaite manuscripts found in Jerusalem. Armed with letters of support from the Russian tsar and a firman (royal decree) from the Ottoman sultan, the seventy-six-year-old scholar was allowed to search for manuscripts at the Haram al-Sharif.[44] His extensive purchases saved a great number of Jewish manuscripts from extinction.

During the Jordanians' conquest of East Jerusalem in 1948, the Karaite synagogue was looted and severely damaged. A photograph taken in that period shows squatters in the ruins. Only stone inscriptions remain in the walls. Contemporary Karaite communities in Ramla, Ashdod, Bat Yam, and Beersheba (many with origins in Egypt and Syria) remain determined to preserve their customs. Jerusalem's Karaites today number just a few families; they rarely open their synagogue. But one morning, Rabbi Ovadia Murad, after cautioning that menstruating women could not enter (in accordance with biblical tradition) and instructing us to remove our shoes and wash our hands, ushered us down a long narrow staircase into the carpeted subterranean synagogue. Such was its age that it stood more than a floor below current street level. As he led us underground, Murad quoted a verse from Psalms: "Out of the depths have I cried unto thee, O Lord" (130:1).

Murad, born in Egypt, immigrated to Israel in 1957, after the 1956 Sinai campaign. He showed us a prayer book, a distinct liturgy developed by Aaron ben Joseph Ha-Rofe, known as Aaron the Elder, and what he claimed was an eighth-century deerskin Torah scroll (though scholars doubt that dating). In Murad's view, it was "our brothers the Rabbanites" who deviated from Jewish orthodoxy.

Islam's arrival in Jerusalem added great monuments to the cityscape, most prominently the Dome of the Rock and the al-Aqsa Mosque, but it also brought the Arabic language, which many of the city's Christians and Jews adopted. The language of theology had changed too. Translations of the Bible into Arabic carried out independently by Christians and Jews (both Rabbanites and Karaites) allowed Jerusalemites to talk about God in new ways and to add fresh chapters to the city of the book.

CHAPTER THREE

MEDIEVAL MINGLING

1099 to 1244

Jerusalem's texts disclose a city that sometimes resembles a living tree of cultural exchange, in which one tradition is grafted onto another. At certain periods in its history, Jerusalem has served as a nexus not only of Levantine and Near Eastern cultures but also of Western and Eastern influences. Ninety years of Frankish rule in Jerusalem introduced Romanesque architecture and Gregorian chants as well as Western-style scriptoria where scribes from as far away as Britain copied manuscripts using Latin calligraphy. A great variety of people speaking different languages and dialects from western and northern Europe came to the city as pilgrims or Crusaders.

They were drawn, in part, by the ways the Christian tradition had added its own heft to the imagination of celestial Jerusalem. In Revelation 21, for instance, the author, Saint John, is taken by an angel to see Jerusalem. "Now I saw a new heaven and a new earth, for the first heaven and the first earth had passed away. Also there was no more sea. Then I, John, saw the holy city, New Jerusalem, coming down out of heaven from God, prepared as a bride adorned for her husband." Paul in his letter to the Galatians (4:25) distinguishes earthly Jerusalem, "in slavery with her children," from heavenly Jerusalem, "our mother."

A great many medieval Christians projected their millennial longings onto a spiritualized Jerusalem they had never set eyes on. More than a thousand years after the crucifixion, the city's scriptural sites—Golgotha, the Holy Sepulchre, the Mount of Olives—kept a firm grip on the imagination of Christian Europe.[1] Urged on by a papal appeal in 1095, a few thousand feudal knights, sons of nobility, joined by clergymen, traders, and tens of thousands of peasant volunteers, ventured eastward on one of the most audacious military campaigns in history. The Crusader knights reached Muslim-ruled Jerusalem in 1099, ready to die for Christ in the city in which he died for them. They took David's words (Ps. 79:1) as a rallying cry: "O God, heathens have entered Your domain, defiled Your holy temple." Against all odds, they succeeded. After a five-week siege that summer, the First Crusade ended four centuries of Muslim rule in Jerusalem and liberated the Church of the Holy Sepulchre, built at the time of the first Christian Roman (Byzantine) emperor, Constantine the Great, in the fourth century, on the hill where his mother, Helena, had identified the site of Jesus's tomb.

We have no reason to whitewash the Crusaders or the cruelties they inflicted on the Holy City. Here, for instance, is the twelfth-century chronicler William of Tyre's reflection on the massacre of Muslims and Jews by the Crusaders: "It was impossible to look at the large number of slain without horror; everywhere lay fragments of human bodies, and the very ground was covered with the blood of the slain. It was not alone the spectacle of the headless bodies and mutilated limbs strewn in all directions that roused horror in all who looked upon them. Still more dreadful it was to gaze upon the victors themselves, dripping with blood from head to foot, an ominous sight which brought terror to all who met them."[2] Yet for all its bloodshed, Crusader Jerusalem also ushered in some enduring multicultural mixtures.

After the Crusaders' conquest of Jerusalem, a kingdom was established with its own king and queen, princes, counts, and vassals. Frankish churchmen added a liturgy of liberation to commemorate the return of the earthly Jerusalem to the new Israelites, the Crusaders. They recited the liturgy of the Feast of the Liberation of Jerusalem each year on the anniversary of the capture, July 15. The feast itself included a procession from the Holy Sepulchre to the site of the ruined Temple and back.

In this way, Latin made its way back to Jerusalem seven centuries after Jerome. The Crusaders aimed to translate religious longing into political fact, and heavenly aspiration into earthly victory. When they arrived, Jerusalem was inhabited not only by Muslims and Jews (Karaites and Rabbanites) but also by an astonishing array of native Christians. The pilgrim John of Würzburg's account from Jerusalem sixty-five years later lists twenty-one Christian groups, including Greeks, Latins, Germans, Georgians, Armenians, and Egyptians (Copts), "and many others whom it would take too long to count."[3]

The *Typikon of the Anastasis,* a Greek liturgical manuscript for the Church of the Holy Sepulchre dated 1122 (from the collection of the Monastery of the Holy Cross at the Greek Orthodox manuscript library, catalogued as Stavros 43), advocates the translation of homilies into Arabic, "so that those who do not know how to read Greek may be comforted, and that all the people may have joy, exultation, and merriment, both the small and the great."[4] At about the same time, Fulcher of Chartres, a chronicler of the First Crusade who stayed on in Jerusalem, described life there as a kind of miracle of cultural cross-fertilization:

> Consider, I pray, and reflect how in our time God has transformed the Occident into the Orient. For we who were Occidentals have now become Orientals. He who was a Roman or a Frank has in this land been made into a Galilean or a Palestinian. He who was of Rheims or Chartres has now become a citizen of Tyre or Antioch. We have already forgotten the places of our birth; already these are unknown to many of us or not mentioned any more. . . .
>
> People use the eloquence and idioms of diverse languages in conversing back and forth. Words of different languages have become common property known to each nationality, and mutual faith unites those who are ignorant of their descent. Indeed it is written, "The lion and the ox shall eat straw together" [Isa. 62:25]. He who was born a stranger is now as one born here; he who was born an alien has become as a native. . . .
>
> Therefore why should one return to the Occident who has found the Orient like this?[5]

To glimpse the mingling of Occident and Orient in this city, we need look no farther than a manuscript commissioned for the only woman to rule Jerusalem in her own right.

Queen Melisende's Psalter

The exquisitely illuminated Melisende Psalter—itself a blend of Eastern and Western styles—was created in the twelfth century at the scriptorium of the Holy Sepulchre. Along with other surviving manuscripts created in this workshop, it bears witness to what had become a deep cultural interchange, a unique Jerusalemite synthesis of Byzantine art and Latin liturgy. Queen Melisende's monarchy helped bring the Orient into the European consciousness, and vice versa. A luxurious gift commissioned for Queen Melisende by her husband and co-regent, King Fulk, the psalter features beautifully carved ivory covers decorated with Byzantine iconography, while miniatures embroider the Latin text. Examining the miniatures decorating her psalter, the art historian Jaroslav Folda remarked on the "obvious ties to the Byzantine artistic tradition, a visual language that Melisende, raised in the Greek Orthodox Church and a woman of deep piety, would especially appreciate."[6] In her day, the Psalms were often copied out separately from the rest of the Bible, preceded by a calendar of feast days. This psalter was the queen's most intimate possession; its calendar marks, among other dates, those of the deaths of her parents. Jerusalem receives a special place, its liberation day marked on July 15.

Today this testament to Jerusalem's confluence of cultures is housed in the British Library, its original ivory covers still intact. For 350 pounds sterling, the British Museum bought it in 1845 from the London antiquarian booksellers Payne & Foss, who purchased it for 180 pounds from an Italian aristocrat and bibliophile, who got it from the director of the Palais-des-Arts in Lyons, who in turn acquired it from the monastery of Grande Chartreuse in the mountains above Grenoble. Nobody knows how it got there from Jerusalem.

The woman who gave the manuscript its name was born in the Frankish colony of Edessa (modern-day Urfa, Turkey) in 1105. At age thirteen, Melisende came to Jerusalem with her French father, Baldwin II, recently chosen as king of the city and the young kingdom. Her Armenian mother, Morfia, had borne four daughters, one of whom became a powerful abbess outside Jerusalem, while the two others married royals from Antioch and Tripoli, the realms surrounding the kingdom of Jerusalem. Melisende, the eldest, had the most prestigious dowry to offer: the throne of the kingdom of Jerusalem.

Melisende was brought up in Jerusalem as the heir to her father. He chose for her a distinguished French husband, Count Fulk of Anjou. When Baldwin II died in 1131, Melisende and her husband were jointly crowned. In 1143, after Fulk's death in a riding accident, Melisende had her second double coronation at the Church of the Holy Sepulchre, this time beside her thirteen-year-old son Baldwin III. As long as her son remained a minor, the queen exercised sole rule by hereditary right. The greatest theologian of the day, Bernard of Clairvaux, wrote to her from France: "On you alone the whole burden of the kingdom will rest. You must set your hand to great things and, although a woman, you must act as a man."[7] Ten years later he wrote to her again, describing her as "a strong woman, a humble widow, a great queen."[8]

Melisende proved equal to the task. She "was a woman of great wisdom who had had much experience in all kinds of secular matters. She had risen [so] far above the normal status of women that she dared to undertake important measures. It was her ambition," wrote William of Tyre, "to emulate the magnificence of the greatest and noblest princes and to show herself in no wise inferior to them."[9] Numerous iconographic representations of her are included in illuminated copies of William of Tyre's *History*. After Melisende's second coronation, William described her as "a queen beloved of God."[10]

William's masterful twenty-three-book history of the Latin kingdom of Jerusalem became the major early source not just for our knowledge of Melisende but for Western histories of the Crusades.[11] Born to a family that had settled in Frankish Syria, William knew French, Latin, Greek, and some Arabic. In Jerusalem, he served as tutor to Baldwin, son of King Amalric I. When Baldwin succeeded to the throne as Baldwin IV in 1174, he appointed William chancellor of the kingdom and then archbishop of Tyre. William's history is a testimony to a deteriorating kingdom, in which he compared the Jerusalem of his time, sinful, immoral, and weak, to that of its glorious past, embodied by Queen Melisende.

With her dual heritage, Melisende bridged the Frankish Latin culture and the Eastern Christians of Byzantium and Greater Armenia. She renovated the nunnery of Saint Lazarus in Bethany, a gift to her sister Yveta, whom she made the mother superior. William of Tyre records that she endowed the nunnery property and made many gifts of

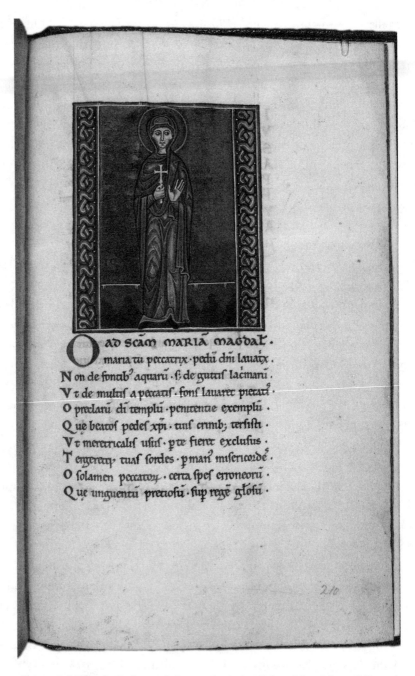

O ad scām maria magdał.
maria tu peccatrix · pedū dīn lauatx ·
Non de fontib’ aquarū · ſ; de guttiſ lacmarū ·
Vt de multiſ a peccatiſ · fonſ lauaret pietatī ·
O preclarū dī templū · penitentie exemplū ·
Que beatoſ pedeſ xp̄i · tuiſ crimb; terſiſti ·
Vt meretricaliſ uſuſ · p̄ te fieret excluſus ·
Tergterctx tuaſ ſordes · p mati miſericorde ·
O ſolamen peccatorx · certa ſpeſ erroneorū ·
Que unguentū pretioſū · ſup rege gloſū ·

chalices, ornaments, "sacred vessels of gold and silver adorned with gems," and books.[12]

But Melisende's true project was Jerusalem itself, and much of her work is still visible. She built covered streets, connecting a spice market with the money changers' square, completed the restoration of the Church of the Holy Sepulchre, and endowed the embellishment of the Dome of the Rock as it was converted into a church. Saint Anne's church, which she sponsored and possibly rebuilt, is still renowned for its astonishing acoustics.[13] The entrance of the Syriac church of Saint Mark shares the same gadrooned arches as Saint Anne's and the facade of the Holy Sepulchre. The Armenian cathedral church of Saint James is today identified as another church she sponsored.[14] And she oversaw the development of religious-military orders such as the Hospitallers and Templars.[15]

Melisende also prepared her city for the jubilee year of its liberation, celebrated in sumptuous style on July 15, 1149. In consolidating the Latin church in Jerusalem, she cultivated relationships with eastern Christian communities, including the Armenians, Syrians, and Georgians. Traveling her kingdom from Tyre (in modern-day Lebanon) to Jaffa on the Mediterranean coast, she dispensed royal favors, issued charters, and concluded treaties. And at a time when Byzantine, Islamic, and European artistic traditions began to mingle, she made herself a patron of the arts.

When Melisende died, at age fifty-one, she was buried beside Mary's tomb at the foot of the Mount of Olives. William of Tyre noted that her much-tested rule "had been wise and judicious." Two decades later, in the wake of the disastrous Second Crusade, Saladin was at the city gates. The Christian rule of Jerusalem had endured fewer than ninety years.

Stolen Illuminations

In our quest to photograph one of Jerusalem's finest Armenian manuscripts, we applied to His Beatitude Nourhan Manougian, elected in 2013 as the ninety-seventh Armenian patriarch of Jerusalem; he granted us an audience in his private chambers. In part we sought his permission to allow photography, but our conversation turned from his hopes for his community in Jerusalem to the imminent threats to his family. Manougian was born in Aleppo, where his family was still trapped in the ongoing clashes between Syrian president Bashar al-Assad's army, Russian bombers, and Islamic State militants.

On the appointed day, Father Shrork Paloyan invited us in silence into the church of Saint Toros, hidden in the recesses of the Armenian Quarter. With its nearly four thousand manuscripts, the Armenian manuscript library housed there is the most extensive of all the libraries in Jerusalem's Old City. Built in the thirteenth century in memory of Prince Toros (Armenian for "Theodore"), the church was restored and given its present form in the first half of the eighteenth century.[16] In 1897, the Patriarchate adapted it to host the manuscript collection.[17] It opens to worshippers only once a year, on the Feast of Saint Theodore the Warrior, the first weekend of Lent. The church has no electricity; on the rare occasions a scholar receives permission to consult a manuscript, Father Shrork stretches a long extension cord from a nearby house.

The treasure we had been allowed to see that day, manuscript 2555, is a stunning Gospel on parchment, decorated with fantastical birds, peacocks and others, which begins with a vividly colored page of the genealogy of Jesus.[18] All we know for certain about it is that it was created by a priest named Krikor (Gregory) and donated to the Patriarchate in 1872. Norayr Bogharian, the editor of the library's eleven-volume catalogue, classified it as a tenth-century manuscript. An Armenian scholar at Columbia University, Krikor Maksoudian, believes that it dates to the eighth century. If he is right, this would be the oldest illuminated codex in Jerusalem (see plate 2).

The Saint Toros library also houses Cilician illuminated manuscripts from the golden age of Armenian book production (the twelfth through fourteenth centuries). Three of them have signed illuminations by the most celebrated medieval Armenian artist, Toros Roslin, whom Kevork (George) Hintlian described as "an extraordinary master of motion and gesture," who "can be considered, by all standards, the greatest of his age." The Armenian art historian Sirarpie Der Nersessian noted "the compositional design, the delicate modeling of the individual figures, and the subtle color harmonies" that show Roslin's work at its best, "equaling in artistic quality some of the finest Byzantine miniatures."[19] Pious Christians have long criticized the ostentatious ornamentation of books. As Saint Jerome

Nourhan Manougian, the ninety-seventh Armenian patriarch of Jerusalem, in Saint James Cathedral. (Photo by Frédéric Brenner, 2016; courtesy of the photographer / Howard Greenberg Gallery.)

complained, "Parchments are dyed purple, gold is melted into lettering, manuscripts are decked with jewels, while Christ lies at the door naked and dying."[20] Yet in the collection kept by the Armenians of Jerusalem, texts are unabashedly treated as treasures: encased between gold-work covers studded with precious stones.

For less valuable texts, the Armenian Quarter houses a second, more accessible library. The Gulbenkian Library, named after its benefactor, the oil baron and philanthropist Calouste Gulbenkian, opened in 1932. It contains Armenian incunabula dating from 1512 to 1850, and newspapers from the eighteenth to the early twentieth century, including unique newspapers in Armeno-Turkish.

Yet some of Jerusalem's Armenian manuscripts are so precious that even the Saint Toros library is not deemed sufficiently secure. These reside, along with priceless reliquaries and gifts offered by pilgrims over the past thousand years, in the carefully guarded Treasury. Here there is no reading room, no online catalogue, no visiting hours. The patriarch had told us that the Armenian treasures were not entrusted to any single person. Three keys—held by two senior members of the clergy and a lay representative—were needed to enter the Treasury. Today it is almost impossible to arrange access to the Treasury, let alone steal from it.

On our visit that day, an archbishop unfurled one of the Treasury's manuscripts for us in a blue-tiled chapel next to the Saint James Cathedral. It is a thirty-foot-long illuminated firman signed by Saladin in 1187 granting the Armenians the right to stay in Jerusalem. Experts tell us that this firman dates to the Mamluk period (1250–1517); it is perhaps a copy made from the original for safekeeping.[21] Armenians, like other eastern and oriental Christians, continued to live in Jerusalem under Muslim rule. The Ethiopian and Georgian communities, in particular, flourished under Mamluk rule.

In 1910, two leaves were torn from the Treasury's most stunning manuscript and one of the most beautiful products of the golden age of Armenian manuscript illumination: the Queen Keran Gospel (Arm. Patr. MS 2563). The Gospel, completed in Cilicia in 1272, was bound in Jerusalem in 1727 in gold repoussé work by the monks of Saint James, the cathedral at the heart of the Armenian Quarter. According to the colophon, the illuminations—13 full-page illustrations of the life of Christ and 103 miniatures—were entrusted to "a man skilled and honored in the art of the scribes." One of the last leaves depicts the Armenian queen Keran, her husband Levon II, and several of their sixteen children kneeling in front of the Deisis (Christ with the Virgin Mary and John the Baptist). The illustrations, the oldest-known portraits of the Armenian royal family in the world, are the work of Toros Roslin. Jerusalem is home to the largest number of his works in the world.

One of the pages stolen in 1910 portrays Saint Mark the evangelist; the other depicts Christ's ascension. The Armenians of Jerusalem felt a profound urge to make the book whole again. Vrej Nersessian, the former curator of the Armenian Collections in the British Library, noted that Armenian scribes "placed a moral obligation on future generations to recover manuscripts carried off as booty, by ransom or other means. Captured manuscripts were never referred to as booty, but rather, like human beings, they were either carried off into captivity or they were rescued or purchased from captivity."[22]

The rescue would come from a most unexpected direction.

Although the thief has never been identified, the missing pages of the Queen Keran Gospel resurfaced in the collection of an antiquities collector and smuggler named Michel van Rijn. In 1988, a Greek shipping magnate, Thanassis Martinos, bought Rijn's collection, including the two stolen leaves. In May 2011, Timothy Bolton, the medieval manuscript expert at Sotheby's London, asked Vrej Nersessian for an expert opinion on the provenance of the two miniatures. Nersessian reported his findings:

> The numberings still in place at the back of the two leaves (folio 115v and folio 284v) leave no doubt in my mind that these two miniatures once belonged to the magnificent Armenian manuscript of the four Gospels in the collection of the Armenian Patriarchate of St. James, Jerusalem, as MS. 2563 called the Queen Keran Gospels. The two miniatures in your collection belong to the Queen Keran Gospels, copied by the scribe Avetis and illuminated by the celebrated artist Toros Roslin in 1272 AD in Sis, the capital city of the Armenian Kingdom of Cilicia. . . . On behalf of the Armenian people and the Brotherhood of St. James, Jerusalem, we will forever be grateful for the return of these two leaves "back to its place."[23]

In late 2011, Martinos returned the two pages to the Jerusalem Patriarchate where he felt they belonged and where future generations could take pleasure in them. Given the centuries-long bitter rivalry between Jerusalem's Armenians and Greeks, this gesture of return was no simple action.

"The first time I saw her [the Queen Keran Gospel]," the Jerusalem-born Armenian journalist Arthur Hagopian wrote that year, "I could not even bring myself to touch her with my own hands. She looked so ineffably fragile and sacrosanct, I was terrified I would be committing a sacrilege. I could only gaze at her in wonder—an 800 year old masterpiece I had been one of the privileged few to have seen or examined close up."[24]

To steal a book is to imperil the wisdom it contains, so it comes as no surprise that in religious terms such theft is considered a sin. Maimonides once commented on the ethics of buying stolen books. "It is forbidden to buy a stolen object from a thief, and it is a serious sin, for [the buyer] thereby abets the wrongdoer and causes him to steal in the future. For if he can't find anyone to buy, he won't steal. And of this it is said, 'Whoever shares with the thief hates his own soul' [Prov. 29:24]."[25] If possible, Maimonides explained, stolen books must be ransomed as though they were human captives and returned to the original owners.

One frequently encounters in Jerusalem's libraries the language of ransom and redemption.

When Jerusalem's Karaite synagogue was plundered during the First Crusade, the most important Jewish biblical codex—known as the Aleppo Codex, or the Crown of Aleppo—was held ransom along with other priceless manuscripts. A letter in Judeo-Arabic found in the Cairo Genizah (the most remarkable repository of Jewish manuscripts ever discovered) remarks that money borrowed from Alexandria was used to "buy back two hundred and thirty Bible codices, a hundred other volumes, and eight Torah Scrolls."[26] After the high ransom was paid, the codex was transferred to the Rabbanite synagogue in Fustat (Old Cairo), where it was consulted by Maimonides.

When the Queen Keran Gospels was made whole again, Verj Nersessian expressed his wonder in similar tones: "After 35 years of curatorship in the British Library in charge of the Armenian collections, I have saved from 'captivity' 114 manuscripts. My last and final act in the li-

PLATE 1. Armenian manuscript library inside the church of Saint Toros.

PLATE 2. Gospel on parchment, Armenian Patriarchate Ms. 2555.

PLATE 3. Greek Orthodox manuscript library with H. B. Theophilos III (left) and Archbishop Aristarchos, director of the library and general secretary.

PLATE 4. Book of Psalms, 13th century, Psalm 50 (51), Greek Orthodox
manuscript library (Taphos 51), fol. 108v.

PLATE 5. Jerusalem's "bird mosaic," 5th–6th century.

PLATE 6. Mar Saba in the Judean desert south of Jerusalem.

PLATE 7. Rabʻa, Qurʾan box, gift of Sultan Abu al-Hasan al-Marini of the Maghrib, 1344, al-Aqsa Mosque Islamic Museum.

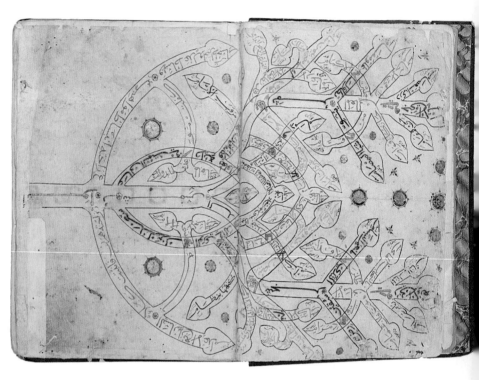

PLATE 8. A manuscript at the Khalidi Library of the Andalusian Sufi poet ʿAbd al-Munʿim Ibn ʿUmar Ibn Hassan al-Ghassani al-Andalusi al-Jeliany (Ms. 1631).

PLATE 9. Conrad Schick's model of the Haram al-Sharif, first displayed at the
Ottoman Empire pavilion at the Vienna World's Fair, 1873.

PLATE 10. Stephan Illes's model of Jerusalem, first displayed at the Ottoman
Empire pavilion at the Vienna World's Fair, 1873.

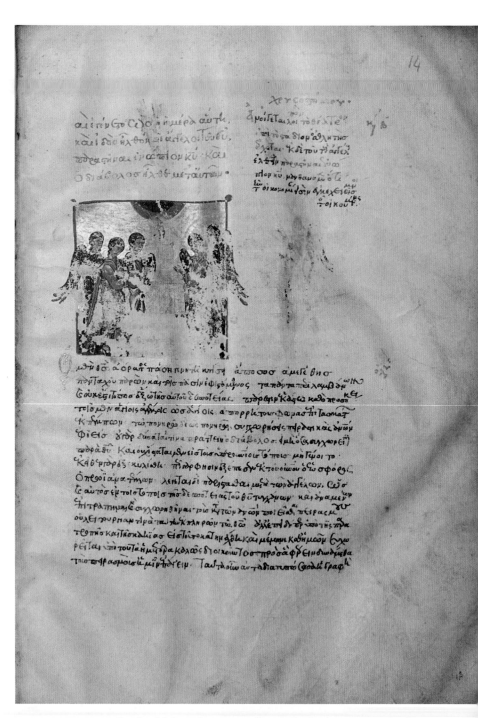

PLATE II. Book of Job, 13th century, Greek Orthodox manuscript library
(Taphos 5).

brary was negotiating and facilitating the return of these two miniatures to the Armenian people in my capacity as Curator in Charge of the Armenian Section in the British Library. I left the library on August 31, 2011, and I could not dream of a more befitting gift than the return of these two leaves to Jerusalem."[27]

In one colophon of an Armenian manuscript, the scribe writes: "I have saved from captivity this precious garden, this fragrant orchard, this pure and shining book in memory of myself and of my parents, my wife, and my children." To rescue books from captivity and bring them back home for the sake of one's own memory or a neighbor's is perhaps a quintessentially Jerusalem act of mercy, a theme to which we shall return in our epilogue.

In the meantime, we suggest that to gauge the distance between theft and return is to measure the poles on which the axis of the history of the book in Jerusalem spins.

Jerusalem's librarians fear both material loss and the destruction of memory, and for good reason. In this sense, a library may be a consolation in exile, a portable homeland. As the exiled Prospero wistfully says in Shakespeare's *The Tempest*, "My library / Was dukedom large enough." A library may serve as a mark of trust in the survival of the word even as men and women perish.

Each year on April 24, Armenians commemorate the genocide. On that day in 1915, 250 Armenian intellectuals and leaders were arrested in Istanbul, and later executed. Over the next three years, more than a million and a half Armenians were massacred by the Ottoman Turks while the world stood silent ("Who, after all," Hitler is reported to have asked two decades later, "speaks today of the annihilation of the Armenians?"). Thousands of refugees were taken in by the Patriarchate in Jerusalem. They entered the monastery and were given rooms or entire apartments. A school was built for the children as well as a health care center, which still today provides free consultation. The monastery was thus turned into a residential area. Many of the residents of Jerusalem's Armenian Quarter today are descendants of the refugees. Having served for centuries as a hospice for pilgrims, the monastery became a refuge for the dispossessed, and the small Armenian community of Jerusalem grew from 1,500 to 5,000 people. Today it numbers about 2,500 in Jerusalem. The

Armenians are anything but foreigners there; they have been part of the city fabric since the fourth century.[28]

Seven and a half centuries before the violence of the First World War, the Armenian Quarter had also served as a refuge, for people and books alike. The Arabic work *The Churches and Monasteries of Egypt*, attributed to Abu Salih al-Armani, records a journey that took place in 1172 when Saladin and his troops invaded Egypt. The Armenians, fearing for their lives and the fate of their books, escaped to the Latin Kingdom of Jerusalem: "On account of ruin brought upon the Armenians by the Ghuzz [Turks] and the Kurds, their patriarch left Egypt and departed to Jerusalem. He took with him seventy-five sacred books, among which was a copy of the Four Gospels with illuminations in colors and gold, repre-senting the miracles of Christ, to whom be glory!"[29]

The textual treasures in Jerusalem, as Krikor Maksoudian told us, also encode a more recent and more fearful history. Maksoudian was born in 1941 in Beirut. His family originated in Adana, the site in southern Turkey of a massacre in 1909, a rehearsal for worse to come. For a year and a half, before he was forced to leave by the 1948 war, his father lived in Jerusalem. Maksoudian earned a doctorate in Armenian studies and Byzantine his-tory from Columbia University, where he taught for many years. For his doctoral dissertation he worked on translations of a tenth-century Armenian author, six of whose manuscripts are in the Jerusalem library.

Maksoudian recounted that during the Armenian genocide, refugees and high-ranking clergy brought their most precious manuscripts with them, swelling the manuscript library in Jerusalem from some eighteen hundred to four thousand manuscripts, in the years during and after World War I. Bishop Papken Guleserian, for example, later the Catholicos in Lebanon, rescued manuscripts from Aleppo and brought them to Jerusalem for safekeeping. Among Jerusalem's guardians of memory, the fear of loss remains acute.

Frederick II, Emperor of Peace

Just after the Franks surrendered Jerusalem to Saladin in 1187, they sent envoys calling for a new crusade. To support their initiative the pope added a prayer to the daily mass, *Clamor pro Terra Sancta*, "A Cry for the

Holy Land," thereby adding Catholic lamentations to the city's liturgical cacophony.[30] (What other city has liturgies written to celebrate its liberation and mourn its destruction?)

This cry was heard and to some small degree answered. Further crusades were launched in the attempt to regain Jerusalem. Only with the arrival of Frederick II, the Holy Roman Emperor, would Frankish rule in Jerusalem—and its capacity for cultural exchange—once more briefly reassert itself. In 1229, following the signing of the Treaty of Jaffa by Frederick and Ayyubid Sultan al-Kamil, Jerusalem passed without bloodshed into the hands of the Franks, who would govern it for the next fifteen years. Frederick achieved by diplomacy what no other Christian ruler had managed by force since 1099: the liberation of Jerusalem. He wrote to al-Kamil: "The Muslims have destroyed it [Jerusalem]; therefore for them it has no economic significance. If the Sultan, may God strengthen him, could decide to confer on me the capital of the land with the right to visit the other holy places, this would show his wisdom and I would raise my head among other kings."[31] True, the city's walls were in ruins and its streets largely abandoned. The terms of the treaty did not allow Frederick to rebuild its defenses, and Muslims remained in control of the Dome of the Rock, the al-Aqsa Mosque, and the rest of the sacred esplanade. Pope Gregory IX, who had earlier excommunicated Frederick for his refusal to participate in the Fifth Crusade, viewed the treaty as a setback for Christendom.

Al-Kamil, facing similar criticism from Muslims for handing over the city, issued a justification: "We have only conceded to them some churches and some ruined houses. The sacred precincts, the venerated Rock and all the other sanctuaries to which we make our pilgrimages remain ours as they were; Muslim rites continue to flourish as they did before, and the Muslims have their own governor of the rural provinces and districts."[32]

Shortly after concluding the treaty, the emperor visited Jerusalem, accompanied by the *qadi* (magistrate) of Nablus. On his first morning, Frederick complained about not hearing the call for prayers. "This humble slave prevented them," the qadi said, "out of regard and respect for Your Majesty." "My chief aim in passing the night in Jerusalem," the emperor replied, "was to hear the call to prayer given by the muezzins, and their cries of praise to God during the night."[33]

Visiting the Dome of the Rock, the emperor had his own brush with the polemics of the place. He noticed an inscription dated A.H. 27 Rajab 585 (October 2, 1187): "Saladin purified this city of polytheists" (a reference to Christians). Having grown up with Arabs in Sicily, Frederick read Arabic quite well. Bemused, he asked who these "polytheists" might be.[34] Finally, at the Holy Sepulchre, Frederick approached the altar and placed the Crown of Jerusalem on his own head in a gesture of self-coronation (perhaps imagining himself as a new King David).[35]

Frederick II's Jerusalem flourished long enough to renew the scriptorium of the Holy Sepulchre. It was there that great masters produced the beautiful Riccardiana Psalter (now in the Biblioteca Riccardiana in Florence). Its lavish beauty suggests that Frederick commissioned the masterpiece himself, probably for his third wife, Isabella, sister of the king of England. The initials beginning major divisions of the psalter are sumptuously decorated with scenes from the life of Christ. One folio features an image of Templum Domini (Latin for the Hebrew phrase "Temple of the Lord"). With its Western layout and Byzantine, perhaps Sicilian, iconography, it too represents a mixing of traditions.[36] The Latin translations in Western calligraphy graced by miniatures depicting events in Jerusalem in the Byzantine style of the Riccardiana and Melisende Psalters highlight an underappreciated feature of medieval Jerusalem: a hybridity of East and West.[37]

After the conquest of 1244, Jerusalem remained in Muslim hands until 1917. In the intervening centuries, Jerusalem acted for Christendom as "the goal and goad of European longing," as the Catholic author James Carroll writes, a defining point of reference, and the intersection, in medieval Christian cartography, of Europe, Asia, and Africa.

Yet the Frankish influence persisted in Jerusalem's polyglot cityscape long after Frederick's death. In the late fifteenth century, a pilgrim named Arnold von Harff composed an Arabic-Frankish lexicon, using the local French dialect of the Latin East written in Coptic letters; to this lexicon he later added Hebrew.[38]

In time, much like Palestinian Aramaic before it, Frankish faded from the streets of Jerusalem as a spoken language. For the city's Muslims, as for many of its Christians and Jews, Arabic regained its former dominance.

Custodians of the Holy Land

For centuries, the Catholic presence in Jerusalem was limited to the Order of Friars Minor, better known as the Franciscans. The order took its name from Francis of Assisi, who in 1219 joined the Fifth Crusade heading for Jerusalem. The *cordati*, or "Brothers of the Cord," as they were called, were formally recognized in 1333 as the representatives of the Catholic Church in Jerusalem, and in 1342 Pope Clement VI placed in their hands the Custody of the Holy Land (Custodia Terrae Sanctae).

On our visits to the Library of the Franciscan Custody of the Holy Land, we found that the history of the Franciscans' presence in the Holy Land was materially consigned to us in the form of more than five hundred manuscripts dating from the eleventh century to the present day. The library contains, for example, a collection of medical books which served the Franciscan Pilgrim Hospital and were used by the monks to treat the sick, including non-Christian inhabitants of Jerusalem, from as early as 1335.[39] The oldest collections came from the library of the convent of Mount Zion, from which the Franciscans were expelled in 1551. (The historian Michele Campopiano has found manuscripts that were once at the library of Mount Zion dispersed in libraries in Pisa and The Hague, the Bibliotheca Augusta in Lower Saxony, and Versailles.)[40] Over the next decade, the library was moved to the Franciscan Convent of San Salvatore at the northwest corner of the Old City, where it remains today.

Jerusalem friars compiled guidebooks for pilgrims which described local Christian customs and beliefs. A compilation now in Versailles, for example, ends with a scribal note: "Here terminates a very useful booklet on the heresies and the lies of the Greeks, written on the 20th of April 1346. Transcribed by me in Mount Zion, 1471, 24 January." Jerusalem's Franciscans have accumulated since then dictionaries of theology, liturgy, archaeology, Holy Scripture, canon law, ecclesiastical history, and geography; court verdicts, bills of sale, and titles of ownership; papal bulls from the thirteenth century to the present; incunabula from 1472 to 1500; and eight thousand letters in Arabic exchanged between the Vatican and Islamic rulers of the Holy Land since the year 1290.[41]

Separate from the library, the Franciscan archive houses more than eight hundred feet of folders. Father Sergey Loktionov showed us a 1230 papal bull, examples of firmans issued by Ottoman sultans, and a 1671 *Biblia Sacra Arabica,* the first Vatican translation of the Scriptures into Arabic, with woodcut headings and Arabic text and Latin Vulgate text in parallel columns. He also brought out books Franciscans rescued from a synagogue that had been destroyed during the war of 1948. The archive also holds a firman signed in 1309 by the Mamluk sultan Baybars II recognizing the Franciscan friars' rights as custodians of Christian holy sites in Jerusalem. In 1333, following the intervention of Robert of Anjou, the king of Naples, the Mamluk sultan al-Nasir Muhammad granted Franciscans the right to keep a presence in the Church of the Holy Sepulchre.

We came across "Itineraria ad loca sancta," accounts of journeys to the Holy Places from the fifteenth to eighteenth centuries. While the archive's primary goal was to keep all official documents that could be useful at future disputes, the library was established to serve pilgrims and guide them both physically and spiritually. A medieval pilgrim could find at Mount Zion useful guidebooks by Burchard of Mount Zion, historical excerpts by Jacques de Vitry, and even Bede's *Ecclesiastical History of the English Nation.* Jerusalem guidebooks written by pilgrims mixed practical advice with religious reflection. A Christian pilgrim named John Phocas, writing in 1185, remarks that he hopes his account will benefit others, but if not it may "remind me of those Holy Places, so that I may be sweetly refreshed in imagination by the remembrance of them."

Such books were sometimes written by people who had never seen Jerusalem. In the thirteenth century, for instance, a Benedictine monk in Saint Albans, England, named Matthew Paris drew a seven-page map charting the itinerary from London to Jerusalem accompanied by detailed descriptions in Anglo-French. He himself had never left the shores of England; neither did many of his readers, but they loved imagining this journey and read stories about the Crusades and their ancestors' journeys, real or imagined, to Jerusalem.

In June 2015, we visited an exhibition mounted by the library of Saint Savior's Monastery. It featured books rescued from the Franciscan Monastery of Aleppo, including a sixteenth-century edition of works by Thomas Aquinas, and, aptly, *A Journey from Aleppo to Jerusalem* (1732) by an Oxford don named Henry Maundrell, who made the trip in 1697. Also on display: a manuscript gifted to the Franciscans in Jerusalem by the future King Henry IV of England in 1392–1393. Fittingly, it is an antiphonary, a liturgy for two voices responding to one another.

Another manuscript at the library exemplifies the city's linguistic heterogeneity: a fourteenth-century Latin translation of medical treatises by Abu Bakr Muhammad Ibn Zakariya al-Razi, a medieval Persian scientist. This is an encounter in the form of translation, which recasts Arabic into Latin. It is commonly known as *Liber Almansoris,* from the name of al-Razi's patron, Manṣur ibn Isḥaq al-Samani. It is a large in-folio manuscript from the end of the thirteenth century, with the Latin translation of the Arabic work, decorated with beautiful miniatures in red and blue. It was used by the Franciscan doctors and nurses of Mount Zion.

The order founded by Saint Francis has enjoyed a continuous presence in Jerusalem since the fourteenth century, and the Franciscans continue to serve as "custodians" of the Holy Land. But as we had discovered, the Custodia Terrae Sanctae also guarded a patrimony of Jerusalem's unlikely textual juxtapositions.

CHAPTER FOUR

FROM MAMLUK PATRONAGE TO OTTOMAN OCCUPATION

The Thirteenth to the Nineteenth Century

Some of the Jews expelled from Spain in 1492 brought their literary riches to Jerusalem. Although Jews remained a marginal presence during the Mamluk period, an extraordinary number of Jewish manuscripts are known to have been produced and copied in Jerusalem in the sixteenth century. This flourishing was aided by a remarkable edict issued in 1508 by the head of the Jewish community in Egypt: given the unique blessing books conferred on the city, he prohibited the removal of any manuscripts from Jerusalem.[1]

The trail of manuscripts from Mamluk and Ottoman Jerusalem led us ineluctably to the private library of the scholar and manuscript collector Meir Benayahu. Benayahu was the son of Yitzhak Nissim, who served as chief Sephardic rabbi from 1955 to 1972. (He adopted his middle name as a family name.) A prolific author of thirty-two books and countless articles, Benayahu pioneered the investigation into the fates of manuscripts of the Sephardic community in Jerusalem. He painstakingly searched for the remaining books in old synagogues and bought them from families who had lost interest in them. He used to escort his father on his journeys abroad and buy manuscripts. In the 1950s, along with President Yitzhak Ben-Zvi, Benayahu founded the Institute for the Research of Jewish Communities in the Middle East (now the Ben-Zvi Institute), where he served as academic director. "The man lived as much in the sixteenth and seventeenth centuries as he did in the twentieth and twenty-first," the historian Matt Goldish writes. "His unique and instantly recognizable prose style reads more like elegant early modern rabbinic composition than modern Israeli Hebrew."[2]

One afternoon we met with Meir Benayahu's son, Hanan Benayahu. He was accompanied by his friend Moshe Hillel, a young expert in Hebrew manuscripts and the son of Rabbi Yaakov Hillel (an Indian-born Kabbalist of distinguished Iraqi lineage who himself amassed a private collection of some five thousand manuscripts). Both sons inherited their passion for manuscripts from their distinguished fathers, who were also friends, and whose manuscript libraries are still surrounded by a veil of mystery.

Hanan Benayahu showed us a small manuscript from his father's collection. Its pages are thin and unnumbered, and its faded letters fill the pages almost to the side margins. The top line of each page nearly touches the edge of the page, but the author left wide margins at the bottom. Perhaps he had intended to add commentary at some later date. Drawings and diagrams punctuate the pages.

"This is Rabbi Sayyah's own handwriting," Moshe Hillel explained. "I recognize it from his other writings." He was referring to Rabbi Joseph Ibn Sayyah, who lived in Jerusalem in the sixteenth century, during its transition from Mamluk to Ottoman hands, and acted as a link between Arabic mysticism and Jewish Kabbalah. At a time when most of Jerusalem's Jewish scholars belonged to the newly arrived Sephardic exiles from Spain, his family had much deeper roots in the city. Ibn Sayyah descended from a family of *Musta'aribun*—a nickname given to local Arabic-speaking Jews by Ladino-speaking Jews who came to Jerusalem from Spain.

The manuscript Benayahu showed us (Benayahu, Ms. K 84), written in Jerusalem in 1537, was a volume of Jewish mysticism called *Even Hashoham* (Onyx Stone). According to the scholar Jonathan Garb it was a source of major influence on the next generation of Jewish mystics including Isaac

Luria (commonly known as Ha'ari, the acronym of the Hebrew phrase "divine Rabbi Yitzhak") and his Kabbalist circle.[3] Ibn Sayyah's *Even Hashoham* is written in riddles and hints intended to daunt and discourage the untrustworthy reader. The author describes techniques of meditation and instructs the Kabbalist to "bow his head like a servant between his knees until his sensory perceptions are abolished, as his senses are absent." Once the practitioner reaches a state of sensory withdrawal, he can then obtain a clear and stable vision: "and then he will behold the higher sights, constantly and not in riddles."[4]

How Meir Benayahu acquired this manuscript we do not know. Nor did his son. But we can identify one of its previous owners. Moshe Hillel shared with us a page from *Hazvi*, the weekly newspaper edited by Eliezer Ben-Yehuda, known as the father of modern Hebrew. The page, published in 1886, lists 109 manuscripts that the weekly's publisher Rabbi Isaac Hirschensohn kept in his library in the Old City. "Encouraged by many who believe that the manuscripts in Jerusalem should be printed," Hirschensohn tried to raise money to print them. The rest of the page features letters of support from distinguished rabbis across the world. Number 28 on the list: Ibn Sayyah's *Even Hashoham*. The manuscript has never been printed. But in accordance with that edict of centuries ago, neither has it been removed from Jerusalem.

The Khalidi Library

According to André Raymond, former director of the French Institute for Arab Studies in Damascus, Jerusalem's Khalidi Library (known in Arabic as the Khālidiyya) ranks as "one of the foremost private libraries open to the public in the Arab world."[5] Housed in a thirteenth-century Mamluk building on Chain Gate Street ("Bab al-Silsila," in Arabic) next to a passage leading to the Western Wall, it takes its name from a distinguished Jerusalem family of judges, diplomats, and scholars who trace their presence in the city at least as far back as Saladin's conquest in the twelfth century, and perhaps even earlier. Several members of the family held the position of *qāḍi al-quḍāh*, or chief justice, during the Mamluk dynasty, which controlled what is now Egypt and Syria from 1250 to 1517. Others included Yūsuf al-Khālidi (1829–1906), a mayor of Jerusalem and author of the first Arabic-Kurdish dictionary. Prominent members of the family today include the historian Walid Khalidi, formerly of Oxford University, Tarif Khalidi of the American University of Beirut, and Rashid Khalidi of Columbia University.

Our first visit to the library began next door, at Haifa Khalidi's home. Following the Six-Day War, a sharia court had assigned Haifa's father, Haidar Khalidi, custodianship of the family's properties, including the library. To visit her we had to talk our way past the soldiers guarding the street; the door to her house was on the section of the street leading to a gateway of the Haram al-Sharif through which only Muslims are allowed to enter. We found her smiling broadly from the top of the stairs— a woman in light summer clothes, trousers and a blouse, with no hair cover. She lived alone in the old family house and took care of the library next door. She reminded us of the great patronesses of Islamic libraries and learning of the past.

One term for "librarian" in Arabic is *amin al-maktabeh,* "the one entrusted with the library." An amin is a guardian who can be trusted to keep secrets. Several years ago, Haifa and the rest of the Khalidi family turned to just such an amin, a former librarian of the al-Aqsa Mosque, to guard their invaluable collection. Ever since, Khader Salameh—a former sheikh, a historian, and the winner of an international archivist award offered by the Scone Foundation—has presided over the largest private collection of manuscripts in Jerusalem.

Before introducing us to the library, Khader Salameh took us to a village in the Judean foothills from which his family had been evicted in June 1950.[6] Zakariyya, southwest of Jerusalem, lies adjacent to the biblical city of 'Azeka, overlooking the Elah valley ("Wadi al-Sunt," in Arabic). 'Azeka is mentioned by both Flavius Josephus and Eusebius of Caesarea; it is marked (as Beth-Zachar) on the sixth-century Madaba map in present-day Jordan. Today the abandoned village mosque, built over the ruins of a Byzantine church, is surrounded by the red-roofed homes of a Jewish village called Zecharia.

As we approached the forsaken minaret, Salameh told us about his youth in the al-'Aroub refugee camp, between Hebron and Bethlehem, and then in the Dheisheh refugee camp outside Bethlehem. He read Tolstoy and Dostoyevsky in Arabic translation. He studied Islamic law

Khader Salameh, former director of the al-Aqsa Mosque Library and Islamic Museum, currently chief librarian of the Khalidi Library. (Photo by Frédéric Brenner, 2015; courtesy of the photographer / Howard Greenberg Gallery.)

and theology in Jerusalem's Tankiziyya—a fourteenth-century building used as an Islamic school well into the fifteenth century, and subsequently as a law court and the residence of the head of the Supreme Muslim Council; it is now an Israeli police station. After serving for three years as a trainee sheikh at the al-Aqsa Mosque, Salameh attended a teachers' training college in Ramallah, worked in a Saudi library, studied library science at the Hebrew University, and finally returned to the mosque as director of its library and museum. When he was not at the Khalidi Library, he spent a day a week correcting the catalogue of Arabic litera-ture at the Hebrew University library on Mount Scopus.

As a specialist in Ottoman Turkish and medieval Arabic, Salameh was passionate about Jerusalem's inscriptions, many of which he alone could decipher. To watch him piece together broken inscriptions was like seeing a broken heart mended. But that day Salameh seemed disillusioned. Ancient inscriptions he discovered in the mosque had since been covered over with gaudy marble. The al-Aqsa library had been reduced in size to make room for a women's mosque. Few in Jerusalem care for scholarship or learning, he noted. "Books in themselves are dead. They come alive only in the hands of their readers."

Not long after our visit, Salameh persuaded the Khalidi family to grant us entry into the library itself. Before his death, in 1726, the Khalidi family patriarch, Muhammad Ṣunʿ Allah, had endowed 560 manuscripts as a private waqf. In the late nineteenth century, his descendant Raghib Efendi gathered together the manuscripts dispersed among branches of the family and chose a magnificent location for the library: the second-oldest Mamluk building in Jerusalem. The Khalidis inaugurated the library in 1900.

In 1978, the adjacent building, overlooking the Western Wall, was appropriated for a yeshiva by Rabbi Shlomo Goren, the first head of the Military Rabbinate of the Israel Defense Forces (subsequently the Ashkenazi chief rabbi of Israel). Walid Khalidi submitted renovation plans for the library to the municipality, and work began in November 1987. A month later, Rabbi Goren obtained a court order to stop the work, claiming that the renovations would both block the yeshiva's light and raise security concerns. For the ensuing five years of legal battles (during which Professor Amnon Cohen and the archaeologist Dan Bahat testified in favor of the Khalidi family), the library was closed to the public. Renovation was allowed to resume in 1992.

Khader Salameh showed us some of the Khalidi treasures: legal writs and Ottoman firmans in slanting calligraphy dating back to 1643 (including an edict from the Turkish sultan's favorite wife, Roxana, commissioning a soup kitchen for the poor to be established in Jerusalem); the library's polyglot guestbook, which in itself could tell the story of Jerusalem's cultural life in the 1920s and 1930s (we noticed the signatures of Louis Massignon, the great Catholic scholar of Islam, and Gideon Schocken, the son of the founder of the Schocken Library). The library also holds *ijazahs,* diploma licenses certifying that the bearer had the authority to transmit a particular teaching. Many of these holdings were painstakingly conserved with help from the Wellcome Institute in London. In addition, the library spent seventy thousand dollars to restore about a hundred manuscripts.

But the most impressive volume Salameh took out for us contained a manuscript from the year 1201 presented to Saladin's family in tribute to his triumphs. It is part of the Khalidi collection of *makrumahs,* presentation copies, originally made for royal libraries. This book is grandiloquently titled *The Spacious Lands of Commendations and the Garden of the Glorious and Praiseworthy Deeds Among the Merits of the Victorious King* (MS 1691; plate 8). Its author, whose full name is 'Abd al-Mun'im Ibn 'Umar Ibn Hassan al-Ghassani al-Andalusi al-Jeliany, was a philosopher, a Sufi, and an artist. The first folio—a thing of startling, seductive beauty—depicts a poem in the shape of a tree. The reader's eyes climb its branches to the right and to the left of the verse that serves as its trunk, and follows words grafted onto words.

The Khālidiyya is one of numerous schools built as endowments in Mamluk-era Jerusalem. Other Mamluk buildings—constructed in alternating stones of red, white, and black—house the Budeiri library, the al-Aqsa manuscript restoration lab, and many other *madaris* (plural of *madrassa*) that families endowed to the city, some of which continue to house Jerusalem's numerous collections of astronomy and science, law and medicine.

Guidebooks to the Imagination

Our best guide to the Mamluk cityscape is Mujir al-Din, born in Jerusalem in 1456 to a family of respected Hanbali judges that traced its roots to Caliph 'Umar Ibn al-Khaṭṭāb. During the transitional years between Mamluk and Ottoman Jerusalem, Mujir al-Din set down his masterful history of the city, *al-Uns al-Jalil bi-Tarikh al-Quds wal-Khalil* (The Glorious History of Jerusalem and Hebron). In the introduction to that work, he explains his objective:

> Some scholars have written something connected with *faḍā'il* [the merits] alone; others have undertaken mention of the conquest by 'Umar and the buildings of the Umayyads. Still others have limited themselves to the conquest by Salah al-Din [Saladin], without mentioning what happened thereafter, and other scholars have written a history citing some of the totality of notables of Bayt al-Maqdis from which there is no great benefit. Therefore I would like to combine [the] discussion of construction, merits, conquests, and biographies of notables with mention of some noteworthy events, so that there will be a complete history.[7]

Drawing from a great variety of Islamic sources, Mujir al-Din recounted the pre-Islamic and Islamic history of Jerusalem from the time of Adam to his own day, running through the monotheistic prophets who preceded Muhammad, the Crusades, the conquest of Jerusalem by Saladin, the Mamluk restoration of the city to Islam in 1260–1261, biographies of Mamluk rulers, and descriptions of the Muslim shrines and landmarks of the al-Quds of his day. Although he does not mention Christian or Jewish books, and cites neither Flavius Josephus nor William of Tyre, he was well versed in Jewish and Christian traditions through the faḍā'il literature.

One afternoon at the National Library of Israel, we came across a sixteenth-century Kabbalistic *siddur* (prayer book, MS. Yah. Heb. 94) written for Joseph Ibn Sayyah, author of *Even Hashoham*, who taught Kabbalah as well as magical practices.[8] The volume was purchased by the Jerusalem-born polymath Abraham Shalom Yahuda. The son of an Iraqi father and German mother, Yahuda studied in Germany with the renowned Orientalists Theodor Nöldeke and Ignaz Goldziher. He taught at the Hochschule für die Wissenschaft des Judentums (Higher Institute for Jewish Studies) in Berlin, was the first professor of Judaic Studies at the University of Madrid, and ended his career at the New School for Social Research in New York (as part of its "University in Exile" during the Second World War).

Yahuda spent decades purchasing rare books and manuscripts from patrician families in Cairo, Damascus, Aleppo, Baghdad, Tunis, and Fez, and from private mosques and libraries in Palestine, Mesopotamia, Turkey, Persia, and Yemen. In 1924, he arranged for the National Library's purchase of the 6,000 volumes that made up the "Goldziher library," amassed by his former teacher. Yahuda sold manuscripts to the British Museum and to Robert and John Garrett on behalf of Princeton University. The rest—including 1,186 manuscripts in Arabic script (primarily in Arabic, with 350 in Persian and 250 in Ottoman Turkish), 240 manuscripts in Hebrew script, and 7,500 pages of Isaac Newton's theological writings—he wished to bring to Jerusalem.[9] Weeks before his sudden death in 1951, Yahuda informed Curt Wormann, the head of what was then known as the Jewish National and University Library (JNUL), that his collection was packed and ready to be shipped to Jerusalem.

Following Yahuda's death, his wife, Ethel, worked on cataloguing the collection in preparation for its transfer to Jerusalem. In 1953, at a luncheon in her honor with President Yitzhak Ben-Zvi and Hebrew University officials, she reiterated her commitment to donate the collection to the JNUL. Ethel Yahuda died in 1955 without completing the donation. The Yahuda Collection, including the pilgrimage manuscript we were shown that afternoon, finally arrived in Jerusalem in 1967 and has been painstakingly catalogued by Ephraim Vust. Raquel Ukeles, curator of the National Library's Islam and Middle East collection, which today contains close to half a million volumes, calls it "undoubtedly one of the most valuable and significant bequests ever received by the National Library of Israel."[10]

At the National Library we were reminded that Mamluk and Ottoman Jerusalem was home to extensive collections of minority religious groups. Two of them attracted our particular interest. The Serbians, an independent (autocephalous) church within the Orthodox world, has no presence in today's Jerusalem, but its history is folded between great volumes on the city's bookshelves.

Milka Levy-Rubin, curator of the National Library's Humanities Collection, showed us Jerusalem's most remarkable example of a literary genre called Proskynetarion (Ms. Var. 186 = 38).[11] It is a Serbian illuminated translation of a Greek guidebook for pilgrims. Its colophon testifies that it was copied in Jerusalem by Gavriil Thadich in the year 7170 (after creation), or 1662 CE. Far from attempting a realistic depiction of Jerusalem, Thadich suspends Slavic blue and black onion domes over the city's red houses and gates.

In 1230, Saint Sava—diplomat, prince, and founder of the Serbian Church—visited Jerusalem. He established his church at the site of Saint John the Evangelist on Mount Zion. A century later, when the roof collapsed, pilgrims record celebrating mass in the church's ruins.[12] Nonetheless, the Serbs remained, and in the early fifteenth century they reached the apex of their influence in the city. Based in Jerusalem's monastery of Saint Michael the Archangel, they were also in possession of Mar Saba monastery. A series of Ottoman firmans confirmed their rights until 1625, when bankruptcy forced the Serbs to sell both properties to the Greek patriarch, who serves as the head of all the Orthodox churches in Jerusalem. We were reminded, too, of the Georgians, who under similar circumstances sixty years later lost their holdings in Jerusalem—and hundreds of manuscripts from the monastery of the Holy Cross—to the Greek Orthodox Patriarchate.

African Zion: From Ethiopia to Jerusalem

As recently as 1975, very little was known about the Ethiopian monastic collections in Jerusalem. That year, Ephraim Isaac (later director of the Institute of Semitic Studies at Princeton) was granted permission to catalogue the 300 manuscripts of the Ethiopian Orthodox library. "To my great surprise," Isaac wrote, "I discovered 764 manuscripts instead of the 300 that I had been told existed in the library. Each day dozens of new manuscripts emerged from behind rows of printed books or other manuscripts as well as from hidden boxes." Isaac concluded that "the Holy City is one of the best centers in the world for Ethiopic studies."[13]

Since that time, little has changed. One reason the collections still prove so difficult to access is that Jerusalem's Ethiopian abbots have lost numerous manuscripts—most written on parchment with ink made of soot—to thieves or buyers who offered extravagant sums. A remarkable codex of the books of Samuel and Kings made in 1344, for instance, is now at the Vatican Library (Borg. Et. 3). A colophon notes that King Amda Seyon I (r. 1314–1344) gave it to "the Church of the Virgin" in Jerusalem. (The Ethiopian term for the codex is *muṣḥaf,* later adopted by Muslims to describe Qur'anic volumes.) Both the Greek Orthodox manuscript library and the Armenian library hold Ge'ez manuscripts, and we learned that the National Library owns fifty-one manuscripts in Ge'ez, both Jewish and Christian. Today, the custodians of Ethiopian memory in Jerusalem, lamenting what they have sold and lost, treat visitors with extreme caution.

Our attempts to track down Ethiopian manuscripts began at Deir al-Sultan, the Ethiopian monastery on the rooftop of the Church of the Holy Sepulchre. One of the cells there has been converted into a shop selling small memorabilia and icons imported from Ethiopia and sold mainly to Ethiopian pilgrims. But the shop also contained copies of old charters that the monks had painstakingly managed to collect and copy from various archives after their own was consumed by fire. The monks at Deir al-Sultan sent us to Dabra Gannat (Mountain of Paradise), the nineteenth-century monastery completed by Emperor Menilek II on Abyssinia (now Ethiopia) Street outside the Old City. In 1888, the community bought this plot of land with treasure which Emperor Yohannes had captured from the Turks. The distinctive round church they built was made famous by the scene of Paul Newman's escape from his British Mandatory police pursuers in the film *Exodus* (1960). The first dictionary of modern Hebrew was compiled in a modest apartment in a two-floor building across the street by Eliezer Ben-Yehuda, who lived there between 1881 and 1921.

At the monastery we met the abbot, Abba Fessiha Tsion (meaning "Joy of Zion"), and the learned Abba Tesfa, who was in charge of the library. Both were fluent in Hebrew and Amharic. Several girls playing in the monastery courtyard boasted that they too spoke Amharic and Hebrew, but the monastery manuscripts written in Ge'ez made a challenge that was too difficult for them. Ge'ez ceased to be a spoken language in the tenth century, though it is still used as the liturgical language of the Ethiopian Christians. The monks admitted that they could not help us; we first needed to obtain the archbishop's permission.

At last we were granted an audience with His Grace Archbishop Abuna Enbakom on the top floor of his residence on Ethiopian Monastery Street in the Old City. The compound, given to the Ethiopians in 1876, accommodates the Ethiopian Orthodox Church administration, a chapel dedicated to Saint Philip the Evangelist, and a dark, single-room library in a state of disrepair. Of the more than 750 manuscripts it contains—one of the most extensive collections outside of Ethiopia—the largest group consists of 150 volumes of Psalms in Ge'ez (called *Mazmura Dawit*) from the fifteenth to the twentieth century. The room also holds several sixteenth-century Gospels in Ge'ez, homilies (called *dersana*), horologia (books of hours), and the Lord's Prayer in Ge'ez (*Abuna Zabasamayat*).

On the wall above the archbishop's door hung a mural with the phrase "Ethiopia extends her hands to God," in Ge'ez, Arabic, and English. In the antechamber, portraits of the previous archbishops—each called *mamher*, or teacher—looked down on us. After a devastating cholera epidemic of the 1830s, Jerusalem's Copts took over the monastery and burned the archive containing the documents that validated the Ethiopians' claim to the Deir al-Sultan monastery. The Ethiopians managed to recover Deir al-Sultan with British support only after the First World War. The archbishop insisted that all the Ge'ez manuscripts in the Armenian and Greek libraries of Jerusalem had been stolen from Deir al-Sultan.

Archbishop Enbakom communicated with us through a translator, Getachew Hailu, who later passed his verdict too. To visit these collections we had to follow the full pilgrim's passage. To obtain permission to enter the library in Jerusalem we first made our way to Addis Ababa to meet His Holiness Abune Mathias I, Sixth Patriarch and Catholicos of Ethiopia. Trying to tell the history of Ethiopian learning and the Ethiopian book collections in Jerusalem proved to be our most demanding challenge, in itself a lesson in the meaning of devotion.

At eight thousand feet above sea level, the patriarchal See in Addis has one of the highest-altitude libraries in the world. We imagined to ourselves the many monks who walked from there to Jerusalem across the mountains and deserts carrying their Bibles and psalters and other beautifully illuminated manuscripts bequeathed to the holy city.

We arrived in Addis on September 16, a few days into the Ethiopian new year, and were greeted by Abba Kaletsidk Mulugeta, who was in charge of the church's foreign relations worldwide. Ethiopia is the only African country that has been Christian since Christianity became the state religion in 330.[14] It kept that faith even when neighboring countries converted to Islam. The Ethiopian church adheres to a purely solar calendar with twelve months of thirty days, and a leap year every four years. The main Christian holidays, however, are celebrated with other churches according to the old Julian calendar. In the Ethiopians' calculations, Jesus was born on January 7 in the year 7 CE (marked by a holiday called Genna), and the New Year (Enkutatash) is celebrated annually on September 11 (or 12). The Ethiopians bring yet another timetable to Jerusalem's busy calendar, where on almost any given day one of the communities is celebrating a holiday.

Abba Mathias was happy to see faces from Jerusalem and greeted us with the little Hebrew he remembered from his many years in the city. "We wish to do justice to our portrait of Ethiopian intellectual life in Jerusalem before its decline under the Ottomans." In Africa too, after many years of prosperity and learning, the early Ottoman period had seen a major setback. "Why is Jerusalem so difficult?" he whispered to Abba Kaletsidk in Amharic. He was referring to Jerusalem's Ethiopian monks, but we felt that his words applied to the city as a whole. Abba Kaletsidk promised to produce an official letter for us, register it in the church's records, and have it signed by the synod's secretary and the patriarch. Only then could we take it back to the archbishop in Jerusalem. He promised us a copy by email.

One day, after spending a couple of hours waiting in vain for the archbishop at the monastic courtyard of Saint Philippos, we were approached by a white-haired deacon of the church named Girma (Amharic for "majesty"). With a wide smile he invited us to call him Jimmy, and welcomed us into the small, unpretentious chapel. There on the gospel stand we found a brightly illuminated but water-damaged manuscript in Ge'ez from the seventeenth century. *Dersane Mikael*, as the book was called, embellishes the miracles of the archangel Michael and includes a homily for the annual commemoration of the archangel on November 21 (12 Hedar in the Ethiopian calendar).[15]

Deacon Girma with the manuscript of *Dersane Mikael*, Ethiopian Orthodox Church of Saint Philippos. (Photo by Gali Tibbon, 2017; courtesy of the photographer.)

As Father Girma guided us through the small church, we learned that Jerusalem plays an important role in the Ethiopian imagination. Although the Ethiopian people converted to Christianity in the fourth and fifth centuries, they trace their legacy back to King Solomon and the Queen of Sheba: "Now when the Queen of Sheba heard of the fame of Solomon, she came to Jerusalem to test Solomon with difficult questions" (1 Kings 10:1). According to Ethiopian tradition, the queen returned home pregnant by Solomon; their son Menelik became the first emperor of Ethiopia. Father Girma added that Menelik traveled to Jerusalem as a young man to learn more of the wisdom of Solomon. According to the national myth recorded in the *Kebra Nagast* (Glory of the Kings), he returned home to his capital, Aksum, with the Ark of the Covenant, dancing before it as his grandfather David had in bringing it to Jerusalem, its presence confirming his empire as a New Israel.

According to Saint Jerome, Ethiopians were already making pilgrimages to Jerusalem by the end of the fourth century. Several centuries later, Emperor Lalibela (r. 1181–1221) carved eleven churches out of rock in a symbolic re-creation of Jerusalem: they carried names like Cavalry, Golgotha, and the Mount of Transfiguration. Beginning in the late thirteenth century, rulers of the so-called Solomonic dynasty took names such as Yagbea Seyon (He Shall Bring Back Zion) and Amda Seyon (Pillar of Zion). Their golden age in Africa, and by proxy also in Jerusalem, lasted until the rising of the Ottoman power. In 1516 an estimated 800 pilgrims came to celebrate Easter in Jerusalem, a journey of nearly twenty-five hundred miles across mountains and deserts. But in the fall of that year the city (as indeed the whole region) was taken by the Ottomans, and the roads were no longer safe for travelers. A group of 336 pilgrims who made their way in 1520 was attacked by Bedouins and almost everyone massacred.[16] Ottoman-Somali raids resulted in the destruction of churches and the burning of numerous manuscripts. In Jerusalem, Ethiopian Christians lost forever their chapels inside the Church of the Holy Sepulchre.

But Ethiopian monks and pilgrims have never ceased to dream of Jerusalem and yearn for it. They carried manuscripts—such as the one of the archangel Michael—to Jerusalem, some of which we saw when we were at last granted access to the tiny library. Some libraries are defined by order: standardized call numbers, carefully arranged volumes on methodical shelves. But this library seemed to us a place of nonlinear chaos. Finding anything in it became a fortuitous accident. Then again, the same could be said of Jerusalem itself.

Oriental Scripts

At the permanent collection in the Jewish Communities wing of the Israel Museum, we saw another example of journeying: a miniature set of tefillin that made the hajj to Mecca concealed in the turban of a Persian Jew.

Jews were allowed to settle in the Shiite city of Mashhad in northeast Iran in 1734 because the Persian rulers wanted their help in turning the city into a commercial center. After a blood libel in the spring of 1839, however, the Jews of Mashhad, numbering about two thousand, were coerced into converting to Islam. Known as *Jadid al-Islam,* or in Judeo-Persian as *Jedidim,* these crypto-Jews continued to live their Jewish lives in secret. Many took both Hebrew and Persian names: Solomon/Suleiman, Shimon/Sha'aban, Yehezkel/Abu Samad, and so forth. They married according to Muslim customs, but they also covertly held a ceremony under a *chuppa.* They used two marriage contracts: a Jewish *ketuba* (written in Aramaic) and a Muslim *qabaleh* (in Farsi). They lit candles every night of the week so as not to raise suspicions when they lit Shabbat candles on Friday nights. On Friday mornings they gathered at the mosque and worshipped facing Mecca, and on Friday evenings they congregated in basements and prayed toward Jerusalem.

In the 1890s, a number of these Jedidim made the hajj to Mecca in order to allay suspicions about their fidelity to Islam. One of them, Mattityahu, concealed his tefillin beneath the folds of his turban. On his way back, Mattityahu dropped out of the caravan and made his way on foot to Jerusalem. There, for the first time in his life, he could be openly Jewish. Known as Haji Mehdi, he settled in the new Bukhara neighborhood designed by the architect Conrad Schick, in which his family established a synagogue named after him. In 1908 the family funded in Jerusalem a unique prayer book, featuring Hebrew alongside Judeo-Persian.[17]

Hajj Mattityahu's great-grandson Efraim Halevi welcomed us into the archives of the Sephardic community in the basement of the Jerusalem municipality. There we learned that the history of Jerusalem's poor is inscribed not on archways or monuments but on the pages of community archives.[18] Finding community archives is not always simple. In the context of Jerusalem's long history, Ottoman archives are considered recent, dating back no more than five hundred years. One such archive belongs to the Sephardic Council, once the sole Jewish representative at the Ottoman municipal and imperial courts.

Jerusalem's Sephardic Council kept its minutes and books in an archive in the Palestine Post building on Ha-Solel (now Ha-Havatzelet) Street, off Zion Square. In February 1948, a car bomb struck the three-story building. Some of what could be salvaged was transferred to the National Library and the Ben-Zvi Institute. But the oldest records, hardly known to scholars, now reside in the basement of the Jerusalem municipality, opposite the northwest corner of the Old City. The municipal archive, containing council records going back nearly five hundred years, was organized into an English filing system during the British Mandate, then handed over to the Jordanians in 1948 and finally to the Israelis.

A great deal was in the meantime spirited away, but in the section of the archive presided over by Efraim Halevi—fifteen hundred folders that encapsulate the story of Sephardic life in Jerusalem—not much had changed. Jerusalem's Sephardic leaders negotiated with the Ottomans in Turkish and with their Arab neighbors in Arabic. For several centuries of Ottoman rule, the Jewish community of Jerusalem was represented by the chief rabbi of the majority Sephardic community—the Hakham Bashi, as the Turks called him. The first Hakham Bashi was appointed in 1452; the last completed his term under the British military government in 1920 (the post was abolished to make room for the creation of the Chief Rabbinate in 1921). Ottoman empowerment, as well as the large size of the community, made the elected Sephardic Council the most important government agency of the Jewish community.

Yet most of its records were written neither in Turkish nor in Arabic but in Ladino, the language of the Jews exiled from Spain. To complicate matters, many of the documents in Ladino are written in Solitreo, a Sephardic cursive script (known as Nisf-Qalam in Arabic and Hatzi

Kulmus in Hebrew) that few can read today. As a boy, Halevi studied Solitreo with an Aleppo-born rabbi, David Laniado. Today Halevi is one of the last people in Jerusalem who can read it, and he is often called upon to help researchers decipher the meaning of documents.

Halevi showed us his archive's oldest notebook, which includes correspondence from the office of the qadi of Jerusalem concerning visits to religious sites like Rachel's Tomb. Beginning in 1759, it charts the Sephardic community's sometimes fractious relationships with the Ashkenazi community and the Muslim authorities—another layer of Jerusalem's long experience with cultural mediation.[19]

Collections in Ge'ez, Ladino, Georgian, and Serbian added to the amalgamation of Jerusalem's libraries and archives that have since Mamluk times enriched the city with distant cultures. They remind us of the journeys taken by people from across the world, long before the days of air travel.

Sultan Suleiman I, commonly called Suleiman the Magnificent, was among those who felt special affinity for Jerusalem without ever visiting it. The Mamluks surrendered the city to his father, Selim I, in 1516, and he inherited the title "possessor of the first Qibla." But his true vocation came from imagining himself walking in the footsteps of King Solomon and building Jerusalem's walls, citadel, and sanctuaries. Two of the thirty-five inscriptions that adorn the monuments he bequeathed to Jerusalem bear the title "Suleiman al-Thany," "the Second Solomon." At the citadel in Jerusalem we found a more elaborate description:

> The order to restore this blessed fortress was given by the Great Suleiman, the Great Hakan [Turkish for "ruler"], the possessor of the necks of all nations, the employer of people of sword and pen, the servant of two holy harams and of the Holy Land. . . . Suleiman the Second, may Allah perpetuate his existence as long as the Dome above the Rock.[20]

CHAPTER FIVE

DRAGOMANS AND THIEVES

The Nineteenth Century

In its wanderings through several languages, the now archaic word *dragoman* enacts its own meaning: it entered the English language from the French, which borrowed it from Greek, which in turn adopted it from the Aramaic and Akkadian words for "translator."[1] Jerusalem's dragomans, fluent in the language of whatever regime happened to be ruling the city, served (and still serve) as mediators adept at crossing the city's linguistic fracture lines. They smooth the way of comprehension between tongues and customs, between "local" and "foreign." If the city, as psalm 122 has it, is "joined together," its translators are the joiners. Yet since translation can never fully transfer meaning from one language to another, its failures also reveal how far Jerusalem's communities remain from one another.

In the nineteenth century, dragomans functioned much as not always beloved "fixers" do today. "Nearly invariably," a French Jerusalemite noted in *Macmillan's Magazine* in 1875, the European traveler to Palestine "has to hand himself over to the mercy of the inevitable dragoman, an obstructive animal, peculiar to the social fauna of the Levant, and combining the functions of interpreter, *maître d'hôtel*, guide, and courier."[2] According to the English traveler Robert Curzon—the peer who acquired Greek manuscripts from Mar Saba in the 1830s—"The newly-arrived European eats and drinks whatever his dragoman chooses to give him; sees through his dragoman's eyes; hears through his ears; and, although he thinks himself master, is, in fact, only a part of the property of this Eastern servant." In the 1890s, a short-lived attempt was made to impose a system of certification on the profession. "All Jerusalem dragomans are now required by the municipal government to pass an examination as to what they are to tell visitors to the holy places," a correspondent for the Palestine Exploration Fund reported in 1895. "The examiners are said to be the *effendis* of the *mejlis*—i.e. the magistrates of the bench—and those who pass successfully are to receive a diploma!"[3]

As colonial powers sought to gain footholds in the Middle East, the mid-nineteenth century brought a rush of consulates to Jerusalem, including those of Britain (established in 1839), Prussia (1842), France (1843), the United States (1844), and Austria (1849). The Prussian and the British consular libraries imported research literature to Jerusalem. Each consulate employed one or more dragomans, who could negotiate in Arabic, Hebrew, Turkish, French, Yiddish, and Ladino. They translated correspondence with Ottoman officials, judges, and heads of religious communities, secured travel permits, and smoothed over property disputes.

Other dragomans functioned as local guides. Rolla Floyd, for instance, a dragoman for Thomas Cook & Son, led tours of Jerusalem for dignitaries including General Ulysses S. Grant. In 1882, Floyd reported that a dragoman serving the American consulate had cheated the Spafford family, founders of the American Colony, in a rent deal. "Oh," the devout Presbyterian Horatio Spafford replied, "we will pray that God will make a better man of him." Floyd later sent wealthy tourists seeking accommodation the Spaffords' way, and the American Colony Hotel was born.[4]

Eliezer Ben-Yehuda described the Jewish dragoman of the pasha in Jerusalem, Joseph Krieger, as "a simple man, an ignoramus [*am ha'aretz*] in every sense, but his ability to converse and write French and Turkish were enough to appoint him a dragoman in Turkey. And in those days a dragoman of the Pasha was almost the king's right-hand man. The Pasha was in the dragoman's hands like clay in the hands of a skillful potter; the dragoman influenced the Pasha to follow all his whims."[5]

The dragoman as a chargé d'affaires figures in many of Jerusalem's religious titles and documents. The annual Calendar of Easter Religious Ceremonies, for instance, published by the Greek Orthodox Patriarchate Printing Press, announces that on the morning of Good Friday, "The Chief Dragoman, accompanied by clergy," will proceed from the Patriarchate to the Basilica of the Holy Sepulchre. The current dragoman, Metropolitan Christodoulos, remains third in the hierarchy of the Greek Orthodox Patriarchate after the patriarch himself and his chief secretary. In effect, he serves as the community's foreign minister, in which capacity, naturally, he must demonstrate a command of the city's languages.

As we shall see, the keepers of Jerusalem's libraries have often served as dragomans who shuttled between languages and interpreted one culture for another.

The nineteenth century, the golden age of book plunder in Jerusalem, offered striking case studies of custodianship gone awry. Jerusalem's book thieves, like plenty of other Jerusalemites, belong to a self-righteous class. Whether acting in self-interest or on behalf of a state, they justify their appropriations as a form of rescue. As Milton asserts in his "Areopagitica," "Books are not absolutely dead things, but do contain a potency of life in them to be as active as that soul was whose progeny they are." To rescue books is to touch that potency and partake of their promise. Perhaps this explains why both Maimonides in the Middle Ages and the Karaite rabbi al-Gamil today regard stolen books as equivalent to human captives who require ransom and redemption.

Some of the book thieves in Jerusalem are driven by pious love. They share their avarice with the medieval relic-mongers who practiced *Furta Sacra*—the theft of relics, or "holy theft," as it is commonly known. Patrick Geary, an authority on the medieval cult of relics, suggests that such thefts were more often countenanced than condemned. "Far from condemning them as aberrations or as sins against the fellow Christians from whom the saint was stolen," he writes, "most people apparently praised them."[6] Even when relics were legitimately acquired, Geary notes, stories of heroic theft were occasionally invented. These raiders of

tombs and churches who stole the remains of saints persuaded themselves and others that they were fulfilling the secret wishes of the saint. If
a saint did not wish to be removed, then no power on earth could spirit
away his or her relics. A successful abduction of a saint's relics thus confirmed and conferred the saint's implicit approval.

Books were not immune to the kind of treatment usually reserved for
relics. In the nineteenth century, Robert Curzon heaped contempt on the
idolatrous monks he encountered at the clifftop monastery of Varlaam in
Greece. "The monks themselves . . . cannot read either Hellenic or ancient Greek; but they consider the books in their library as sacred relics
and preserve them with a certain feeling of awe for their antiquity and
incomprehensibility."[7]

The same awe persists today. In October 2015, the earliest complete
copy of the New Testament—dating to the fourth century—went on display at the British Museum. The Codex Sinaiticus, written in Greek, was
displayed beside the First Gaster Bible, a Hebrew text written on parchment in Egypt or Palestine in the ninth century. The incomprehensibility
of these texts to most visitors did not inhibit their reverence for the
volumes' antiquity.

Our forays into Jerusalem's libraries confronted us with some less than
clear-cut moral dilemmas, in which theft masquerades as rescue and private ownership is challenged by national claims. But they have also given
us glimpses of thefts returned, losses regained, and exiled texts repatriated.

Bishop Uspensky, God's Bee

A manuscript may take the name of the place where it was discovered,
the monarch who commissioned it, or its author or illustrator. Only
rarely is a manuscript named after its thief. In the Greek Orthodox
manuscript library, we encountered the stories of two such manuscripts:
the Uspensky Gospels and a palimpsest called Codex Porphyrianus. Both,
in fact, bear the name of the same person: the theologian and thief
Porphyri Uspensky.

Despite numerous audiences and a collegial relationship with His
Beatitude Theophilos III, Greek Orthodox Patriarch of Jerusalem, our
petitions to access the library were repeatedly deferred. Several times we

visited the well-appointed waiting room of Archbishop Aristarchos, the secretary-general and librarian, and sat beneath a large document with the signatures and inked fingerprints of the workers hired by the Patriarchate to renovate the rotunda and edicule of the Holy Sepulchre in 1809–1810.

We pondered the reasons for the hesitation until one day Reverend Aristovoulos Kyriazis, a scholar and senior member of the Brotherhood of the Holy Sepulchre, offered us an explanation for the suspicion that barred our way: the dubious heritage left more than 150 years ago by Uspensky. "We keep our library closed because of Uspensky, because he was proud of his theft and because in Russia he is considered a hero to this day. Generations of thieves follow in his footsteps." In the Patriarchate, "Uspensky" serves as a kind of code word, a name whispered behind doors that remain bolted fast. It also serves as a caution: "Be careful, remember Uspensky."

Bishop Uspensky, who founded the Russian Ecclesiastical Mission in Jerusalem in 1847, was a born collector. He once jotted down a little poem about himself:

> Why do I walk the earth so long?
> To bring, like a bee,
> Beautiful honey to my hive,
> I am a God's bee, and Russia is my hive.[8]

Born in 1804, Uspensky took his monastic vows after graduating from the Saint Petersburg Ecclesiastical Academy. By thirty, he had been promoted to the rank of archimandrite (literally, "chief of a sheepfold"), and was on track to being made a bishop.[9] Yet Uspensky first came to Jerusalem neither as a scholar nor as a clergyman. Disguised as a simple pilgrim, he was sent as a spy in 1842 by the synod of the Russian Orthodox Church in conjunction with the Asiatic Department of the Russian Foreign Ministry, an appointment that required Tsar Nicholas's approval. His instructions were explicit: "Perform faithfully the duties of a pilgrim. Do not give any reason to others to suspect that you are a secret envoy dispatched by the government."[10] He was not to alarm the Sublime Porte in Istanbul or upset the delicate balance between the communities in Jerusalem. His mission was to assess the state of the Christian churches, to

Portrait of Porphyri Uspensky, oil, 19th century. (Fond 118. Inv. 1. Folder 197; courtesy of Saint Petersburg Branch of the Archive of the Russian Academy of Sciences.)

establish why the Latin and Protestant churches there were so successfully proselytizing, and to win the confidence of the eastern clergy (namely the Arab Orthodox).

What did Jerusalem look like when Porphyri Uspensky arrived in 1844? The city's life was confined within the walls built in the sixteenth century by Suleiman the Magnificent. Scattered cemeteries—Jewish and Muslim, ancient and modern—surrounded the walls, and small tanneries and cattle markets clustered outside the gates. Farmers from nearby villages brought their fruit and vegetables to sell in the market held inside the moat surrounding the misnamed Tower of David. Orchards were protected by watchtowers (*qasr*), like the one built by Jerusalem's mufti Sheikh Khalili in 1711, which can still be seen behind the Rockefeller Museum. The rapid expansion beyond the confines of the walls did not begin until the 1860s, shortly after Uspensky had left the city for good.

Uspensky first resided in the Saint Abraham monastery, near the Holy Sepulchre, which had hosted male Russian pilgrims since 1841. Russia's offers to purchase this monastery, as well as Saint Theodore's (for female pilgrims), had been turned down by the Greeks, who grew suspicious about Russia's intentions in Jerusalem. It took twenty more years and a major war (the Crimean War, 1853–1856) before Russia was permitted to purchase lands and begin the construction of compounds along Jaffa Road, on the Mount of Olives, in the village of Ein Kerem, and within the walls of the Old City.

Paying little heed to his instructions, Uspensky never bothered to conceal his identity or mission. He trailed trouble. Greek monks publicly accused him of inciting the Arab Christian Orthodox population against them. He repaid the antagonism. In his diary he refers to the Greek monks as "religion-mongers." He reported on the "unfriendly" relationship between the Greeks and the Arabs in the Orthodox Church and the poor levels of education in both communities. The Brotherhood of the Holy Sepulchre, he noted, was infiltrated with "worldly habits." Celibacy was not practiced. Positions "were bought and sold." He sent his recommendations back to Russia: a Russian bishop (perhaps himself) should be installed in Jerusalem. Russians should open schools and promote the education of the Orthodox community in Arabic, "the national language of the Arab community." Russian books ought to be translated into Arabic. He also recommended that the Greek Orthodox patriarch reside permanently in Jerusalem rather than oversee the community remotely from Istanbul.[11]

Uspensky traveled extensively in the region, tracing oral histories and hunting for ancient Greek, Arabic, and Slavonic manuscripts, both in

Jerusalem and in the desert monasteries of Mar Saba and Saint Catherine. Before setting off from Russia on a trip in 1858 he wrote in his diary (which he titled *The Book of My Existence*): "I will search for ancient texts of the Greek Bible." He complained about insufficient funds and asked the Russian government and individuals to donate money for the purchase of books. He noted that he bought many manuscripts "in Greek, Slavonic, Arabic, Georgian, Coptic, Ethiopian and Armenian" out of his own pocket.[12]

On March 27, 1860, Uspensky arrived at Mar Saba for the last time. He stayed just three days. "I took from there a Greek gospel of the year 835, and from the Justinian tower a Greek Prophytologos of 1054 and one fat [large] Georgian manuscript in 12 parts, that while binding, I divided into three parts." He probably knew that he was walking away from Mar Saba with the world's oldest dated manuscript of the New Testament, written in minuscule Greek script. A rare colophon by the scribe, boxed in naive decorations of dots and exes, bears the date 6343 *Etos Kosmou* (to the creation), equivalent to the year 835 CE. Uspensky brought it to the Imperial Public Library in Saint Petersburg (which the Soviets renamed the State Public Library and is currently known as the National Library of Russia). Catalogued as Gr. 219, the manuscript is simply called the Uspensky Gospels.[13]

There it rests alongside a palimpsest that Uspensky obtained (or stole) at the same time. Codex Porphyrianus (Gr. 225), as it would become known, features a fourteenth-century text written over a ninth-century Greek text of the Acts of the Apostles and Paul's letters. Uspensky lent this manuscript to the German scholar Constantine von Tischendorf (famous for "rescuing" the Codex Sinaiticus at Saint Catherine's) in 1862 to produce a facsimile edition. The German scholar and the Russian clergyman had a long history of rivalry and mutual dislike but also some degree of cooperation. It was Tischendorf who in tribute to Uspensky named the manuscript Codex Porphyrianus.

Shortly before his death, Uspensky sold 435 manuscripts to the Imperial Library—legitimately purchased ones alongside stolen ones.[14] The page dedicated to him at the National Library of Russia website offers a justification for his actions: "He was convinced that the manuscripts may be purchased from private persons only, but should be borrowed from monastery libraries only for temporary use, for study and reproduction. However, he did not always follow this principle, fearing that precious Christian books would find 'wrong owners' or be lost. He was always led by his warm heart and an unquenchable thirst for knowledge."[15] Uspensky, loyal to God and his fatherland, never expressed regret for his thefts. He was God's bee, hovering among the flowers of the Holy Land. But the hive to which he inevitably returned was always Russia.

The Russians have never apologized for the theft, a fact which infuriates the Orthodox population of Jerusalem almost as much as the theft itself. The Greek Orthodox library of Jerusalem had lost the oldest manuscript in its collection to a trusted member of the clergy, a fellow Orthodox bishop. Uspensky's thefts left a lasting legacy of suspicion. After learning of them, the late-nineteenth-century Greek Orthodox Patriarch Nicodemus decided to gather hundreds of manuscripts from monasteries throughout the Judean desert into a single well-guarded library at the Patriarchate in Jerusalem.[16]

Uspensky was far from alone in his predations. Motivated by passion for the Word of God, manuscript hunters—men and women, meticulous scholars and unscrupulous thieves—flocked to Jerusalem in search of biblical authenticity.

Abraham Firkovich, Yaakov Saphir, and the Aleppo Codex

We hoped to travel to Saint Petersburg to search for the Christian Orthodox trove of manuscripts deposited there by Uspensky. Another good reason to go on a manuscript pilgrimage to Saint Petersburg would have been to view Jewish manuscripts taken from Jerusalem. In 1948 the Jordanians captured the Old City and the remaining Jewish manuscripts were looted or destroyed. Among the ones that escaped are manuscripts from the Abraham Firkovich collection, which the historians Menahem Ben-Sasson and Zeev Elkin described as "one of the most important collections in Jewish studies in the world."[17]

In the centuries before the arrival of the first Crusaders in 1099, Jerusalem's Karaites left the city an astonishing literary legacy. None of it, however, remains in Jerusalem. A collection of ten thousand of their manuscripts and fragments is kept today in the National Library of

Russia. They got there by virtue of the obsessions of Firkovich, a less than scrupulous Ukrainian-born Karaite historian and collector.

As a penniless young man, Abraham Firkovich found work as secretary to a Karaite noble, one of the richest men in Crimea, Simcha Babowicz. Firkovich began to trade in books and in leather for tefillin. In 1830, he accompanied Babowicz to Jerusalem, where he bought manuscripts from Karaites and Rabbanites and unearthed hitherto unknown manuscripts that had been deposited in the ancient Karaite synagogue of Jerusalem. He chose the better ones. "And I removed them from Jerusalem without regard for the great anathema, as I relied on the verse 'For out of Zion shall go forth the law.' For the sake of heaven I removed them from the darkness of the storerooms in order to enlighten the land and benefit the many."[18]

Firkovich had made himself an expert in synagogue architecture design and cemeteries, and thus he was able to identify locations of hidden rooms of forgotten genizahs. Guided by Judaism's reverential regard for—and fidelity to—the dignity of the written word, many Jewish communities, even now, keep a genizah, or repository for discarded sacred texts, where the manuscripts gather dust or disintegrate. Such repositories, often in synagogue attics or cellars, hold anything bearing the name of God, texts with scribal errors or physical damage, or sometimes anything written in Hebrew characters. These storerooms have functioned both to protect a text's sanctity and to hide heretical texts. They conceal both the sacred and the censored. The Hebrew word *ganuz,* in fact, like the Arabic *janaza* (funeral), suggests burial, and later evolved to connote concealment.

On the way back to Crimea, at the end of 1830, Firkovich, now forty-three, settled in Istanbul. For two years he taught two dozen Karaite students, continued to acquire manuscripts, and led the team that translated the Torah into vernacular Turkish (a copy of which is now in the Ben-Zvi Institute library in Jerusalem).[19]

When he returned to Crimea, Firkovich and his patron Babowicz set up the first Karaite printing press. Among the books it produced were his own polemical works *Massah U-Meriva* (Test and Quarrel, 1838), and *Chotam Tokhnit* (Seal of Perfection, 1836). In the latter, he accuses Rabbanite Jews of killing "our master, Anan Hanasi," and killing "the righteous, pure, upright, God-fearing Jesus, the son of Miriam . . . who was of the race of the Sons of the Scripture [i.e., Karaites]."[20] (The

Karaite leader Anan ben David died around 795, more than a thousand years before Firkovich made this charge.) The book was banned by the government censor, and Babowicz tried to recall and destroy all copies. Firkovich later told his student and secretary Ephraim Deinard that he regretted his vilification of the rabbis, and he apologized in the introduction to a later book, *Avnei Zikaron* (Stones of Memory, 1871).

Beginning in 1839, the bibliomaniac Firkovich devoted his years to hunting for manuscripts through Crimea, the Caucasus, Damascus, Cairo, and Jerusalem. He unearthed tombstones and documented the history of his community using fading inscriptions. In the introduction to *Avnei Zikaron*, his book on Jewish cemeteries, he speaks of his "great desire to search, explore, and excavate the past." He gained in social stature, began to dress like a biblical patriarch, and was invited in 1856 to the coronation of Tsar Alexander II in Moscow. He presented the new monarch with a poem he composed in Hebrew to commemorate the occasion.

Firkovich gathered his harvest into three collections. The first two contained Jewish manuscripts in Hebrew and Arabic; the third became the largest collection of Samaritan manuscripts in the world.

The Imperial Russian Library bought the first collection in 1862 for 125,000 rubles. It included 18,000 manuscripts and fragments. The website of the National Library of Russia boasts that "thanks to Firkovich and Archimandrite Antonin (1,180 items) the collection of Jewish (or, to be precise, Judaic) manuscripts in the National Library of Russia is one of the largest in the world." The greatest manuscript he obtained for the library is the Leningrad Codex, dated 1008–1009 CE, which fills in major gaps about missing pages from the Aleppo Codex. (Firkovich's personal archive, including his correspondence, most of it in Hebrew, is also kept in the National Library of Russia.)[21]

In October 1863, Firkovich returned to Jerusalem, flush with money, letters of recommendation from Russian officials, and Ottoman firmans. With his own funds he rebuilt the Karaite Anan ben David synagogue and bought manuscripts from Yaakov Saphir, an ethnographer and one of the only Jewish book collectors in Jerusalem itself, who had just returned from Yemen.

In 1859, Saphir had been on his way to British India to raise funds for the construction of the Hurva Synagogue in the Jewish Quarter. The

Hurva (lit., "Ruins") Synagogue was nothing but a plot of land owned by the Ashkenazi community and left empty since their first failed attempt to construct a synagogue on the site in 1701. Lack of funds and debts to Muslim neighbors had determined its fate as a ruin for more than one and a half centuries (hence its nickname). But when the synagogue was finally built it was glorious. The largest sum came from Sir Moses Montefiore, but Saphir was one of the few leading local Ashkenazi Jews who worked for its reconstruction until its completion in 1864. The result was a grand synagogue (now reconstructed) in an enclosure with adjacent schools and a yeshiva, containing "a trove of books" (*otzar sfarim*), according to Avraham Luncz, a Jewish traveler who visited it in 1890. Herbert Samuel was invited to visit when he became the First High Commissioner of Palestine. In 1948 the synagogue was blown up by the Royal Jordanian Army, and it was not reconstructed and inaugurated until 2010.[22]

Saphir was not a traveler or ethnographer by choice. In fact, he sub- scribed to the belief of some Jews that once in Jerusalem, Jews should not leave their city. But he needed work, and his language skills made him the most suitable candidate to go to India. Along the way, he fell victim to a scam and found himself penniless and stranded in Aden, Yemen. During his nine months with the Jewish community there, he grew more and more impressed by the members' literacy, their skillful precision in recit- ing the Torah, and, above all, the great abundance of manuscripts they held. Jews in Yemen had enjoyed a centuries-long scribal, literary, and epistolary tradition. Biblical commentaries by Rabbi Shlomo Yitzchaki (known by his acronym, Rashi), the leading medieval exegete, were cop- ied by Yemenite Jewish scholars at the end of the twelfth century. Heads of the community in Aden exchanged letters and theological treatises in Judeo-Arabic with Maimonides, the great theologian living in Egypt.[23]

Meanwhile, Firkovich had come to Aleppo from Jerusalem. Before he left, Yaakov Saphir handed him a page containing a copy of the Dedication Inscription of the tenth-century Aleppo Codex. The inscrip- tion had been copied into a Bible manuscript from 1322 housed in the Karaite synagogue in Jerusalem. Saphir asked Firkovich to compare the copy with the original. On his return, Firkovich gave the page, with marginal corrections, back to Saphir. Saphir, who relates the story in his book *Even Sapir* (Sapphire Stone), was stunned by one emendation.

According to the codex's Dedication Inscription, the name of the scribe who wrote the manuscript was Shelomo ben Buyaa, whereas Firkovich had amended it to ascribe the crown to the Karaite scholar Shelomo ben Yeroham.[24]

Whether this was another of Firkovich's inventions must remain, for now, an open question.

From Aleppo, Firkovich went on to Cairo and rummaged through the Cairo Genizah thirty years before the Cambridge scholar Solomon Schechter first entered the same storeroom. But his primary passion was directed to the Karaite manuscripts that he found in abundance in the genizah of Cairo's Karaite synagogue.

Some regarded Firkovich as a charlatan who forged colophons, tombstone inscriptions, and dates of manuscripts in order to lend credence to his theory that the Karaite minority—rather than the Talmud-worshipping Rabbanite majority that had split off a millennium earlier—were the true Jews. His erstwhile secretary, Ephraim Deinard, set himself to "removing the mask off this man's face," and declared, "I find all his writings and discoveries a lie."[25] Another of his critics, Abraham Harkavy, was a graduate of the renowned Volozhin yeshiva (the jewel in the crown of rabbinic learning in eastern Europe) and for more than four decades head of the oriental manuscript collection at the Imperial Public Library of Saint Petersburg. A prolific polyglot scholar, Harkavy wrote books in Russian, German, Hebrew, and French. He convinced the directors of the library to buy Firkovich's collections, but he was also the first to show that Firkovich's skills as a forger equaled his skills as a scholar and collector.

The Imperial Public Library purchased Firkovich's collections—over sixteen thousand mostly Hebrew manuscripts and fragments—at an astonishing price. They remain a source of pride to the National Library of Russia, which is currently collaborating with the National Library of Israel to digitize them and make them available online.

Jerusalem's Master Forger?

One morning, Alegre Savariego, a curator at the Israel Antiquities Authority since 1995, ushered us into the cramped basement storerooms of the Rockefeller Museum. Built on a perch of land called Karm al-

Sheikh that is pocked with tombs (mapped by the French archaeologist Charles Clermont-Ganneau in 1874), the white limestone museum overlooks the northeast corner of the Old City. It is said that Godfrey of Bouillon, the leader of the First Crusade, set up camp there in 1099. The Prince of Wales (soon to be King Edward VII) camped there in 1862. The museum was built next to a villa constructed in the eighteenth century for Sheikh Muhammad al-Khalili.

Alegre Savariego plucked from the shelves a clay jar the size of a watermelon. It was covered in oddly angled ancient Hebrew lettering. Despite its apparent patina of antiquity, she said, the artifact was in fact by several centuries the newest among the thousands shelved here. It was a nineteenth-century forgery from the collection of Jerusalem's most notorious antiquities dealer and book hunter, Wilhelm Moses Shapira.

We recognized the name at once; few of our protagonists has attracted as much worldwide attention. At the British Library, we had come across several manuscripts from Shapira's astonishing collection, including a book of Karaite liturgical poems (*piyuttim*) from the seventeenth or eighteenth century. Its colophon reads: "Written here in the Holy City, Mount Zion, beloved of God, may He establish it for eternity. May it be rebuilt soon, in our times. Amen. [In the year] 5504 to the creation."

Shapira was born in Kamenets (in today's Ukraine) in 1830. Baptized at age twenty-five, he arrived in Jerusalem in 1856. After apprenticing at the vocational school run by Jerusalem's Anglican mission, the first Protestant church in the Middle East, Shapira opened a souvenir shop offering pressed flowers "from the Holy Land," mother-of-pearl necklaces, photographs, and olive-wood Bible covers. Baedeker's *Guide to Palestine and Syria* (1876 edition) recommended the shop to pilgrims.[26]

Beginning in 1871, riding the gathering wave of interest in biblical archaeology aiming "to prove the Bible right," Shapira expanded to antiquities. He amassed a collection of ancient Moabite statuettes, fertility figurines, and vessels with indecipherable inscriptions, such as the one at the Rockefeller. Nothing like them had been seen before. In two consignments, Shapira persuaded the Royal Museum in Berlin to purchase sixteen hundred of the pieces for an amount—partly donated by the German Kaiser himself—that made him one of the richest men in

Jerusalem. The London *Daily News* reported on "the transfer of a goodly sum from the gorged money bags of Berlin to the lean and hungry coffers of Jerusalem."[27] With his newfound fortune, Shapira moved his family into one of the first villas built outside the old city walls (later known as the Ticho House).[28]

But Shapira's high ambitions would soon crash into low realities. The renowned archaeologist Charles Clermont-Ganneau started his career in the Middle East as a dragoman for the French consulate in Jerusalem. He exposed the Moabite collection as what he called a colossal deception, clumsily fabricated by Shapira's partner, Salim al-Qari. Shapira insisted that he had sold his collection in good faith and that he himself had been duped by his erstwhile partner.

To rehabilitate his reputation, Shapira began purveying hundreds of genuine Hebrew manuscripts to the British Museum, including rare volumes he had acquired from Jews in Yemen and from Karaites in Iraq and Egypt. He proudly added a title in gold letters on the white sign above the shop door in the Christian Quarter: "Correspondent to the British Museum."

Shapira visited Yemen's Jewish communities in 1879. Four years later, several Yemenite Jews who had recently arrived in Jerusalem sought the help of Horatio Spafford, founder of the American Colony. "He lived among them when he was in Yemen," Bertha Spafford Vester, Horatio's daughter, writes in her memoir, "joining them in their synagogue until he had won their confidence." During a holiday, "Rabbi Moses," as he called himself, spotted a valuable old Torah scroll. "He offered to buy it, but they said they would rather part with their eyes or their lives than with their beloved manuscript." According to what was reported to the Spaffords, Shapira returned with Ottoman soldiers and "forcibly took the Temanite [Yemenite] scroll, leaving a nominal sum of money."[29]

The Yemenite rabbi Yihye Kapah, in his *Wars of God* (*Milchamot Hashem*), tells a similar story:

> Many of our multitudes sold old books that they had inherited from their ancestors to uncircumcised people who came to Yemen, such as Moshe ben Netanel [Shapira], who dwelt in the house of our master and teacher Avraham Salah. He himself sold him a Taj of Prophets and Writings with

the Targum of Yonatan ben Uzziel on the Prophets and Saadia Gaon's Arabic translation of Isaiah and the Writings. Also a Mishnah, Seder Kodashim, with Maimonides' commentary in Arabic in a beautiful script, including drawings of our holy and glorious Temple and its holy vessels. I saw it in his hands with my own eyes . . . and we were powerless to take it away from him. . . . Many ancient manuscripts were sold to him and to others cheaply.[30]

So rich was his haul that before his death Shapira would supply price-less Yemenite manuscripts to the British Museum, to Baron David Ginzburg in Saint Petersburg, and to Abraham Firkovich. Between 1877 and 1882 the British Museum purchased from him nearly 300 manu-scripts, mostly Karaite. Of these, 145 were purchased in one transaction in July 1882. "At one stroke" wrote the museum's specialist on Hebrew and oriental manuscripts in 1935, this purchase "raised the Karaite sec-tion of the Hebrew manuscripts to one of outstanding importance, only surpassed by the Firkovich collection in Leningrad."[31]

Still, Shapira's ambitions vaulted higher. A decade after the Moabite scandal, Shapira claimed to have come into possession of a hitherto un-known version of Deuteronomy, some two thousand years older than any known biblical manuscript. In Shapira's telling, Bedouin tribesmen had taken refuge in a limestone cave overlooking Wadi Mujib, on the east side of the Dead Sea. "They found there several bundles of old black linen," Shapira said. "They peeled away the linen, and, behold, instead of gold, which they expected to find, there were only some black inscribed strips of leather."[32] Written in ancient Canaanite Hebrew script (also called Paleo-Hebrew or Phoenician) on fifteen seven-inch-long strips of leather, this "short unorthodoxical book of the last speech of Moses in the plain of Moab," as Shapira called it, purported to date from the First Temple period.[33] It departed from the traditional text, including an altered ver-sion of the Decalogue.

As his daughter would write in an autobiographical novel, Shapira and his family put great hopes in the discovery. "Now, at last, he would be free to shed his humble bookseller's garb. No more need to spend long days in the stuffy shop, engraving texts on olive-wood covers for prayer-books and albums! . . . He would be given a chair in some European university as an Orientalist; and last, but by no means least, he would score a victory over that insolent dragoman [Clermont-Ganneau]." The Shapira household began to spend lavishly in anticipation of a large profit. "Is it not so, Papa," his daughter asked, "that when you have sold the Deuteronomy you will buy all Palestine?"[34]

In 1883, Shapira took his find from Jerusalem to Berlin and presented it to a group of scholars. In ninety minutes they reached their verdict: the manuscript was a "clever and impudent forgery."[35] They refused to purchase the manuscript for the Royal Library (now the Staatsbibliothek).

Undaunted, Shapira hastened to London and offered his scrolls to the British Museum. His asking price: £1 million (about $250 million today). He first approached Sir Walter Besant, secretary of the Palestine Exploration Fund. Besant recounted: "A certain Shapira, a Polish Jew converted to Christianity but not to good works, came to England and called upon me mysteriously. He had with him, he said, a document which would simply make students of the Bible and Hebrew scholars reconsider their ways; it would throw a flood of light upon the Pentateuch. . . . It was nothing less than a contemporary copy of the book of Deuteronomy written on parchment."[36]

The scrolls caused a sensation. Two of the fragments, displayed at the British Museum, attracted enthusiastic crowds. Prime Minister William Gladstone came to inspect the texts and to meet Shapira. The *Times* of London featured translations.

Once more, however, Shapira's euphoria would be cut short. Two experts—a leading Bible scholar, Christian David Ginsburg, and Shapira's nemesis Clermont-Ganneau—denounced the manuscripts as forgeries inked on strips cut from the blank lower margins of old Torah scrolls. Worse, the debunkers implied that Shapira, now caricatured in the satirical magazine *Punch* with a hooked nose as "Mr. Sharp-Eye-Ra," was himself the forger. Ganneau concluded that the forger

> took one of those large synagogue rolls of leather, containing the Pentateuch, written in the square Hebrew character, and perhaps dating back two or three centuries, rolls which Mr. Shapira must be well acquainted with, for he deals in them. . . . The forger then cut off the lower edge of this roll—that which offered him the widest surface. He obtained in this way some narrow strips of leather with an appearance of comparative antiquity, which was still further heightened by the use of the proper

chemical agents. On these strips of leather he wrote with ink, making use of the alphabet of the Moabite stone, and introducing such "various readings" as fancy dictated, the passages from Deuteronomy which have been deciphered and translated by M. Ginsburg, with patience and learning worthy of better employment.[37]

The scrolls and the man both stood accused of having passed themselves off as something they were not. The cunning baptized Jew had forged himself. Disgraced and humiliated, Shapira abandoned his spurious specimens at the British Museum and fled to Holland. Before leaving, he sent a note to Ginsburg: "I do not think that I will be able to survive this shame."[38]

But the shame outlived him. Six months later, in March 1884, Shapira shot himself in a seedy hotel in Rotterdam. "What cost him his life," his daughter wrote, "was the thought of being viewed in the eyes of the world not as the deceived but as the deceiver." He was buried in an unmarked pauper's grave.[39]

As we mentioned in an earlier chapter, six decades later, a Bedouin shepherd followed a stray goat into a cave at Qumran, near the Dead Sea. There he discovered seven scrolls of animal hide, wrapped in linen and stuffed into an ancient jar. Struck by the remarkable similarities between the Qumran documents and the Shapira Deuteronomy, scholars includ-

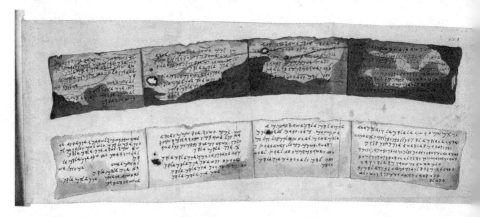

Shapira's Deuteronomy scroll, lithograph by Dangerfield Lith, Covent Garden, London, 1883. (British Library, Add. MS. 41294, fol. 35r. British Library, London, UK, © British Library Board. All Rights Reserved / Bridgeman Images.)

ing Menahem Mansoor and John Marco Allegro reopened Shapira's case, wondering whether his scrolls had been too hastily dismissed. J. L. Teicher of the University of Cambridge went so far as to argue that in light of the discovery of the Dead Sea Scrolls, we are led to "the inescapable conclusion that the Shapira manuscripts were genuine."[40]

Others disagreed. "Since several scholars have compared the new Scrolls to the so-called archetype of Deuteronomy, offered by the notorious forger Shapira to the British government for a million pounds," said William F. Albright, dean of biblical archaeologists, and the expert who authenticated the Dead Sea Scrolls, "it should be emphasized that there is nothing whatever in common between them except the fact that texts of the Hebrew Bible written in ancient scripts are involved."[41] However, as recently as 2017 scholars continue to debate the question of authenticity of Shapira's Deuteronomy.[42]

In the meantime, the evidence that might have vindicated Shapira, the scrolls themselves, had mysteriously vanished. After Shapira's suicide, the scrolls were auctioned at Sotheby's to a London book dealer named Bernard Quaritch for a mere 10 pounds, 5 shillings. Quaritch displayed them at the Royal Albert Hall, and then put them up for sale. In his catalogue, the fragments, "which led the religious world of England to sing hallelujahs," are advertised for 25 pounds.[43]

Some conjecture that Quaritch sold them to Sir Charles Nicholson, whose estate north of London, scrolls perhaps included, burned down in 1899. Others suppose Shapira's widow took them from Jerusalem to her house in Stockhausen, Germany, also destroyed by fire that year. With the help of a fellow sleuth in Australia, the journalist Chanan Tigay traced them instead to Philip Brookes Mason, a natural history enthusiast from Burton-on-Trent, England, who exhibited the fragments in 1889. But there the trail runs cold. Tigay did find what he believes to be the scrolls' negatives—parchments of Torah scrolls with margins cut out in exactly the same way as Charles Clermont-Ganneau suspected that they were produced.[44]

Perhaps we can understand Shapira as a product of a modern fetish for authenticity, and of a rivalry of European nation-states obsessed not just with colonial expansion but with their own origins. In Shapira, their obsessions were made visible.

Strait-laced Victorians may have regarded forgers as a menace to history. But not all falsifications are equally unforgivable. The irony is that Deuteronomy, the fifth and final book of the Torah, may itself be a kind of inspired forgery, miraculously "found" in the reign of King Josiah in the late seventh century BCE (reported in 2 Kings 22), and attributed to Moses to enhance its authenticity.

That morning in the Rockefeller, we wondered why the museum kept Shapira's Moabite forgeries among its genuine treasures. Perhaps because the history of a lie is itself a truth. Like any forger, Shapira imprinted the pattern of his own period on a past he hoped to make real. In archaeology as in psychology, we come to know ourselves by understanding our self-deceptions. What is forgery, after all, if not the intimacy of knowledge and deception?

CHAPTER SIX

DREAMERS AND VISIONARIES

Between Two Centuries

After you have visited the library ten times to look at books, go once to
look at the readers.
—*Martin Buber, "Advice to Frequenters of Libraries"*

Not all those enchanted by Jerusalem tried to empty the city of its textual treasures. As the nineteenth century turned into the twentieth, some
set their minds to enriching the city's coffers and forging it in the shape of
their dreams. We discovered some beautifully esoteric collections from
the numerous libraries and archives established in Jerusalem in this period; some destined to disappear into larger libraries and one that we
were among the last to visit before it was auctioned off piecemeal.

One morning we climbed a ribbon of road up the terraced hillside of the
Mount of Olives toward the Augusta Victoria hospital, built by Kaiser
Wilhelm II, the last German emperor. Looking back, we took in a sweeping
view of the Old City's clustered domes and minarets, which seemed to glow
with a gauzy light. We had come to visit a pallid stone house tucked away
behind the compound, which held the eclectic collection of Gustaf Dalman,
a German Orientalist and scholar of Semitic languages, who produced an

authoritative grammar (1894) and dictionary (1901) of postbiblical Aramaic.[1] Dalman also revised an early translation of the New Testament into Hebrew (published in Leipzig in 1877), before the modern revival of the Hebrew language.

Under the auspices of the German Protestant Institute of Archaeology, founded in Jerusalem in 1900, Dalman gathered ceramics and ossuaries, herbs, native songbirds, and two exquisite models of Jerusalem made by Conrad Schick. "There is no aspect of the country and its life with which Dalman has not familiarized himself," W. F. Albright said in 1938. "He knows the geography and topography, the rocks, animals, and plants, the life of the people, their dialects, their poetry and their proverbs, their customs and their crafts."[2] From 1902 to 1917, Dalman also served as director of the library which the Prussian consulate had founded in Jerusalem in 1847. According to Dov Schidorsky, an expert on libraries in Ottoman Palestine, "Most probably it was the first research library in Palestine." In the hands of Dalman and other scholars, Schidorsky adds, "German librarianship had a decisive impact with long-term effects on the development of libraries in Palestine."[3]

Dalman ultimately returned to Germany and ended his career at the University of Greifswald. But when he was first offered the Greifswald job he turned it down, as he said in a telegram, because "my heart is drawn toward Jerusalem."[4]

In *Jerusalem: The Biography*, Simon Sebag Montefiore writes: "Throughout her history, Jerusalem existed in the imagination of devotees who lived far away in America or Europe. Now that these visitors were arriving on steamships in their thousands, they expected to find the exotic and dangerous, picturesque and authentic images they had imagined with the help of their Bibles, their Victorian stereotypes of race, and, once they arrived, their translators and guides."[5] For both those who viewed it from afar and those who viewed it from within, Jerusalem has served to trigger figures of the imagination. In both cases, the words and texts that nourished the imagined Jerusalem, past or future, loomed larger than the city's physical topography and outward surface. The keepers of Jerusalem's libraries and archives thus registered the city's imagination.

Some visitors to Jerusalem find it nearly impossible to see the city unmediated by a textual tradition of one kind or another: scriptural texts, liturgy, homilies, or guidebooks. Some seem to believe that Jerusalem—more a narrative space than a physical one—can be explored using the Bible as a guidebook. They see the city through the eyes of faith. Father Pakrad Berjikian of the Armenian Patriarchate illustrated this tendency with a linguistic example. Armenian pilgrims to Jerusalem, he told us, called themselves *Mahdesi*, "I experienced death." By following the footsteps of Christ through his passion, crucifixion, and resurrection, they could imagine that they too were entering the heavenly Jerusalem where all the Just live.

In this ever-elusive city, a city more invented than known, the gap between real and imagined leaves other visitors with a sense of vertigo. In the summer of 1867, Mark Twain recorded his first sight of the city: "At last, away in the middle of the day, ancient bits of wall and crumbling arches began to line the way—we toiled up one more hill, and every pilgrim and every sinner swung his hat on high! Jerusalem! . . . I think there was no individual in the party whose brain was not teeming with thoughts and images and memories invoked by the grand history of the venerable city that lay before us, but still among them all was no 'voice of them that wept.'"[6]

Three decades after Twain's visit, Theodor Herzl, the father of modern Zionism, jotted down his impression of the city in his diary: "When I remember thee in days to come, O Jerusalem, it will not be with pleasure. The musty deposits of two thousand years of inhumanity, intolerance, and uncleanliness lie in the foul-smelling alleys. . . . If we ever get Jerusalem and I am still able to do anything actively at that time, I would begin by cleaning it up!"[7]

But even Herzl, in his utopian novel *Altneuland* (Old-New Land, 1902), could not help imagining a different future for the capital:

> In the old days they had had to endure many disgusting sights before they could reach their shrines. All was different now. There were no longer private dwellings in the Old City; the lanes and the streets were beautifully paved and cared for. All the buildings were devoted to religious and benevolent purposes: hospices for pilgrims of all denominations. Moslem, Jewish, and Christian welfare institutions, hospitals, clinics stood side by side. In the middle of a great square was the splendid Peace Palace, where international congresses of peace-lovers and scientists were held, for Jerusalem was now a home for all the best strivings of the human spirit, for Faith, Love, Knowledge.[8]

The twelfth-century Toledo-born poet Yehuda Halevi is said to have dropped dead on setting foot in Jerusalem. Others stopped at the threshold of the city, hesitant to let reality intrude on the purity of their imagination. They did not want to see the real Jerusalem. In their thwarted love, they preferred the imagined encounter to the thing itself. In the sixth century, a Georgian pilgrim named David Garejeli resolved to set out on the perilous journey to Jerusalem in order "to pray at the Holy Places and worship at the life-giving sepulchre of our Lord Jesus Christ." After an arduous journey, he reached a hilltop overlooking Jerusalem, fell on his knees, and could go no farther: "I judge myself unworthy even to approach those holy places." He picked up three stones and turned back. That night, it is said, the patriarch in Jerusalem dreamt that someone had stolen the city's grace. The next day he sent his men to seek the culprit. They took two stones from David, and allowed him to keep the third, which he brought back with him to Georgia. There he founded a monastery southeast of Tbilisi, near the present-day border with Azerbaijan. To this day, the faithful believe that visiting the David Gareja Monastery three times is the equivalent of making a pilgrimage to Jerusalem.[9]

Robert Curzon first laid eyes on Jerusalem in 1833.

> It was curious to observe the different effect which our approach to Jerusalem had upon the various persons who composed our party. A Christian pilgrim, who had joined us on the road, fell down upon his knees and kissed the holy ground; two others embraced each other, and congratulated themselves that they had lived to see Jerusalem. As for us Franks, we sat bolt upright upon our horses, and stared and said nothing; whilst around us the more natural children of the East wept for joy, and, as in the army of the Crusaders, the word Jerusalem! Jerusalem! was repeated from mouth to mouth; but we, who consider ourselves civilized and superior beings, repressed our emotions; we were above showing that we participated in the feelings of our barbarous companions. As for myself, I would have got off my horse and walked bare-footed towards the gate, as some did, if I had dared: but I was in fear of being laughed at for my absurdity, and therefore sat fast in my saddle.[10]

Still others preferred the thrall of imagination to Jerusalem's mundane reality. The German Jewish lyric poet Else Lasker-Schüler, who lived in the city from 1937 until her death in early 1945, effused somewhat unconvincingly that residents of Jerusalem were compelled "to behave solemnly and courteously, so as not to startle the devout spirit of the exquisite, exalted city."[11]

The gap between the real and imagined cities, between myth and metropolis, lies at the root of the peculiar form of madness known as Jerusalem Syndrome (first clinically described in 1937 by Heinz Herman, a pioneering Israeli psychiatrist). Afflicted visitors, seduced by the city's sacred spaces, imagine themselves as self-appointed prophets, messiahs, or redeemers. They can no longer distinguish reality and fevered imagination. (Today a barefoot Jesus in white robes can often be spotted wandering the Old City. He hails from Texas.)

How has Jerusalem been imagined from a distance? Believers are exhorted not to forget Jerusalem. But how to remember something you have never seen except by an act of imagination? How did images of Jerusalem that had little to do with the real city become so pervasive? And how has Jerusalem been imagined in Jerusalem itself? To get a feel for the texture of a city woven from its own imagined communities, we delved into basements where contemporary and historical models of Jerusalem were kept alongside esoteric archives of communities that now exist only in the imagination.

Jerusalem in Replicas

It is not uncommon to long for an imagined Jerusalem even in the real Jerusalem. In his novella *The Hill of Evil Counsel* (1972), the Jerusalem-born writer Amos Oz has a character say, "I have been living in Jerusalem for three years and I continue to yearn for it as though I were still a student in Leipzig. Surely there is a paradox here."[12] The habit of imagining Jerusalem has become so deeply ingrained that its momentum continues in Jerusalem itself. What else explains the paradoxical abundance of copies of Jerusalem in Jerusalem?

Conrad Schick, a German-born missionary, architect, carpenter, and archaeologist who lived in Jerusalem until his death in 1901, created models of the city unsurpassed in the intricacy of their design and craftsmanship. He also planned the Mea Shearim neighborhood and designed his own house, Beit Tabor, which still stands on Prophets Street in central Jerusalem, around the corner from the Ethiopian monastery (which he also designed). When we visited the monastery, we noticed that Schick had incorporated into his house a copy of the boundary inscription from Gezer, an important biblical city, and a stone set into the lobby wall inscribed in Second Temple Samaritan script (a descendant of the ancient Hebrew alphabet).

Schick taught carpentry on behalf of the London Society for Promoting Christianity Amongst the Jews at Christ Church. This two-hundred-year-old Anglican mission in Jerusalem's Old City (and the first Protestant church in the Middle East) houses two of his works: a model of the Holy Sepulchre (highly recommended by the 1876 Baedeker travel guide) and a model of the Haram al-Sharif commissioned by Turkish authorities for display at the Ottoman pavilion at the 1873 World's Fair in Vienna (plate 9).[13] It is also home to what has been named the Conrad Schick Library, with glass negatives, some hand-colored, a few thousand books, and a vast archive with rich material on Schick, Shapira, and other members of the mission. In 1872, Schick became one of the only non-Muslims ever allowed to explore the subterranean spaces beneath the Islamic shrines on the sacred esplanade; in his models he re-created what he saw both above and below ground.

In the basement of Schmidt's College, a Lutheran school across from Damascus Gate, we marveled at Schick's model of Solomon's Temple built on the basis of biblical descriptions. Though it attracts few visitors these days, the model has patiently resided there for some time. In 1923, a Franciscan friar named Barnaby Meistermann insisted that Jerusalem "should not be left without seeing the exact model of the Temple made from painted wood by Mr. Schick."[14]

Many model makers would follow in Schick's footsteps. The Tower of David Museum inside Jaffa Gate devotes an entire room to a remarkable model of nineteenth-century Jerusalem made of strips of beaten zinc mounted on a wooden platform to a scale of 1:500 (plate 10). It was created by a Hungarian Catholic, Stephan Illes, who worked as a bookbinder in Jerusalem from 1860 to 1880 and displayed his model (alongside Schick's) at the 1873 World's Fair.[15] Mobile models of Jerusalem traveled across Europe. In the exhibition room at Christ Church in Jerusalem, one such model folds neatly into a suitcase.

A short walk away from Christ Church, in a house in the heart of the Jewish Quarter, sits a 375-square-foot model of Jerusalem in the First Temple period, built by the archaeologist Dan Bahat under the auspices of the Ben-Zvi Institute. A 1:50 scale model at the Israel Museum, designed by archaeologist Michael Avi-Yonah and updated by Yoram Tsafrir, re-creates the cityscape as it looked in 66 CE, the year in which the Great Revolt against the Romans broke out.[16] Steps from the model, the museum gift shop offers a 637-piece do-it-yourself Third Temple model kit. The real blurs into the imagined.

Even the most accurate models of Jerusalem, however, carry an element of the imagination. The materials engineer Nataly Ostrovsky ushered us into the basement of the municipality building on Safra Square, which houses an expansive room that at first glance resembles a large playground. It is filled with an astonishingly accurate—and continuously updated—1:500 scale model of the modern city. To aid urban planners, the American-born architect Richard Harvey began constructing this Lilliputian Jerusalem in 1978 and dedicated twenty-one years of his life to it. Ostrovsky and her small team have continued his work and keep the model current, piecing together houses, balconies, and even palm trees. "Our model is intended primarily as a tool for architects, developers and planners, as well as for those involved in the municipal decision-making process," commented Kobi Ariel, former director of the Jerusalem Center for Planning in Historic Cities. "Architects with specific projects in mind can try out their ideas on the model."[17] Near the model of Santiago Calatrava's 1,200-foot-long light-rail bridge arching over the entrance to the city, laser-cut transparent Plexiglas constructions rise above the familiar buildings and roads, marking the future plans for Jerusalem's western entrance area, approved in August 2012. They reflect a vision of the not yet built future city.

We reflect on the correlations between these models and the archives and libraries that house them, as though the models give three-dimensional expression to the dreams of building Jerusalem that inhabit so many of the books beside which they rest.

Past Imperfect, Future Messianic: The American Colonists

The archivist and curator Rachel Lev welcomed us into the serene and spacious ground-floor apartment in the Palm House of the American Colony Hotel in which Valentine Vester, matriarch of the American Colony, lived until her death in 2008. Lev had invited us to examine the Colony's exceptionally rich archives, which paint a portrait of a group of ardent believers who from their Jerusalem perch witnessed the death throes of the Ottoman Empire, the arrival of the British in 1917, and the upheavals that would remake the Middle East. She brought down albums that documented the 1915 locust plague, the battles between the Turkish and the British armies, the 1927 earthquake, and the 1929 Arab riots, as well as hand-painted idyllic pastoral scenes of shepherd boys with wooden flutes and girls with clay pitchers. The archives, and how they got there, offer a window into the long-standing American Christian preoccupation with envisioning Jerusalem.

On departing Spain for his great expedition, Christopher Columbus wrote to his royal benefactors, "I propose to Your Majesties that all the profit derived from this enterprise be used for the recovery of Jerusalem." Early Americans, on the other hand, envisioned themselves as building a new Jerusalem—"a city on a hill." William Bradford, the first governor of the Plymouth Colony, stepped off the *Mayflower* and declared, "Come let us declare in Zion the word of God."[18]

The ideal of Jerusalem would prove fruitful, at least as a rhetorical flourish, through the Protestant Social Gospel movement, which peaked in the late nineteenth and early twentieth centuries. "Here, if anywhere," Washington Gladden, one of the movement's early leaders, proclaimed in 1890, "is to rise that city of God, the New Jerusalem, whose glories are to fill the earth." In an ongoing gesture of self-definition, hundreds of towns across the American continent would be named Jerusalem, Salem, or Zion, and a number of nineteenth-century American public figures (Ulysses S. Grant, William T. Sherman) and writers (Mark Twain, Herman Melville, Ralph Waldo Emerson) would make the pilgrimage to the original city.[19]

Nineteenth-century Christian Restorationists in both America and Britain, on the other hand, ardently wished to restore the Jews to Jerusalem. On a visit to the Ben-Zvi Institute, we learned that its library contains the diaries and letters of James Finn, a nineteenth-century British Consul in Jerusalem and member of the London Society for Promoting Christianity Amongst the Jews. The head librarian showed us a remarkable letter from 1857 in which Finn recommends to the earl of Caledon that Jewish farmers immigrate to Jerusalem to work the land.

In 1881 a group of messianic Christians from Chicago arrived at the city, where they planned to await Jesus's imminent return. Not one brought a guidebook. Instead, they brought Bibles. They called themselves Overcomers, for their attitude toward sin. Soon joined by two groups of Swedish settlers led by Olof Henrik Larsson, the Overcomers set up a utopian commune, known as the American Colony, with cows and pigs and chickens and a bakery—and a hostel for pilgrims. Their leader was Horatio Spafford, a lawyer, and his charismatic wife, Anna. Jerusalem's Protestant missionaries, as well as the American consul, regarded the newcomers with suspicion. There was talk of unorthodox theologies and sexual practices.

Before the turn of the century, the American colonists moved into an estate on Nablus Road built by Rabbah Daoud Amin Effendi al-Husseini, who had lived there with his harem of four wives. In 1902, the Jaffa hotelier Plato von Ustinov (grandfather of the British actor Peter Ustinov) was looking for a place to put up some guests and asked the Spaffords to accommodate them. Soon afterward, the Spaffords began transforming the house into Jerusalem's favorite hangout of diplomats, foreign correspondents, and spies. T. E. Lawrence stayed here. Ingrid Bergman was filmed in the sitting room playing Golda Meir for a television movie. John le Carré wrote one of his spy novels here.[20]

Disillusioned by internal divisions, by inheritance disputes, and perhaps by Jerusalem itself, many of the Swedish colonists returned to Sweden. There they created their own sort of replica: a play in which they reenacted their own story of passion, love, and suffering in Jerusalem. The *Ingmar Play* (*Ingmarsspelen*) is a dramatized version by Rune Lindström of part 1 of the novel *Jerusalem* by Selma Lagerlöf, based on events which took place in Nås between 1890 and 1896. It is staged annually at Nås on July 4. Similar plays at Christmas and Eastertime dating from medieval days were the oldest forms of bringing Jerusalem to Christian audiences around the world.

More recently, the American Colony has become embroiled in the divisive politics of the city. In 1999 dozens of Israeli police officers briefly surrounded the hotel during a showdown between Israeli and Palestinian security officials over who should guard the British foreign minister, Robin Cook. The minister was meeting with Faisal Husseini, the Palestine Liberation Organization's representative in Jerusalem and head of the Orient House, the PLO headquarters, located around the corner from the hotel. After the Orient House was locked up in 2001 by the Israeli police during the Second Intifada, the hotel became the unofficial headquarters of Palestinian representatives in Jerusalem. In 2004 the hotel's head bartender, Ibrahim Zeghari, was barred from Jerusalem because he resided on the wrong side of Israel's newly constructed security barrier. Several years later, the Interior Ministry ordered Munther Fahimi, the Jerusalem-born owner of the American Colony bookshop, the best bookstore in East Jerusalem, to be deported on the grounds that he had lost his residency rights after spending several years in the United States.

In April 2014, the American Colony Hotel celebrated the public inauguration of its archives, containing photographs and previously unknown diaries, letters, and other historical records dating back to 1840. These include biographical records of Bertha and Horatio Spafford; the letters of Jacob Eliahu Spafford, the adopted son of Horatio and Anna, whose Sephardic biological parents were among the first Jews in Jerusalem converted by the London Mission Society for Spreading Christianity Among Jews (a precursor of the London Society for Promoting Christianity Amongst the Jews); family photo albums; geopolitical maps; and glass negatives documenting the Colony's aid projects and communal life from the 1890s to 1934. Following the death of Valentine Vester in 2008, Rachel Lev discovered thousands more documents in her apartment.

As we pored through this archive, it became apparent that the American Colony photographers had documented both the life of their own community and pivotal moments in the city's history. Elijah Meyers, a Jew born in Bombay (Mumbai) who converted to Christianity, founded the American Colony Photo Department in 1898. He photographed the visit of Kaiser Wilhelm II in the same year. The following year, Theodor Herzl commissioned him to photograph Jewish settlements.

The colonists collected photographs by local photographers, such as Khalil Raed and Garabed Krikorian. Elijah Meyers trained fifteen Colony teenagers in the art of photography. Foremost among his young students were Lewis Larsson, later the Swedish consul general in Jerusalem, and Eric Matson, the first person in the country to use stereoscopic cameras. Matson continued to use the trade name of the American Colony long after he left Jerusalem. He gave some thirteen thousand negatives and eleven albums of contact prints to the U.S. Library of Congress in 1966 and in 1970 donated a group of negatives that he had hidden away in the basement of the Jerusalem YMCA. During the first half of the twentieth century, the Colony's photographers produced the most important collection of photographs of Jerusalem ever created. Attracted to the city by the forces of messianic anticipation and imagination, the colonists stayed to document its realities.[21]

Dominican Discourses: École Biblique

Entering the École Biblique et Archéologique, a few streets away from the American Colony Hotel, in the heart of East Jerusalem's bustle, one day, we found ourselves in a sequestered garden of pine-lined paths leading to the courtyard of Saint Stephen's priory (known also by its French name, Saint-Étienne). It is one of the residual reminders of the nineteenth-century competition among the European powers to stake a claim to the city and assert custodial rights. The École was founded in 1890 by Father Marie-Joseph Lagrange, a French Dominican who wished to ground biblical study in the text's original geographical context. "One cannot understand the Bible without placing oneself in its atmosphere," he said at the opening ceremony. As his biographer summarized, "In order to understand the Bible, we must draw on the land of the Bible." When Lagrange came to Jerusalem, he could at last read the Scriptures against the landscape. "I had so loved the Book and now I contemplate the Land!" he exclaimed.[22] At the time of his arrival, the Dominicans lived in a humble plot outside Damascus Gate (known to the Crusaders as Saint Stephen's Gate). But that year they laid the foundations for the impressive Dominican monastery on the ground where tradition said Saint Stephen, the first Christian martyr, was stoned to death.[23]

Much to the concern of his more traditional contemporaries, Lagrange was one of the first Catholic scholars to adopt the new scientific approaches to the Bible aimed at shedding light on the text through historical and critical exegesis, archaeological research, and the study of geography. "At that time," reported Father Pierre Benoit, one of Lagrange's successors, "Catholic attitudes toward the Bible were a little, let us say, childlike, too simple—taking each word of the Bible as divine truth, for example, to say that 600,000 Israelites came out of Egypt or that the world was created 6,000 years ago, or that each word of the Gospel is exactly what Jesus said. Father Lagrange gave scholars some liberty to understand how God used man, with his own way of thinking and speaking, in what we call in France *genre littéraire*, the fashion of writing history in the past. For some scholars and some theologians, that was scandalous. Lagrange was attacked."[24]

Pope Leo XIII defended Lagrange's unorthodox approach, but his successor Pope Pius X added some of Lagrange's writings, including his commentary on Genesis, to the index of forbidden books. Even today the École's library has only a photocopy of Lagrange's first book. In 1909, Pius sent Jesuits to Jerusalem to establish a counter institute, the Pontifical Biblical Institute. Three years later, Lagrange was forced to withdraw from the school for a year. Rather than back down, however, he struggled to reach an equilibrium balancing "heroism, obedience, and above all, an unflinching devotion to the truth."[25]

Lagrange died in France in 1938. His last words, reportedly, were "Jerusalem, Jerusalem," and he was buried under the choir of the church he founded in Jerusalem. In a history of the Dominicans, *St. Dominic's Family*, he is compared to none other than Aquinas: "He had done for biblical criticism what St. Thomas did for Aristotle."[26] On our visit to the monastery library we asked Father Pawel Trzopek whether Lagrange had been beatified. "Not yet, we're still waiting for a miracle to be attributed to him," he said. "Though if you ask me the real miracle is that he got Catholics to read the Bible again."

Beginning with two books that he brought to Jerusalem—a Latin Bible and a copy of Thomas Aquinas's *Summa Theologica*—Lagrange founded the library at the same time as the École itself. It has since grown to include one of the world's finest collections on biblical exegesis, the archae-

Father Marie-Joseph Lagrange. (Courtesy of École Biblique, Jerusalem.)

ology of the Holy Land, languages of the ancient Near East, and
travelogues by ancient and medieval pilgrims to Jerusalem. Father Pawel
told us that the arrival of crates of books—sent by Jesuits in Beirut, or by
a Dominican publisher in Mosul—often occasioned great celebration.
Some of the volumes, confiscated and taken to Istanbul by the Turks during World War I, still bear the stamps of the Ottoman Imperial Library.
Among its many treasures, the library contains the diaries of the abbots
of the monastery, many of whom, in keeping with the long medieval tradition of monastic annals writing, kept a diary. Today it serves as a research library for scholars and advanced students of biblical studies and
archaeology, and is one of the few institutes open on Saturdays.[27]

The Dominican library also houses some 12,000 negatives, 4,000 glass
plates, and 33 autochromes (early color photographs) currently being digitized by Father Jean-Michel de Tarragon. (The earliest of these negatives
were made by Lagrange himself, who took photographs on his first visit
to Jerusalem in 1890.) Father Jean-Michel, who holds a Ph.D. from the
Sorbonne in cuneiform writing, informed us that the Dominican library
held the world's largest private collection of historic photos of the Holy

Land. He himself had helped other Jerusalem institutions preserve and digitize their negatives, including 2,400 at the Latin Patriarchate, 2,200 belonging to the White Fathers at the Church of Saint Anne, and another 2,200 at the Pontifical Institute Notre Dame across from the Old City's New Gate.

Since Lagrange's death, archaeologists affiliated with the École have done pathbreaking work in biblical studies. In 1943, Pope Pius XII issued an encyclical which encouraged Roman Catholics to translate the Scriptures from Hebrew and Greek texts, rather than from Jerome's Vulgate. As a result, a number of Dominicans and other scholars at the École Biblique embarked once more on the translation of the Bible, with a similar vocation to that of Saint Jerome over fifteen hundred years earlier, to translate the Old and New Testaments so as to make them accessible to people in their spoken, modern French. The product of these efforts was *La Bible de Jérusalem* (1956). This translation served in turn as the impetus for an English translation in 1966, the *Jerusalem Bible*. Both modern translations have been praised as masterpieces of textual accuracy and modern style.

In 1945, Father Roland de Vaux, a professor of Old Testament, assumed the directorship and later led the Jordan-based international team of scholars assembled to study, edit, and translate the Dead Sea Scrolls. Today the library houses an important collection of Qumran studies, along with the critical edition of the scrolls, *Discoveries in the Judean Desert*.

In the library's catacomb-like basement, Father Pawel led us to a shelf of Semitic lexicons and grammars—the very volumes consulted by Eliezer Ben-Yehuda—including two fourteenth-century Druze manuscripts. Ben-Yehuda settled in Jerusalem at age twenty-three. In his autobiography, he writes that although he did not have the privilege of having been born in Jerusalem, he felt "completely a Jerusalemite." In effect, he translated himself to Jerusalem, where he would translate an ancient tongue into a modern idiom and grant classical Hebrew an unlikely afterlife.[28] Part of Ben-Yehuda's yearning for Jerusalem came from the fact that he witnessed people communicating in Hebrew. Jerusalem had already become a city of Jewish migrants, who came from the four corners of the world; Hebrew, as poor as it was as a modern language, was the only language they had in common.

Linguists share a passion that crosses borders and boundaries. Saint Jerome was drawn to the study houses of rabbis in the fourth century when he translated difficult words into Latin. As he labored on the first dictionary of modern Hebrew, Ben-Yehuda was likewise drawn from his house on Ethiopia Street to the extensive collection of dictionaries and lexicons kept by the Dominican fathers.

In late 1893, Ben-Yehuda was arrested by the Turkish authorities on a charge of treason for an editorial that had run in the Hebrew newspaper he edited. Just before the trial began a cable arrived from Constantinople signed by the religious leader of the Ottoman Jewish community (the Hakham Bashi) proclaiming a ban of excommunication, or *herem*, against Ben-Yehuda.

Ben-Yehuda's defense counsel, another man who had been called a heretic, was his friend Father Lagrange. Presenting the court with a translation into Arabic of the disputed editorial, Lagrange argued that there was nothing subversive about it. The court sentenced Ben-Yehuda to one year in prison and suspended his newspaper. In the end, he walked free on bail paid by Shlomo Amiel, a wealthy immigrant from Morocco, and the Hakham Bashi, Rabbi Yakov Elyashar, lifted the ban. Eight months later, Ben-Yehuda was exonerated on appeal.[29]

Creating a National Library

Not far from Eliezer Ben-Yehuda's home on Ethiopia Street stood the Midrash Abarbanel Library, also known as the B'nai B'rith Library. As the city's first free public library, it became the nucleus of what would become the Jewish National and University Library. At the time of its inauguration in 1892, the founders envisioned it as serving the entire Jewish community, but an anathema signed by the rabbinical authorities of Jerusalem against the library rejected what they saw as a symbol of the secular, modern, and partially Zionist. The rabbis objected not because the library was open on Saturday (when else would people have time to read for pleasure?) but because of its secular and therefore morally questionable contents. In his novel *Only Yesterday*, the Nobel Prize–winning writer S. Y. Agnon sends his protagonist, a demonic dog with sarcastic humor, to explore the library:

The dog sees that his luck does not hold, for he is in danger wherever he looks, and he fled inadvertently, lo and behold, to a house full of books. And thus our *schlemiel*, in full compliance, entered the library, Treasure of Science. And there sit wise sages, the finest minds of the ages, concocting word pictures, and correcting the Scriptures, quoting their quotes and writing their notes, their hands holding quills, books piled up in hills, with pamphlets so ample and notebooks to sample, they multiply and increase and grow without cease. A camel who bore them would fall down afraid if a complete total ass didn't come to his aid. And they copy and write avoiding imbroglios, from many old books and some ancient folios, and compose compositions one after another, for the sake of wisdom and the good of their brother. And as they sit, each in his seat, wisdom on his head and knowledge at his feet, a lowly creature did appear, the dog who had fled in panic and fear, their quill pens dropped out of their hands and they trembled, their breath fell off and they scrambled, and the books they were copying they didn't even mention, for to fleeing they turned their attention. And the dog fled too. And not because of a primeval ban on the library, but because he feared that the books would be his tomb.[30]

Joseph Chazanowicz of Bialystok was the leading spirit behind the early collections; he made the first significant donation of books and continued to purchase rare and unique Judaica books and manuscripts for the library until his death in 1919. By the outbreak of World War I he had sent fifteen thousand volumes. In 1900 the cornerstone for the building was laid and in 1902 the library opened to the public.

But the building did not suit its purpose for long. The collection quickly grew beyond expectations. In 1920, the small B'nai B'rith Library was transferred to the World Zionist Organization. In that year, Shmuel Hugo Bergman, an émigré from Prague and friend of Franz Kafka, was appointed its director. In 1925 it merged with the Hebrew University Library, and the building was abandoned. Over the years it served many different purposes, but today it serves once more as a temporary library of the unique collections of the Jerusalem Kabbalist Yaakov Hillel.

In January 1911, Eliezer Ben-Yehuda published an impassioned plea in his Jerusalem-based journal *Ha'Or* (The Light, also known as *Ha-Zvi*). He called on "Zionists and lovers of Jewish wisdom and literature" to re-

Reading room at the Midrash Abarbanel/B'nai B'rith Library. (Photograph by Zadok Bassan, 1925; courtesy of the National Library of Israel.)

deem the library of the recently deceased Baron David Ginzburg (also spelled Günzburg). "Save it and put it in the only deserving place: in the National House of the Books in Jerusalem!"[31] The innovative man who gave modern Hebrew so many of its words thus coined the term *Beit Hasfarim*, the House of the Books. Many years later the House of the Books was nationalized and renamed the National Library of Israel.

The object of Ben-Yehuda's solicitude was an unparalleled collection of two thousand Hebrew manuscripts (many of them unique copies of otherwise lost works), another thousand in Judeo-Arabic and Judeo-Tatar, dozens of incunabula, and more than fourteen thousand rare books (including the oldest known copy of the authoritative code of Jewish law by the eleventh-century North African scholar Yitzhak Alfasi, a 1489 edition of Nahmanides' commentary on the Bible printed in Lisbon, and Yehuda ben Moshe Albotini's 1519 commentary on Maimonides' *Mishneh Torah*). This treasure trove had been assembled in Saint Petersburg in the second half of the nineteenth century by the Russian Orientalist David Ginzburg, scion of a noble family that had made a vast fortune in banking, insurance, and sugar production. Other members of the family had gained renown as pillars of the Jewish community: David's father, Baron Horace Ginzburg, for instance, presided over the building of the famous Grand Choral Synagogue in Saint Petersburg.

Besides his career as a bibliophile, a scholar of Semitic languages, and an editor of the groundbreaking Russian-language Jewish encyclopedia (*Evreiskaia entsiklopediia*), Ginzburg founded the Academy of Jewish Studies, introducing critical scientific scrutiny to traditional Jewish scholarship. Simon Dubnow lectured there on Jewish history, Berl Katznelson on the Talmud. The baron himself gave classes, trailed into the lecture hall by a servant carrying stacks of dictionaries and lexicons. His greatest frustration with his students was that he could not teach them to read Maimonides' *Guide of the Perplexed* in the original because of their ignorance of Arabic. Jewish studies and oriental languages played significant roles in the Russian Empire, and a polyglot scholar of Baron Ginzburg's caliber was esteemed as a cultural mediator.

Shneor Zalman Rubashov, later to take the name Zalman Shazar and serve as Israel's third president, was one of the academy's first students. Shazar recounted that until the inauguration of the academy building in 1909, classes were held at the baron's private library: "His huge library, housed in many rooms and halls, opened onto a darkish, small, intimate sort of room which was his private study—and a private doorway, one might say, to the sanctuary of Jewish and world thought."[32]

In his will, Baron Ginzburg instructed that his library be sold to a Jewish academic institution. After his death, in 1910, his family continued to support his Jewish academy and sought a fitting home for the library. His widow, Baroness Mathilde Ginzburg, originally entered into negotiations with the University of Oxford in England and the Jewish Theological Seminary in New York. But Ben-Yehuda appealed to her to bring the library to Jerusalem, its "only deserving place," where the books were desperately needed as a foundation of the national house of the books.

In May 1917, despite far more generous offers from Europe and the United States, the baroness offered to sell the collection for the modest price of half a million rubles (about $15 million in today's value) to the Midrash Abarbanel/B'nai B'rith Library in Jerusalem. The deal was concluded, and the payment transferred. But as the shipment was being prepared, the October Revolution broke out. In 1920 the baron's books were seized by the Bolsheviks and absorbed into the Rumyantsev Museum in Moscow (later the Lenin State Library, in turn renamed in 1992 the Russian State Library).

Ever since, figures as diverse as Eliezer Ben-Yehuda, David Ben-Gurion, and Albert Einstein have exerted pressure to bring the Ginzburg collection to Jerusalem. "It will be a great sin should the Zionists fail," Ben-Yehuda lamented.

> The library of the late David Ginzburg is extremely valuable, and the likes of it cannot be found in other places. This is a collection that had been gathered slowly over two generations, with love and dedication, and it cost a great deal. . . . There is a real danger that this will be lost or ruined, or at the very least lost to us, to the national library in Jerusalem. And letting this happen would be a great sin. All those who love our wisdom, knowledge and literature . . . must band together and call out: save [the collection], save [the collection]![33]

The efforts almost bore fruit in 1924. The Soviet Union's vice commissioner for education, Mikhail Pokrovsky, agreed to return the collection for a compensation of fifteen thousand pounds sterling to help Russian libraries expand their own collections of German publications. The following year, which saw the inauguration of the Hebrew University, the Zionist movement was short of funds. Albert Einstein, a member of its board of trustees, asked the Soviets to waive the fee. Pokrovsky replied on May 25, 1925: "The issue is not the principle of restitution of the Collection, but about its price, and again note the moderate requests we have made."[34]

These and subsequent efforts have so far been in vain. "From 1917 until the recent *perestroika*," writes Benjamin Richler of Israel's National Library, "hardly any Western scholars were permitted to examine the collection." In 1958, the National Library in Jerusalem managed to acquire microfilms of 200 Ginzburg manuscripts from the Lenin Library, and in 1972 microfilms of 150 more. Racheli Idelman, a granddaughter of Salman Schocken, visited the Ginzburg collection in 1987 and took to the pages of the Israeli newspaper *Haaretz* to call on the Soviets to give the collection to Jerusalem. Elie Wiesel agreed to speak directly with President Mikhail Gorbachev. Finally, in 1992 a National Library team led by Israel Weiser microfilmed over 1,900 manuscripts over a period of four and a half months.

Prime Minister Ehud Olmert raised the matter in his meetings with President Dmitry Medvedev in Moscow in October 2008. Prime Minister Benjamin Netanyahu brought the topic up again in his meetings with Vladimir Putin in February, March, and June 2012. The Israelis' insistence on bringing the collection to Jerusalem, however, has been consistently met with the Russians' claim that Jewish books gathered in tsarist Russia remain part of the Russian patrimony. Since the Russian State Library includes dozens if not hundreds of nationalized collections, moreover, the Russians fear that meeting Israel's request might set off a flood of claims by other heirs.[35]

Yet the hope that the baron's books will ultimately find their rightful place in Jerusalem is kept alive at the National Library. David Blumberg, the current chairman of the library's board, insists that every Israeli prime minister be briefed on the Ginzburg collection and raise it in negotiations with Russian heads of state. Netanyahu told Blumberg that in several of his conversations with Putin the two first topics addressed were nuclear power and the Ginzburg collection. A "Ginzburg Brief" for future prime ministers of Israel is currently under preparation.

In November 2017, the National Library of Israel and the Russian State Library signed a historic agreement. With the financial backing of the Moscow-based Peri Foundation, two thousand manuscripts and thousands of books in the Ginzburg collection will be digitized and made accessible online. Lord Rothschild, a benefactor of the National Library, hailed the agreement: "For many decades now the National Library has lived in hope of having access to the great Ginzburg Collection in Russia. Thanks to the imaginative generosity of Ziyavudin Magomedov [a Russian Muslim billionaire from Dagestan] and the Peri Foundation and with the support of the Russian State Library, this will at last happen. This is of particular sentimental importance to me as I happen to be an Executor of the estate of Isaiah Berlin's widow, born Aline Günzburg, a direct descendant of the Günzburg family."[36]

In the meantime, Jerusalem still awaits the baron's books.

Worlds of the Imagination

Even Jerusalemites who descend from families that have resided in the city for generations often continue to be identified by their places of origin, whether they are Uzbeki Sufis, Christians from Aleppo (Halab), or Jews from Bukhara. But what does it mean to define oneself by reference to a place of origin that no longer exists except in the inherited memory of it? Why might a fifth-generation Jerusalemite define him- or herself not as a Jerusalemite but as, say, a Galician?

We made a visit to the ultra-Orthodox neighborhood of Mea Shearim, where Rabbi Shlomo Fruchthandler invited us into Kollel Hibat Yerushalayim, or Kollel Galicia, a community and learning center housed in a two-story building. On the wall hung a marvelously detailed map of what was once Galicia, a region annexed in 1772 to Habsburg rule, comprising what is now western Ukraine and southeastern Poland. This was the heartland of Hasidic Jewry, the home of the Baal Shem Tov and the Bobov and Belz dynasties, as well as the birthplace of S. Y. Agnon.[37] At the center of the map, the largest dot marks Lviv ("Lemberg" in Yiddish), once a flourishing center of Yiddish literature.

The map, like the archive over which it presides, serves a practical purpose. The kollel exists to assist Jerusalem's Galitzianers, as descendants of Galician Jews are known. In the Old Yishuv (the Jewish community that lived in Jerusalem for centuries before the First Aliyah to Palestine, 1881–1903), each community established its own social support system, known as a *kollel*. Each kollel acted as a kind of embassy in Jerusalem of the home community in Europe. Kollel Galicia, too, takes the name of a long-lost hub of Jewish culture. Indigent Jerusalemites—yeshiva students, brides of impoverished families, the ill, and those in need of food and clothing for Jewish holidays—who can trace their origins to a dot on that map are eligible for charity. Yet those dots mark communities that have not existed since the Second World War.

Fruchthandler opened several cabinets flanking the map, revealing an archive that includes the correspondence and travelogues of *shadarim*—emissaries the kollel sent across Europe to raise funds for Jerusalem's poor—and several boxes of glass-plate photographs of families, which the shadarim used on their trips. Those left in Galicia who yearned to come to Jerusalem were assured that their donations would sponsor learning and prayers on their behalf.

We held some of the plates up to the light. In one, a man named Mordechai Tselnik and his young wife leaned against each other lightly touching. She wore a tilted small cap hat that covered only part of her hair, revealing a flapper hairdo beneath. Even in the black-and-white photo, her makeup was noticeable. Mordechai wore a tie, a pressed white shirt, a dark jacket, and a 1920s-style fedora.

The glass negatives remain undeveloped and undigitized. Since this ultra-Orthodox community defines itself as non-Zionist, a term that alludes to the group's opposition to the establishment of a Jewish state before the arrival of the Messiah, it has an ambivalent relationship with the State of Israel. Ultra-Orthodox, for example, are reluctant to seek help from the National Library, a state institution. Besides, as Fruchthandler explained, Kollel Galicia is more urgently concerned with feeding the poor who arrive on the doorstep every day than with documenting parpers from the previous century.

Deciding to seek the advice of Jerusalem's leading expert on glass negatives, Father Jean-Michel de Tarragon, we walked the several hundred feet east from Mea Shearim to Saint Stephen's Monastery (home to the École Biblique), bringing with us several slides from the Galicia collection. No rabbi from Fruchthandler's community has ever set foot here, and it is doubtful whether Dominicans have visited any of the nearby kollels. We had no great optimism that the two communities would cooperate in the conservation and digitization of the ghosts of Galicia.

In their style of dress, their language (Yiddish), and above all their commitment to Jewish law, the keepers of the kollel's archives dedicate themselves to preserving a link with their origins in a place that no longer exists except in their memories. Fruchthandler's interest in the Galician archive is exceptional: most kollel administrators attach little historical significance to the archives themselves. The majority are not interested in history as such, nor are they moved by a documentary impulse. As we pulled ourselves away from the allure of the archives and stepped out of the kollel into the bustle of Mea Shearim, we recognized that if we were to understand the story of Jerusalem as a uniquely vivid chapter in the human drive to preserve and transmit memory, we would do well to ac-

Glass negative of several portraits of Jerusalem Jews of Galician origin, 1930s.
(Courtesy of Galicia Archives.)

cept that memory is not history. In this part of Jerusalem, at least, memory is expressed in ritual, law, and liturgy; the critical study of history interferes, if anything, with memory.

While Galicians in the diaspora dreamt of Jerusalem, Galician Jews in nineteenth-century Jerusalem held fast to their Galician identity. After the ruptures and upheavals of the world wars, only the imagination remained of one of the hubs of Jewish life in Europe.

An architect envisions what is not yet there. In the archives of the Franciscan Monastery of Saint Savior, belonging to the Custody of the Holy Land, we stumbled across a blueprint for another imagined Jerusalem: Antonio Barluzzi's elaborate fantasy of a Holy Sepulchre basilica.

Following the earthquake of 1927, the al-Aqsa Mosque and the Dome of the Rock required extensive repairs; in fact, most of what we see today is a product of twentieth-century reconstruction. During restoration in 1938–1942, the mosque's Carrara marble columns were donated by Mussolini.[38] The Church of the Holy Sepulchre, too, sustained damage. A British report of 1935 warned of its imminent collapse.[39] The need to renovate the church tempted some architects to consider demolishing the damaged structure and building it anew. Reacting to this notion, Bishop Gustavo Testa, the papal nuncio to Palestine, remarked that sometimes "the craziest ideas become a glorious reality."[40] But this particular idea would have to overcome stiff opposition if it were to be realized. The Italian archaeologist Roberto Paribeni, for instance, expressed horror that the Holy Sepulchre might be demolished:

> No! Leave intact as much as possible this ancient and graceless monument. No purity, no beauty of architectural line will ever compare to the charm of this dark, cumbersome, worn-out, begrimed, and smoky building, where every stone has for centuries imbibed pure and holy human tears, where the most fervent aspirations were placed in Christendom.[41]

Yet in 1940, Antonio Barluzzi and the celebrated Venetian architect Luigi Marangoni constructed a scale model of their vision for a radically new Holy Sepulchre. Barluzzi, an Italian Franciscan monk and architect, served as secretary of the Fascist Party in Jerusalem from 1926 to 1936.

He had already completed the Church of All Nations at Gethsemane, facing the sealed Gate of Mercy; the Catholic chapel of Calvary in the Holy Sepulchre; and the Church of the Flagellation near the beginning of the Via Dolorosa.

Barluzzi hoped to present his model at the Catholic Pavilion of the World's Fair that Mussolini planned to hold in Rome in 1942. One scholar described Barluzzi's blueprint as "a bizarre Orientalist/antiquarian fantasy, detailed with Fascist-like façade arcading, minaret-like belfries, and mosque-like domes."[42] Despite its extravagance, enthusiasm for Barluzzi's design grew in Rome. It was rumored that Pius XI might make the first papal pilgrimage to the Holy Land to consecrate the new church.[43] Fascist priests remained hopeful that Hitler and Mussolini would win the war and Italian forces would take charge of the holy sites in time for the eight hundredth anniversary of the consecration of the Holy Sepulchre by Queen Melisende and the Franks. "Only when the flag of Fascist and Catholic Italy is unfurled over Christ's Sepulchre," proclaimed Monsignor Navvara, bishop of Terracina, "will the Holy Land have received the veneration it deserves."[44]

But by the time the model was finally presented to the public in Rome in 1950, the Axis defeat had reduced Barluzzi's reimagined Jerusalem landmark to a mere curiosity, filed away in the Franciscan archives.

Barluzzi's scheme was not the only one to be scrapped before it could blight Jerusalem's skyline. In 1919, the Scottish architects Patrick Geddes and Frank Mears drew up a Great Hall at the center of the university on Mount Scopus, crowned by a "floating dome" that would have been the largest of its kind in the world. It would echo the Dome of the Rock and serve as a Temple for what Geddes called "a spacious City of Dreams."[45]

One afternoon we got an unexpected tip: one of Jerusalem's most extensive private libraries—the obsession of a leading ultra-Orthodox figure in Jerusalem—was being sold off piecemeal. If we wished to see it, we had to go immediately.

When we at last found the place, it became clear why the owner had been so secretive about his library, and why his family was now so eager to be relieved of it. The library of Rabbi Shlomo Pappenheim, who died at the age of ninety-one in April 2017, seemed somewhat out of place. It was housed in a concrete bomb shelter in the basement of a school for orphaned girls, Bayis Lepleitos. Before it moved to its present address, in the far reaches of ultra-Orthodox Jerusalem, the school stood adjacent to the Ethiopian Orthodox church in West Jerusalem.

We were met at the basement door by Moshe Hillel, whom we had consulted about the manuscripts of Meir Benayahu. Hillel described one of his earlier visits, at which he had walked in on one of Pappenheim's rare invitations. The older man was at his desk, clipping a page featuring an image of a female nude. To Hillel's astonishment, Pappenheim had not bothered to hide the erotic art.

Besides well-curated shelves of German literature (including rare first editions of the works of Kafka, Max Brod, Heinrich Heine, and Kleist), tens of thousands of art books and exhibition catalogues, and postcards (we found one addressed to Pappenheim from his friend Mordechai Ardon, the artist whose stained-glass windows dominate the lobby of the National Library), Pappenheim's library was well stocked with erotica, photographic and otherwise. Pappenheim took special interest in artistic representations of the Bible, and many of his volumes featured images considered subversive or taboo to most members of his ultra-Orthodox community, who adhere not just to the prohibition against graven images but to strict codes of female modesty. Shortly before his death, Pappenheim estimated the value of the collection at four million dollars.

Born in Munich to a family that included Bertha Pappenheim, Freud's patient "Anna O.," Shlomo grew up in the city of Halberstadt. After Kristallnacht, he fled with his brother to London. After a year in London, he came to Jerusalem. Joining the Toldos Aharon community, one of the strictest sects in the city, he served as deputy chairman of the Edah Hachareidit and founded the Bayis Lepleitos.

Shlomo Pappenheim was by no means a conventional ultra-Orthodox rabbi. He stood firmly against the violent demonstrations in the streets of Mea Shearim that were promoted by other leaders of the community. In 2013, he made a controversial declaration about the Hasidic *shtreimels* (hats that became the Hasidic movement symbol): if they were made of animal fur, he ruled, they violated the Jewish injunction against causing needless pain to animals. Perhaps he envisioned an ultra-Orthodox way of life that did not exclude an appreciation for art and literature.

The Israeli sociologist Sima Zalcberg, who has researched Hasidim in Jerusalem, described an interview she had with Pappenheim. She found him to be unusually open in discussing delicate issues such as sexuality in the Hasidic world. Even so, he refused to let Zalcberg meet his wife and daughters; he regarded them as too innocent to hold intellectual conversations with an academic: "They are like children," the rabbi told her. The women of his community were not expected to work. Married women covered their shaved heads with a black scarf, another means of communal identification. Neither the women of the Pappenheim family nor the girls at the school in which the collection was kept had ever stepped into the rabbi's library.

Today, Shlomo's grandson Rabbi Shmuel Pappenheim single-handedly tries to preserve his grandfather's legacy. "I am the only one in the family he would trust," Shmuel told us. "He knew that his collection would be destroyed by his sons, but in his last will he instructed me not to fight them over the collection. Still, I will keep his legacy alive." That legacy is now dispersed. At the behest of Pappenheim's sons—Yaakov Eliezer, the head of a kollel, Gavriel, director of the kashrut division (concerned with Jewish dietary laws) of a Jerusalem ultra-Orthodox organization, and Avrohom—the library was auctioned off. We could not help but wonder whether imagination—even the broad-horizoned imagination of Shlomo Pappenheim—has its limits, whether a library can reflect both a profoundly personal love of learning and the limits of that love.

Scholars, too, number among the dreamers. They weave theories and go to great lengths in search of evidence and truth. Sometimes a dream becomes an obsession. But even a fantasy might find unexpected confirmation in a library.

In the summer of 1958, a Columbia University historian of antiquity (and former Episcopal deacon) named Morton Smith visited Mar Saba's library. He had visited the monastery before, while he was a graduate student at the Hebrew University in Jerusalem during World War II. (He was the first Christian granted a doctorate by that university.) Smith had honed his philological expertise examining Greek manuscripts in monastic libraries on Mount Athos. Now he gravitated not to the great illuminated volumes of medieval manuscripts, which had by then been moved from Mar Saba to Jerusalem, but to bound collections of printed material, which he offered to catalogue. In the endpapers of a book printed in the seventeenth century, Smith discovered a copy of an ancient letter allegedly written by the second-century church father Clement of Alexandria, the teacher of Bishop Alexander, who founded the library of Jerusalem discussed in Chapter 1. Much to Smith's astonishment, Clement's letter quoted two excerpts from the Secret Gospel of Mark.

The Secret Gospel, purportedly suppressed by church authorities, depicts Jesus initiating his disciples with a nocturnal and possibly erotic rite. A youth comes to Jesus "wearing a linen cloth over his naked body," and "he remained with him that night." Jesus initiates the youth into "the mystery of the kingdom of God."

Smith reported that on making the discovery, he felt as if he were "walking on air." He snapped black-and-white photographs of the text and spent the next fifteen years studying it. He argued that the text pointed to the existence of magical elements in Jesus's teachings, and to traces of transgressive sexual rites among Jesus and his disciples.[46]

Many scholars dismissed the Secret Mark manuscript as the work of a modern forger, possibly Smith himself. The paleographer Agamemnon Tselikas concluded it was a twentieth-century forgery of an eighteenth-century script. Smith's student Jacob Neusner called it "the forgery of the century."[47]

In theory, scientific methods could resolve the matter by dating the manuscript's paper and ink. But the manuscript disappeared. In 1976, the Hebrew University professors Guy Stroumsa, David Flusser, and Shlomo Pines, along with the Greek Orthodox archimandrite Meliton, were the last to see it. Stroumsa still believes in the document's authenticity. "It is a well-known fact among scientists and epistemologists," Stroumsa wrote, "that it takes a long time, up to thirty years, before scientific breakthroughs are widely acknowledged and their implications fully recognized. Smith published the account of his discovery in 1973. It seems the time has come to accept it."[48]

This story holds a final twist. Eighteen years before Morton Smith's discovery, the Scottish-born writer James H. Hunter published a novel, an evangelical thriller called *The Mystery of Mar Saba* (1940). Hunter imagined a Nazi conspiracy to undermine Christianity by blackmailing a scholar to forge a manuscript in which Nicodemus and Joseph of Arimathea confess to having secretly moved the body of Jesus from his tomb. In the novel, the forgery, planted at Mar Saba, is discovered there by a British manuscript hunter. The similarity between these stories, some have argued, cannot be a coincidence.[49]

Soon after Stroumsa's visit to Mar Saba, the seventeenth-century volume containing the manuscript was removed to the Greek Orthodox Patriarchate in Jerusalem for safekeeping alongside the rest of the monastery's manuscripts. The two pages with Clement's letter have been cut out and have not been seen since—another enigmatic instance of Jerusalem's erasures.

CHAPTER SEVEN

RESCUE AND RETURN

The Twentieth Century

The acquisition of an old book is its rebirth.
—*Walter Benjamin*

There is no library in Jerusalem that has not suffered theft, and none that has not been touched at one point or another by the wish to restore what has been lost. Abuna Shimon Can, keeper of the library in the Syriac Church of Saint Mark, told us that in 1948 Syriac monks rescued several Torah scrolls from a torched synagogue in Syria and smuggled them to Jerusalem. In 1983 the monks at Saint Mark's were forced to hand them over to a deputy mayor of Jerusalem. He had offered in exchange to help the Syriac community regain the dilapidated Chapel of Saint Joseph of Arimathea and Saint Nicodemus in the Church of the Holy Sepulchre from the Armenians. The promise went unfulfilled. Abuna Shimon felt that returning the holy scriptures to the Jews was just, though he would have preferred to hand them over to Syrian Jews rather than to an officer of the state accompanied by uniformed soldiers. We were unable to track down the scrolls' current home.

The Syriac library, not alone among Jerusalem collections, is defined by what is absent, marked by what is missing. Three centuries ago, Saint Mark's library was looted, and many documents attesting to Syriac property claims vanished. A magnificent Syriac breviary (a book of the prayers, hymns, psalms, and readings for the canonical hours) copied in Jerusalem by a monk named Michael de Mar'ach in 1138 was taken to Aleppo, where it was given to the French consul in 1684. (It is today in the Bibliothèque Municipale, Lyon, Ms. Syr. 001.) Other valuable Syriac manuscripts were transferred from Jerusalem to Damascus for safekeeping on the eve of the Arab-Israeli war in 1948, never to be returned. These included a lectionary written in Edessa in 1222 that was embellished with a series of exceptional miniatures and a Syriac Gospel on vellum dated 994.[1] Have they been among the victims of the ongoing conflict ravaging Syria? "There is no news from our library in Damascus," Abuna Shimon reported with profound sadness. Recalling a Syriac poem on the destruction of Jerusalem by the Romans, his eyes filled with tears, as though it had happened yesterday.

"Return"—to an individual, a community, or a geographical place— numbers among the words that ring with special resonance in Jerusalem's libraries and texts. Jews have prayed for a return to Jerusalem since the Babylonian exile and destruction of the First Temple in 586 BCE. In the classical Jewish imagination, a transcendent Jerusalem (*Yerushalayim shel ma'alah*) hovers until a messianic time when the earthly Jerusalem (*Yerushalayim shel matah*) will be rebuilt. Jewish worshippers, wherever in the world they may be, face Jerusalem, the sacred center, and in Jerusalem they pray facing the absent Temple. Jewish prayer has its origins as a substitute for the Temple rites, whose structure and frequency they echo. A well-known Talmudic teaching relates that since the destruction of the Temple, animal sacrifice was replaced by worship in the heart. "And what is worship in the heart? Prayer" (Tractate Ta'anit 2b). One of the oldest prayers introduced into Jewish practice after the destruction of the Second Temple (70 CE) was the 'Amidah (the standing prayer recited three times a day). It includes the words "May You rebuild it soon in our days as an eternal structure, and may You speedily establish within it the throne of David. Blessed are You, God, the Builder of Jerusalem."[2]

In this sense, the very essence of Jewish prayer encodes lamentation for loss of the real thing, for that which is no longer possible to perform. It is a replica, permeated by memories of the city past and by longings for the future city rebuilt. Prayer is longing at a distance, one might say prayer is predicated on distance. It acknowledges absence. That longing and that acknowledgment have acted as the threads that weave together Jerusalem and its diasporas. We learn to love the place where our longings were born.

"By the rivers of Babylon," as the Psalmist put it, "there we sat down, yea, we wept, when we remembered Zion" (Ps. 137). That term for Jerusalem, "Zion," gave its name to the modern Jewish national movement of return. Israel's national anthem, joining longing and loss, invokes the age-old yearning (Ps. 126:1) of a Return to Zion—a yearning so ingrained that it became its own object, a yearning after yearning. Evangelical Christians, too, prayed for the Jews to return to Zion; the great ingathering of the Jewish people to Jerusalem is said to herald the Second Coming and the advent of the messianic kingdom.

In some cases, the goal of return is joined not to messianic hopes but to a pressing desire to restore justice and set history right. For Palestinian refugees, some still holding keys to homes in Jerusalem they were forced to abandon in 1948, the Right of Return (*haqq al-ʿawda* in Arabic) is a matter of the utmost personal and collective urgency.

But the impulse toward return also animates Jerusalem's librarians and bibliophiles. At the 2016 groundbreaking ceremony for the new National Library, for example, we heard Israel's president Reuven Rivlin invoke the vision expressed almost 150 years earlier by the rabbi of Volozhin (in what is today Belarus): "To establish a Treasure House of Books, a flagship, and collect all of our people's books, miss not a single one, and assemble scattered manuscripts from the corners of the world."[3] Many Israelis today recognize Jerusalem as a natural center for the cultural reconstruction of Jewish life—in other words, as a place of return.

In 1907–1908, shortly before his death at age fifty-three, a Galician Jew named Naftali Herz Imber jotted down a short version of the only poem of his destined to achieve renown. Imber, the first translator into Hebrew of the *Rubáiyát of Omar Khayyám*, had lived in Palestine for some four years, torn between his poetic ambitions and a failing farming career. But he did not stay long on the land he had longed for so ardently. The only surviving handwritten copy of "Hatikvah" (The Hope), later adopted as Israel's national anthem, was scribbled in elaborate cursive on the stationery of a New York hospital. Imber's handwriting wobbles, as if his letters uncertainly dispersed themselves on the page. The original poem reads, "to return to the land of our forefathers." The anthem Israelis sing today includes the words "to be a free nation on our land." The original concludes with the phrase "to the city in which David dwelled." The editors of the anthem changed the ending to "the land of Zion and Jerusalem." Imber's autograph copy was presented in 1936 to the National Library in Jerusalem, then known as the National House of the Books. The poet, like his most enduring poem, was also repatriated; his remains were removed from Mount Zion Cemetery in Queens, New York, and reinterred at Jerusalem's Givat Shaul cemetery in 1953.

Books serve as a portable homeland for peoples in exile. "From days immemorial books played an important, even vital role in our nation's life," said the librarian of the Sholem Aleichem Library in Radomsko,

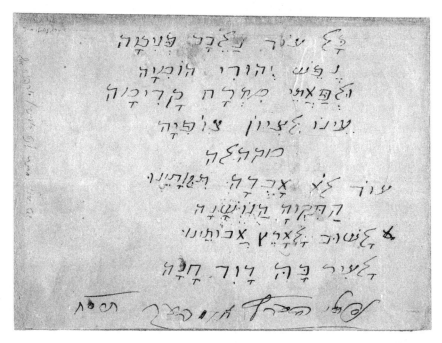

Naftali Herz Imber, "Hatikvah." (Abraham Schwadron Collection [01.01.181], the National Library of Israel; courtesy of the National Library of Israel.)

Poland, before the Second World War. "Rightly we were considered in the Diaspora the people of the book when the book served as a loyal companion of our nation."[4] The Zionist project involved not just the return of exiled Jews to their ancestral homeland and language but also the ingathering of Jewish books and cultural heritage to the land of Israel. Since the founding of the state, Israeli parliamentarians and prime ministers have actively sought to rescue and redeem Jewish books.

Treasures of the Diaspora

Why has Jerusalem seen itself as the rightful heir and home to books that may or may not have been created there or written under its inspiration? What explains this city's centripetal force?

The Israeli prime minister's heavily guarded residence on Balfour Street, built by the German Jewish architect Richard Kauffmann, faces a library boasting the clean lines and rounded balconies typical of Bauhaus architecture. Erich Mendelsohn, Kauffmann's rival, designed the building in the 1930s for the German department-store magnate and publisher Salman Schocken. At the time, the Schocken library was the most modern (and the first air-conditioned) building in the city.

In 1935, as the Nazi menace loomed, Schocken managed to rescue his Berlin collection of more than sixty thousand volumes and hundreds of manuscripts, one of the largest privately owned collections in Europe. Four years earlier, he had donated sixty-four Hebrew incunabula to the National Library in Jerusalem. After forty days at sea, like Noah's ark, the ship bearing the rest of Schocken's library arrived in 164 crates at the port of Haifa, which were then trucked to the building awaiting them on Balfour Street. A diasporic treasure had returned.

In 1933, Schocken described the origins of his collection in the third person in his introduction to the first volume for the studies of the Research Institute of Medieval Hebrew Poetry: "Out of the desire of a Jew to have in his home a well-preserved copy of each of the standard works of Jewish tradition and literature grew, little by little, a collection which at first stressed first editions, rare and early prints[,] and incunabula. It then became the collector's major object to trace the history of the Jewish people as manifested in and by its books." He conceived of his library on Balfour

Street as an elite research institution where scholars could work with the medieval and early modern Hebrew illuminated manuscripts and incunabula, and use them as inspiration for contemporary works of the imagination. Schocken intended it to be a "half private, half public setting," "an extension of the great National Library" that would earn "a place for itself in the breathing life of the city."[5] Jerusalem's leading literary lights, including Gershom Scholem and S. Y. Agnon, frequented readings and literary soirees there. During the 1940s, the American consulate flew the Stars and Stripes over the library to protect it. As we walked through the hallway of what is today an underused library we noticed Schocken's Remington No. 12 typewriter from the 1920s sitting unused atop the card catalogue. Baruch Yonin, a longtime Schocken librarian, described for us the library's fate since its founder's death.

Two years after Schocken's death in 1959, his library, though physically remaining in Jerusalem, was entrusted to the Jewish Theological Seminary (JTS) in New York. Schocken had known Alexander Marx, the librarian of JTS from 1903 to 1953, and had helped rescue the library of Alexander's brother Moses Marx from Berlin and repatriate it to Jerusalem. In 1989, the library of Saul Lieberman, one of the leading Jewish scholars of his generation, was also brought to Balfour Street. Lieberman, who lived in Palestine for years before migrating to New York (where he taught Talmud at JTS for forty years), wanted his collection of ten thousand volumes of rabbinic scholarship to find its final home in Jerusalem.

In recent decades, Schocken's heirs chose to auction off the incunabula collection and six hundred volumes of Hebraica he left to his children. These included Schocken's fourteenth-century illuminated Nuremberg Mahzor (valued at $2–3 million), and the Nuremberg Haggadah on parchment from Germany (before 1449), richly illuminated in sepia by the scribe and illustrator Joel ben Simeon ("the Leonardo da Vinci of Jewish illustrators of the time," according to James Snyder, former director of the Israel Museum in Jerusalem, where the haggadah is on permanent display). Israeli officials objected to the sale, invoking the law that prohibits removing cultural heritage from the country. After protracted legal proceedings, a compromise was reached: the National Library of Israel would be granted the right to choose books to purchase for its collection prior to the public auctions. The remainder were sold at three auctions (in 1993, 2003, and 2005).[6] Here, too, recovery proved anything but straightforward. But it did suggest that Jerusalem is often regarded as the symbolic origin of texts—and communities—that did not in fact originate there.

Dov Schidorsky of the Hebrew University has estimated that some two million Jewish books were destroyed by the Third Reich, a modern form of Savonarola's "bonfire of the vanities" in Renaissance Florence, and a fulfillment of Heinrich Heine's prescient remark in 1823: "Wherever they burn books they will also, in the end, burn human beings." One of numberless reports of the cultural eradication was offered by a Nazi participant in the destruction of the thirty-thousand-volume Lublin Yeshiva library on September 7, 1939: "For us it was a matter of special pride to destroy the Talmudic Academy, which was known as the greatest in Poland. . . . We threw the huge talmudic library out of the building and carried the books to the marketplace where we set fire to them. The fire lasted twenty hours. The Lublin Jews assembled around and wept bitterly, almost silencing us with their cries. We summoned the military band, and with joyful shouts the soldiers drowned out the sounds of the Jewish cries."[7]

Millions more books were systematically looted by the Nazis between 1933 and 1945. Some were intended for anti-Jewish museums that would bear pseudo-scientific witness to a culture destroyed. In 1941, Frankfurt's Institut zur Erforschung der Judenfrage (Institute of Research of the Jewish Question), under the directorship of Alfred Rosenberg, listed some 350,000 volumes, including Hebraica and Judaica from the municipal library of Frankfurt, 11,000 books from the Jewish theological seminary in Breslau, archives of the House of Rothschild, archives of the Alliance Israélite Universelle, and many other collections. The Reichsuniversität in Poznan, Poland, founded by the German government in 1941, held about 400,000 volumes from confiscated Jewish libraries.[8]

After the war, the rescue and restitution of Jewish books created a host of political, administrative, and diplomatic difficulties, and became entangled in struggles over the Jewish past, the memory of the victims, and the connection between the Holocaust and the establishment of the State of Israel. The deeper dilemmas, however, were more ethical than legal or political. Who should inherit heirless books? Should they be repatriated to their countries of origin, even those where the Jewish communities had been eradicated? Should they be sent to the United States, as the American Jewish Joint Distribution Committee argued? Or could Jerusalem lay the greater moral claim to this heritage?

When the Hebrew University set up the Committee for Saving the Treasures of the Diaspora (*Otzrot Hagolah*) in March 1944, Jerusalem was still under British administration. Yet the city was recognized as a natural center for the cultural reconstruction of Jewish life—a place of return. The committee included university faculty and administrators Gershom Scholem, (Shmuel) Hugo Bergman, David Werner Senator, and librarian Curt Wormann. In July 1945, its members were already insisting that it was "a requirement of historic justice that the Hebrew University and the Jewish National and University Library in Jerusalem be made the repository of these remains of Jewish culture which have fortunately been saved for the world."[9] Having failed to save European Jews from extermination, the Zionist movement now wished at least to rescue the literary vestiges of their culture.

Accordingly, Otzrot Hagolah sent emissaries to Europe to rescue books and libraries that now served as ghostly traces of owners who had perished. In 1946, Scholem visited Prague, Vienna, and finally Germany in search of looted books. The same year, Judah Magnes, president of the Hebrew University, wrote: "We are to be the chief country for the absorption of the living human beings who have escaped from Nazi persecution. . . . By the same token we should be the trustee of these spiritual goods which destroyed German Jewry left behind."[10] The rescue was an assertion of the continuity of Jewish culture, but it was also a transfer of the center of gravity of Jewish life from Europe to the capital of the future Jewish state.

Not everyone acquiesced in Jerusalem's claims of inheritance. In May 1946, Hannah Arendt wrote to Gershom Scholem on the letterhead of the Commission on European Jewish Cultural Reconstruction and added a secret memorandum that the commission had submitted to Rabbi Philip S. Bernstein, an American adviser in occupied Germany. The secretary of the commission, Koppel S. Pinson, a historian at Queens College and the editor of *Jewish Social Studies*, warned that "claims from Palestine, a state from which none of this collection originates, and which unfortunately is not recognized as a legal side to this property restitution, are not likely to be accepted and may even enhance Russian claims."[11] Pinson feared that the Soviet Union might lay claim to cultural assets that had come from Russia, Poland, Lithuania, the Baltic States, the Czech Republic, and Russian-occupied Germany.

In April 1947, the New York–based Jewish Cultural Reconstruction was designated the custodian of these hundreds of thousands of books and Torah scrolls, although the Hebrew University and the National House of the Books in Jerusalem were granted the first right to request items missing from their libraries. Jewish institutions in Israel and the United States would each receive 40 percent of the books, with the remaining 20 percent distributed among Jewish communities elsewhere in the world.[12]

Many of the looted libraries were never recovered. Of the 40,000 printed books and 150 Hebrew manuscripts the German S.S. plundered from the Library for Jewish Studies of the Great Synagogue in Warsaw, none survived the war. But thanks to the tireless efforts of Otzrot Hagolah, some half a million books looted by the Nazis found their way to the National Library in Jerusalem.

The story remains unfinished. Today, as part of a German initiative to return property looted by the Nazis to their rightful owners, four German libraries (the University of Potsdam Library, the Stiftung Neue Synagoge Berlin—Centrum Judaicum Library, the Freie Universität Berlin University Library, and the Berlin Central and Regional Library) have published a list of twelve thousand looted books in their holdings.[13] They, too, are awaiting return.

A Hidden Hasidic Library

One Wednesday evening, we were granted an audience with the rebbe of the Karlin-Stolin community, who holds court twice a week. Like other Hasidic groups, Karliners ascribe special holiness to their rebbe. If they cannot see him in person, they jot down their wishes in notes, or *kvitlech,* then place the notes not in the cracks of the Western Wall but between the pages of *Beis Aharon,* their rabbi's book.

The rebbe's waiting room is partitioned; men and women sit apart. As we took our seats the women in the waiting room recommended a quick and direct approach; most audiences, they said, lasted just two or three minutes, and in any case, "the rebbe will read through your wishes and pain." When our turn came, we were sent into the rebbe's chamber right after a nervous young groom who came with a bottle of vodka and a baked noodle dish (*kugel*) to celebrate with the rabbi and get his blessing.

At some point during the course of our forty-five-minute audience, the rebbe turned the tide of our conversation and began to interview us about our encounters with Jerusalem's libraries. Intrigued by the Aramaic-speaking community in Jerusalem, he wondered why the National Library was not doing more to help the Syriac library. He asked whether we had come across anything new concerning the lost pages of the Aleppo Codex. He wondered whether stray pages from the Afghan Genizah were still on the market.

When at last we asked to see his library, he demurred. "It's more like a storehouse than a library. Even I can't always find books easily." We found it hard to believe that it could be in a worse state than other important collections we have seen. Like other Jerusalem libraries, the Karliner library is defined by the gaps on the shelves. Until the Second World War, the Karlin-Stolin community, centered in present-day Belarus, had an extraordinary cache of signed letters from the greatest Hasidic masters: Dov Ber, the Maggid of Mezeritch; Levi Yitzhak of Berdichev; Yisroel of Ruzhin; Avrum Yehoshua Heschel of Apta; and many others. The library held books that had belonged to the visionary wonder-working founder of Hasidism, Rabbi Yisroel (Israel) ben Eliezer, better known as the Baal Shem Tov, "Master of the Good Name." The Karliner library included, for example, the Baal Shem Tov's personal copy of the *Zohar*, the classic work of Jewish mysticism, and of *Sefer Ha-Zoref*, a fourteen-hundred-page volume of Kabbalah.

After the Germans conquered Stolin in the summer of 1941, Nazi forces confiscated the archive and murdered its custodians. The Karliners in Jerusalem today still search for remnants of the collection, so far in vain. At least two rare Kabbalistic manuscripts known to have been part of their collection have surfaced in the murky world of Hebraica dealers—one bought by the Karliners themselves, the other by the National Library. "If the rare manuscripts and books carefully collected and preserved by the Stoliner Hasidim from the early nineteenth century until the 1930s were recovered," writes Yitzhak Melamed of Johns Hopkins, "even in part, it would be one of the greatest Hebraica finds of our times."[14]

Since the Second World War, the Karliners have rebuilt their library to some nine hundred rabbinic manuscripts and printed books. It is housed in the Jerusalem home of Rabbi Baruch Shochat, the current Karliner rebbe, who ascended to the throne of his community at age nine. When the former rabbi died Shochat was asked, despite his youth, to depart from his family home in Brooklyn and move to Jerusalem for training. At age thirteen, after his bar mitzvah, he assumed the role of the community's rabbi. In his early twenties, he asked Rabbi Shimon Schwartz, almost ten years his senior, to help him rebuild the Karliner library.

Schwartz, Jerusalem's leading paleographer of premodern Hebrew books, initiated us into the story of the Karliners' library. Like Abuna Shimon Can, Schwartz had early training as a scribe. He had amassed a lifetime's experience in identifying and dating Hebrew manuscripts. Eyeing a page, he could tell us where the text was written and, give or take a couple of decades, when. He could identify not only styles of script but types of paper and watermarks. In his cluttered office in Mea Shearim he communicated with his assistants in Yiddish inflected with Hebrew. Experts from both the National Library and international auction houses regularly consulted him or asked him to authenticate manuscripts or spot forgeries. He recently judged a late-sixteenth-century Hebrew manuscript by the Gaza poet Israel Najara a forgery, for example, because its signature too perfectly resembled a known signature. (Some manuscripts in Najara's hand, dated 1579, were discovered in 1836 in the ruins of Jerusalem's Hurva Synagogue, next to Nahmanides' synagogue.) For the past several decades Schwartz has also served as the keeper and cataloguer of the Karliner library.

The Karliners had a presence in Jerusalem long before the Second World War. After establishing communities in Tiberias and Safed, a small group of the Karlin Hasidim settled in Jerusalem's Old City in the 1870s. There they established a synagogue called Beit Aharon, after the title of their rabbi's book (first published in 1875). During the 1948 war,

Jordanian forces destroyed their synagogue, and the Karliners relocated to the Beit Yisrael neighborhood, an ultra-Orthodox enclave bordering Mea Shearim.

The oldest book the library held, Schwartz told us, dates from about a hundred years before the expulsion of the Jews from Spain in 1492. Schwartz made no secret of his purchases for the library. In fact, he digitizes each manuscript before he hands it over to the rabbi, and sends a copy of the files to the National Library. Schwartz acknowledged that the market value of a manuscript plummets the moment it is digitized, but the community has no intention of selling its manuscripts. The lessons of a lost library outweigh the material price. He also oversees the publication of a bimonthly journal, now in its 177th number, which publishes annotated versions of the library's holdings.

On closer inspection, however, we discovered that his is a library both open and radically closed. Schwartz declined our request to see the library itself, housed at the rebbe's home. He gestured toward a hard drive on his cluttered desk. "What do you need to visit the library for? It's all here." If you know a text well, he implied, what could seeing a physical manuscript add? As if to console us, he made an astonishing confession: in all these years, he himself had never been inside the Karliner library, the library he knew so intimately. After cataloguing and digitizing new acquisitions, he could access it only by means of a screen. He has been denied the exaltation of a bibliophile among his treasures. For now, the Karliner library, accessible and inaccessible both, remains in a kind of placeless purgatory. It is a "no place."

Schwartz attributed the rebbe's extreme caution to the earlier loss. "The rebbe is afraid that something might happen to the library again." That "again" lingered as we stepped out of his office into the bright sunlight.

We wondered about the ways the physicality of a library—so very different from the convenient immateriality of the digitized book—awakens the senses to the crinkle of paper, the musky perfume of leather bindings, the tangible heft of volumes, the handsome uprightness of columns of type, the marginal scribblings of distant readers, the simple act of flipping pages. In these, too, there is intimacy. "There is no true love without some sensuality," Anatole France wrote. "One is not happy in books unless one loves to caress them."[15]

The esoteric spell cast by the Hasidic movement gave rise to the rationalism of the Jewish "counterreformation," or Haskalah. The founding father of the Haskalah, Moses Mendelssohn, called his major treatise *Jerusalem; or, On Religious Power and Judaism* (1783). In articulating a Jewish political theory that would point toward a just and tolerant society, Mendelssohn did not call that society a utopia, or "no place." He named it Jerusalem.[16]

Property Lost, Property Regained

The world's most significant collections of Jewish manuscripts from Yemen are to be found today not in any Yemenite home or synagogue but in the vaults of the National Library and the Ben-Zvi Institute in Jerusalem. And therein lies a story.

The value of Yemenite manuscripts had long been known in Jerusalem. In 1859, Yaakov Saphir, who had had dealings with Abraham Firkovich over the Aleppo Codex, brought numerous books back from Yemen and dedicated himself to studying the community's rich literary heritage, including rare theological texts unknown elsewhere. Saphir, born in a town in present-day Belarus, moved to Jerusalem in 1836 but traveled widely to collect alms for the city's poor. On returning to Jerusalem, he spent his remaining days in the Hurva synagogue (then the largest in the city) with his closest friend, Rabbi Shmuel Salant, leader of the Ashkenazic community in Jerusalem.

Yet the great dispossession of the Yemenite books did not take place at the hands of nineteenth-century book hunters, but after the Yemenite community immigrated to the Holy Land. In 1881–1882, a first wave of about five hundred Yemenites arrived in Jerusalem. There they formed an unlikely bond with another group that settled in Jerusalem at the same time: the evangelical settlers of the American Colony. The archives of the American Colony, as well as the U.S. Library of Congress, still hold photos of these Yemenites who found shelter and work there.

The American colonists believed the Jewish immigrants from Yemen to be descended from the lost tribe of Gad. When founder Horatio Spafford inquired about their reasons for returning to Jerusalem, "Suddenly, they said, without warning, a spirit seemed to fall on them and they began to speak about returning to the land of Israel." Spafford felt that it was not by chance that he had heard his own call at the same time. Bertha Spafford Vester recalled her father's fascination with the Yemenites: "Father was interested in the Gadites at once. Their story about their un-provoked conviction that this was the time to return to Palestine coin-cided with what he felt sure was coming to pass—the fulfillment of the prophecy of the return of the Jews to Palestine. . . . They had to be helped, and quickly. No time was lost in getting relief started. . . . Every Friday morning the heads of the Gadite families would appear at the American Colony and be given coins in proportion to the number of in-dividuals to be fed." Much to the gratitude of the destitute Yemenites, the Spaffords organized shelter and kosher food.[17]

"The Gadites had a scribe among them who was a cripple," Vester's ac-count continued. "He could not use his arms and wrote the most beautiful Hebrew, holding a reed pen between his toes. He wrote a prayer for Father and his associates, which was brought one day and presented to Father as a thanksgiving offering. They said that they repeated the prayer daily. I have it in my possession; it is written on a piece of parchment." The prayer (inscribed in Horatio's personal copy of the Bible, now at the Library of Congress) reads: "He who blessed our fathers Abraham, Isaac & Jacob, bless & guard & keep Horatio Spafford & his household & all that are joined with him, because he has shown mercy to us & our children & little ones. Therefore may the Lord make his days long . . . and may the Lord's mercy shelter them. In his and in our days may Judah be helped and Israel rest peacefully and may the Redeemer come to Zion, Amen."[18]

In 1883, a group of Yemenite Jews settled just south of Jerusalem's Old City in the village of Silwan, which they called Kfar Hashiloah. By 1929, some 110 Yemenite families had made their homes there. When Arab ri-ots erupted that summer, British authorities evacuated the Yemenites to the Old City, and a permanent police station was installed to ensure their safety. But in the summer of 1938, toward the end of the Great Arab Revolt (1936–1939), it was decided to evacuate the community once more. Men carrying Torah scrolls led the exodus, followed by their wives, chil-dren, and shepherds with their herds.[19]

A far larger wave of immigrants arrived shortly after the Aden riots of 1947, in which at least eighty-two Jews were killed. Between December

1948 and September 1950, almost fifty thousand Yemenites were flown to Israel in an operation dubbed Eagles' Wings (or, in English, Operation Magic Carpet). The name derives from a passage from the book of Exodus: "You have seen what I did unto the Egyptians, and how I bore you on eagles' wings, and brought you unto myself."

Before boarding the airplanes, the Yemenites were asked to deposit their possessions and manuscripts with the transit camp's Israeli personnel, who assured the immigrants that their belongings would be returned on arrival. But families who came to pick up their literary treasures from the customs officials at the Jaffa port or from the Jewish Agency storehouses in Jaffa were told they were not there. Instead, thousands of Yemenite books and manuscripts found their way in the late 1940s and early 1950s to private dealers, collectors, and libraries.

Two of the largest Yemenite libraries, each dating back several centuries, belonged to the Korah and al-Shech families. Rabbi Shlomo Korah, born in Sana'a, Yemen's capital, was told by Israeli port authorities that his family's crates of manuscripts had been destroyed in a warehouse fire.[20] Some of those manuscripts have since turned up in the Vatican Library and on the antiquities market.

In December 1949, Yitzhak Ben-Zvi, at that time a Labor Zionist leader and signatory of Israel's Declaration of Independence, went to observe Operation Magic Carpet in person. Photos from the Hashid camp, fifteen miles from Aden, show Ben-Zvi speaking to Yemenite refugees. Several folders of the Yemenite cases of 1949–1951, classified "confidential," are kept today in the archives of the American Jewish Joint Distribution Committee. In one unclassified memo, Ben-Zvi addresses "the property of the migrants":

> Most migrants carry their Torah scrolls and other books with them. In Aden they hand over their property to a central storage place, where they are packed and guarded until the chance comes to ship them. . . . I opened two or three boxes and found mostly printed material and a few common manuscripts, copies of liturgical books and *diwans* [poetry books]. But it is very likely that among them are valuable manuscripts as well as documents. . . . These [boxes] must be collected into one central basis before [they are] returned to their owners. The objective is to examine if there

may be valuable material to purchase from them for the Centre for the Study of Eastern Jewish Communities, which I am heading, for the purpose of research and publication.[21]

From his first days in Palestine, Ben-Zvi had become passionately involved with the Jews of the Arab world, and of Yemen in particular. "This marvelous tribe has kept its naïveté and solid unity," he wrote, "a tribe that tightly observed forefathers' traditions since the days of the Second Temple, that has memories of the kingdoms of Israel, and that has been keeping its heroic spirit in the worst conditions of exile among the Ishmaelites."[22] In 1949 he described his plan to set up a Center for the Study of Eastern Jewish Communities (today the Ben-Zvi Institute). "The war against Zionism has expanded to include Jews in general. There is great fear that entire cultural treasures and communities will suffer as a result or even be annihilated as a result." Against David Ben-Gurion's vision of an Israeli melting pot, Ben-Zvi worked to preserve the distinct literatures of Jewish communities "before they blur as a result of mixing with the people of Europe and America, 'the Ashkenazi.'"[23] Today, the two-floor Ben-Zvi library specializes in Jewish communities of the diaspora. Its shelves are organized by communities now largely vanished: Persia, Libya, India, and so on.

Ben-Zvi envisioned the ingathering of Jewish manuscripts to Jerusalem from the entire diaspora, a project he would be in a position to carry out when he was elected the second president of Israel in 1952. He dedicated his research to the communities neglected by the Western Jewish world, and he collected hundreds of Yemenite manuscripts—many of inestimable value. Although he intended to return them to their rightful owners, most are still in the institute that bears his name.

Hundreds more Yemenite volumes are stored in the National Library of Israel. In some cases, claimants were unable to prove ownership. In others, they felt that their manuscripts would be better preserved in the library. The library claims that "in cases where private ownership of a manuscript in the library's collection is indisputably proved, the library will return the manuscript to its owners. This is what the library has done in the past and what it will do in the future."[24] But the policy has only rarely been put into practice.

President Ben-Zvi devoted his energies, before and during his tenure, to rescuing Jewish manuscripts. Like many other European-born Israeli leaders of the time, he argued that Judaism's most important books belonged in—and to—the Jewish national home, as the patrimony of the Jewish people as a whole. His successors continue to act on the same impulse. As recently as March 2016, Israel covertly brought in nineteen Jews from war-ravaged Yemen—fourteen from the northern town of Raydah, and a family of five from Sana'a. The rabbi of Raydah carried with him a five-hundred-year-old Torah scroll. The sacred manuscript's departure from Yemen marked the de facto end of a community that had lived alongside its Muslim neighbors for centuries.

Silwan, the neighborhood that slopes downward from the southern wall of the Old City, is today one of Jerusalem's most contentious areas. Israeli archaeologists seek to unearth the city of David as Palestinian inhabitants of the houses above fear their floors might collapse underfoot.

In 1873, members of the Meyouhas family moved to Silwan to escape the overcrowded Old City and expand their kosher meat business. The family traces its ancestry to Spain before the Edict of Expulsion of 1492 but came to Jerusalem by way of Izmir in the sixteenth century. One member of the family, Yosef Meyouhas, became active in both the National House of the Books and Jerusalem's Sephardic Committee, whose archives we visited in the basement of the municipality. Meyouhas writes in his memoirs: "I was a constant guest at the house of the *fellahs* [peasants]. . . . In the evening, when I returned from the *heder* [religious boys' school], or during vacations and holidays, I would always visit Muhammad and Fatma, as well as 'Ali and Khadijah, my favorite neighbors. They fed me their bread, and I drank their water, and sometimes when they honored me with their conversations and stories as 'dessert' late into the night, I would also sleep in their homes, and in this manner all their manners, values, way of life, speech, and the stories I loved, served as my childhood education."[25]

The neighborly relations were dampened by the Arab riots of 1929, but not entirely extinguished. A Muslim family from Silwan, the Guzlans, prevented Arab rioters from harming their Jewish neighbors. When the violence subsided, the leaders of the Jewish community of Silwan pre-sented the Guzlans with a letter of gratitude:

> We wish to express our gratitude to the dear and courageous Mohammad Guzlan . . . for the warm, humane, and exceptional treatment he extended the Jewish residents of Silwan during the 1929 riots, not allowing any harm to befall them by the bands of rioters who paraded through our village. . . . How pleasant was it for our neighbors to personally fulfill the adage of King Solomon: "It is an honor for a man to cease from strife" [Prov. 20:3]. . . . We hope that such relations between us continue in perpetuity and that the good Lord reward the righteous for their deeds.[26]

In 1948, with the outbreak of the War of Independence, the Meyouhas family fled Silwan for the last time. They left three items with the Guzlans: the mezuzah from their home, a book of religious poetry, and their "Book of Remedies," a thick handwritten eighteenth–nineteenth century journal of medical cures in Hebrew in Solitreo script. The book includes "an amulet for those who are afraid at night," "a charm for a time of plague and epidemic," a formula "for every kind of headache," and even "a charm to chase Lilith out of the home of a woman who has given birth."[27]

After the Six-Day War in 1967, the Guzlans returned the "Book of Remedies" to the Meyouhas family.[28] We learned from Ayelet Hillel Cohen-Orgad, a researcher at Jerusalem's Tower of David Museum, that she tracked down the manuscript at the home of Yaeli Meyouhas, a daughter of Yosef Meyouhas. Rather than receiving official recognition for their courage and honorable dealings, however, the Guzlans were evicted from their home in 1999. An Israeli court ruled that their home stood on land that had been Jewish owned in the early part of the twentieth century.

At the Israel Museum, above the Valley of the Cross, a gleaming white dome and a black basalt wall shield Israel's greatest treasures—not bejew-eled crowns but unadorned texts. The Shrine of the Book is among the sites that most tourists feel compelled to include in their tour of Jerusalem. Visitors can descend a steep flight of stairs from the main hall, where the Dead Sea Scrolls are on display, and arrive at a round chamber that houses the oldest and most authoritative copy of the Hebrew Bible, known in Hebrew simply as the Crown (*ha-keter*).

Or so it appears. In fact, the Aleppo Codex, as the copy is known in English—a bound volume of vellum pages is stored in a nearby vault. Only its topmost leaf, the one that viewers see, is from the codex itself. The rest is a dummy, cleverly arranged by the curators to appear real. This illusion is but the first sign that not everything about the codex is as it seems.

In February 2016, UNESCO added the Aleppo Codex to its International Memory of the World Register. (The registry includes only two other items from Jerusalem: the Israel Museum's Rothschild Miscellany, a collection of illustrated fifteenth-century manuscripts, and the Pages of Testimony at the Yad Vashem Holocaust Museum.) But the story of the codex, ably told in a book by the Jerusalem-based journalist Matti Friedman, begins in tenth-century Tiberias, on the shores of the Sea of Galilee.[29] Two master scribes and philologists, facing the widening dispersal of Jewish communities, undertook to preserve the Jewish traditions that derive from the biblical text—derive, that is, not just from each letter but from each vowel, punctuation mark, and cantillation mark. A book, they felt, would serve scholars better than a scroll. This is the meaning of the term *codex*, which in Hebrew is *mitshaf* and in Arabic *muṣḥaf*, both derived from Ge'ez.[30] Through their combined efforts, the scribes aimed to create a copy of the Hebrew Bible of such precision that it would serve as a template for all future versions. For the codex's creators, philology was theology. They knew that layers of meaning can reside in a single syllable and that a single error can render a Torah scroll unusable.

A century later, the already revered codex migrated to Jerusalem and into the hands of Karaite owners, who added a colophon of warning: "Blessed be its guardian and damned he who sells it, damned be he who pawns it. [This book] must never be sold or purchased." Plundered by Crusaders in 1099, the codex was eventually ransomed by the Jewish community in Egypt, where it was consulted by Maimonides.[31] In the fourteenth century, the codex was spirited to the Cave of Elijah, a candle-lit grotto beneath the Great Synagogue of Aleppo. There it would remain for six centuries. For the Jews of Aleppo, the codex was a kind of talisman, protecting its own protectors from harm. Its removal, they believed, would portend the disastrous end of their community.

They were not entirely wrong. In late November 1947, following the United Nations resolution calling for the establishment of a Jewish state in part of Palestine, Arab rioters mobbed Aleppo's Jewish quarter, ransacking synagogues and torching dozens of Torah scrolls. Some six thousand Jews fled. The priceless codex was rumored to have gone up in flames. In fact, Aleppo's rabbis had concealed it in a storeroom in the Old City bazaar, where it remained for the next decade.

In 1957, with the help of a Jewish cheese merchant, the codex was smuggled from Syria to Jerusalem, where it came into the hands of Yitzhak Ben-Zvi. By the time the codex was properly documented, several months after arriving at Ben-Zvi's institute in 1958, nearly two hundred pages—40 percent—were missing, including nearly all of the Torah, four of the Five Books of Moses. The folios have not yet turned up. Some scholars have alleged that other valuable manuscripts have been stolen from the Ben-Zvi Institute, a claim that only adds to the puzzle: How could there have been no state investigation into the disappearance of the Jewish equivalent of the *Codex Sinaiticus*?

There followed a bitter four-year trial over ownership of the codex and, by extension, of the cultural riches of the diaspora. The Jews of Aleppo had not intended to give up the precious codex—the merchant to whom they had entrusted it had no right, they felt, to pass it along to the government. They wanted it back. Israeli authorities argued that the codex would be best served and best protected in national rather than private hands. Matti Friedman remarked on the irony that a book that enjoins against theft and coveting was itself coveted and pilfered. "A volume that survived one thousand years of turbulent history was betrayed in our times by the people charged with guarding it," he writes.[32] For now, the codex's story of loss and recovery—a story mirroring the Jews' fate in the Middle East—is far from over.

From the Silk Road to Jerusalem

"I buy and sell used goods. In other terms, you might say I'm a practical Orientalist." That was how the antiquities dealer Lenny Wolfe, who moved to Jerusalem from Glasgow in 1972, had introduced himself to us, with a wry smile and heavy Glaswegian brogue, the first time we met.

The vaulted basement of Wolfe's home in the Musrara neighborhood, on the seamline between East and West Jerusalem, is crammed with books and artefacts: five thousand bullae and scaraboids (seals in the shape of a scarab beetle, some dating back to the First Temple period); Islamic amulets from the Umayyad period to the British Mandate; and coins of the Bar Kochba revolt. He showed us bowls with magical inscriptions from the fifth to seventh centuries, including one inscribed with Arabic script in Syriac language, and another containing the name of the Abbasid caliph al-Ma'mun (who falsely inscribed himself as the builder of the Dome of the Rock, deleting the name of his predecessor, 'Abd al-Malik). Behind his desk, three of his hats perched on an ancient amphora.

Blending historical erudition and a merchant's canniness, Lenny Wolfe had a way of talking along tantalizing tangents. He peppered his speech with such expressions as "By the beard of the prophet," "By the cooking pot of Abraham," "By the Turban of Joseph," "By the sword of King David," "By whichever of the seventeen heads of John the Baptist you wish." He also possessed the rare ability to negotiate with people of all cultures. In an essay called "On Haggling," he describes spotting a Bedouin peddler in Petra who had a necklace Wolfe wanted:

> I greeted the son of the desert, sat down, introduced myself and asked after his health, his welfare, that of his immediate family, his distant family, and his livestock. I then went on to say how I was taken aback by Petra, and that it was surely the most beautiful spot on God's earth, and that he was very lucky to live here. By this time I was on my second cup of coffee, and we were already like lifelong friends. Like satisfying foreplay I worked my way around the main issue. Finally I brought up, by the way, the possibility of purchasing a necklace. I exercised all the Arabic I knew, words, colorful phrases, proverbs, and finally we consummated the deal, buying what I wanted at the price I wanted. . . . The entertainment made the whole exercise worthwhile. And then he said to me, "By Allah, you are like a Bedouin," typical Middle Eastern flattery, I dare say.[33]

With just such flair, Wolfe had negotiated the purchase of the First Temple–era papyrus fragment, believed to have been plundered from a Judean desert cave, with the earliest mention of Jerusalem in Hebrew.

At last we got around to the reason we had come: we were interested in his acquisition of a hoard of manuscripts discovered along the Silk Road in North Afghanistan, eleventh-century documents from the Jewish communities of Central Asia in Hebrew, Aramaic, Judeo-Arabic, and Judeo-Persian.

When Arab armies conquered the area now known as Afghanistan in the eighth century, they found an established Jewish community known as *al-Yahudan al-Kubra,* or the Great Jewry, which claimed to descend from exiles forced from Jerusalem in 597 BCE. But the newly discovered archive—mundane merchants' letters mixed in with fragments of religious texts—offers a window into Jewish life in the community before the Mongol invasion in the thirteenth century. "Place names mentioned in the documents," Wolfe explained, "suggest that it was probably written in present-day Afghanistan but could have been found in a number of places from a large area encompassing Western China, Afghanistan, Persia, Iraq, and the Central Asian republics that were formerly part of the Soviet Union." The collection includes a page of a previously unknown commentary on Isaiah 34 by Saadia Gaon, written in Arabic in Hebrew letters. (To rule out forgery, part of the material was sent to the Weizmann Institute of Science for carbon dating.) To obtain the Afghan Genizah, as the trove is called, Wolfe traveled across eight countries in the Middle East and former Soviet bloc.

After the Russian-Israeli oligarch Leonid Nevzlin backed out of an offer to buy them, Wolfe sold twenty-nine pages of the genizah to the National Library. "The price I gave them was in effect a donation," he told us. "To make money—even a great deal of money—from antiquities is legitimate, but material of great importance belongs to a national institution. If you're not cognizant of that, you're a *chazir* ["pig" in Hebrew]." For him, bringing the genizah to Jerusalem was far more than a commercial transaction. To describe the thrill of discovering and redeeming it, he used an impassioned vocabulary of return that, as we had begun to realize, he shared with many Jerusalemites who tend to the written word. But ownership of the documents may still be challenged; Omara Khan Massoudi, director of Afghanistan's National Museum, clings to the hope that artefacts and documents that had been smuggled out will eventually return to Kabul.

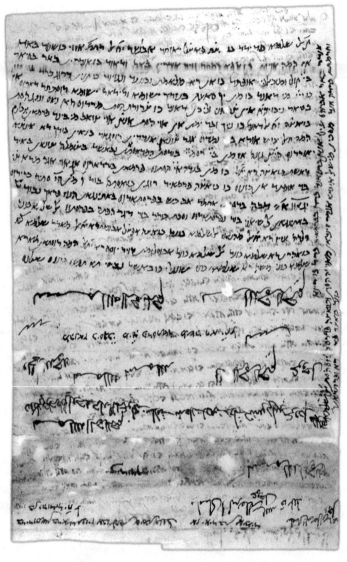

Letter to Abū Naṣr b. Dāniyāl, a page from the Afghan Genizah
(NLI 8333.29=4. PR2 recto). (Courtesy of the National Library
of Israel.)

"Abandoned Property"

One afternoon at the National Library in Jerusalem, we persuaded a reluctant librarian to retrieve several volumes marked with an unusual designation: "AP": "abandoned property" (in Hebrew *nikhsei nifkadim*)—a term that is commonly used to designate homes that were "abandoned" and confiscated by the state after 1948 and again after 1967. The volumes we see, like almost 6,500 others with the designation, legally belong not to the library but to the custodian of absentee property at Israel's Finance Ministry.

In the late 1950s and early 1960s, the National Library overhauled its cataloguing system. Collections of Palestinian books were brought together under the designation "AP." Until then, the books bore the names of the former owners, recorded as abbreviated surnames; for example, "SAK" for "Sakakini," followed by a serial number. As the historian Gish Amit pointed out, the new cataloguing system depersonalized each collection and detached it from individual ownership. What he did not say was that the new designation also prevented the books from being assimilated into the library's collections and losing all trace of their history of acquisition.

During the war of 1948, Jordanian troops demolished nearly all of the Old City's synagogues, including the Hurva (so dear to Yaakov Saphir), often destroying their books and Torah scrolls. Konstantinos Mavrides, an employee of the Greek Consulate in Jerusalem, witnessed the devastation: "After the destruction of the Jewish Quarter, the surrender and removal of the Jewish community, bombing of the Old City from 1 to 9 June concentrated on the Holy Sepulchre Church area and compound, the premises of the Greek Patriarchate and Central Monastery. Mortar fire was also directed at St Vasileios, St Theodoros, the Roman Catholic Casa Nova, the Greek chapel of the Archangel, and other monasteries and chapels, as well as the area near the Library housing priceless ancient manuscripts, parchments, documents, Byzantine and Ottoman archival material."[34]

The writer Shulamith Hareven, born in Warsaw, grew up in Jerusalem from the age of ten. Like Eliezer Ben-Yehuda, she regarded Jerusalem as both her real birthplace and her ineluctable fate. "Born in Europe, all my days there passed in an obscure impatience, as if it were all a mistake, a confinement, like a wretched marriage—until I first saw strong light on rocky hedges on a mountain, a stooping summer olive tree, a well carved in stone and I knew that was it. I had arrived at some deep, palpable ancientness, at the womb of the world, where virtually everything was and will be created. Here were the right light, the right smell, the right touch." Hareven joined the Haganah underground paramilitary organization and served as a combat medic in the War of Independence. Over the next decades she published essays and a book of poems, *Predatory Jerusalem* (1962). In her memoir, published shortly before her death in 2003, Hareven describes the first time she entered one of the beautiful Arab houses.

> That morning we pounced on the desolated wealthy neighborhood like a pack of young and ravenous wolves. The inhabitants had left it the night before in a seizure of fear, a seizure of inevitable error that would paralyze the face of the city for many years to come. . . .
>
> Then twilight came, blood-streaked, the sun sinking like heavy molten metal, which together with the sweat and fatigue made it almost impossible to keep the eyes open. The commander divided us among the houses. My squad was assigned to Anton 'Awad's house. I recognised the name: one of the 'Awad Brothers Ltd. . . . We climbed the stairs, over the pretty dim-colored carpet, and stormed into the bedrooms. I did not take off my shoes. I was too tired. I remember the heavenly, sensual quality, under my dirty hands, below my arm, where my flesh touched the yellow silk bed-cover. I stroked it with my fingers. Slept for awhile.

Hareven describes the ensuing party in the house; the fighters drank Italian vermouth discovered in the cellar, tried on shoes and clothes, broke into an empty safe box, and finally stepped into the room of the family's teenage son, Joseph 'Awad. On his desk, she found a copy of Shakespeare. "I crouched on the bed of 'Awad junior and read sonnets out loud."[35] When she left the house the next morning, she took the book with her. It continued to haunt her for many years.

If a book can serve as a portable homeland it can also serve as a reminder of the impossibility of return. After the 1967 war, Shulamith Hareven looked up the young Jerusalemite whose name was inscribed in the edition of Shakespeare she had taken from the bedroom of a Palestinian home in 1948. "When I found the name of Anton 'Awad in the phonebook, I could not stand having that Shakespeare with me for a moment longer. I felt as if for twenty-one years I had been bearing within me a hidden unrest that would be soothed and be calmed only when I returned the book to its owner." She resolved to return the book to Anton 'Awad in person:

"Look," I said in English, although I understand Arabic, "the fates of war brought me a book with your name on it."

"I don't understand. What book?"

I became tongue-tied. "This book. It belongs to you, and I want to return it to you. I found your name in the phonebook. A few days ago. It was in your former home."

"My former home?!" His entire head blushed darkly. A torrent of words streamed from his mouth. He won't hear a word of this. Let them return it all. They looted property worth tens of thousands of liras. I must give him my name and address, I must be one of the looters. He'll sue, he . . . [36]

'Awad's refusal to accept the book brings Hareven's story to an end.

In the meantime, even as the fighting raged, official complaints about looting at the hands of Jewish soldiers and commanders in Jerusalem were aired in the Knesset. Yitzhak Ben-Zvi, the first to condemn these actions, demanded immediate action from Prime Minister Ben-Gurion. Ben-Zvi failed to mention that those collecting the greatest numbers of books from Palestinian homes were acting on behalf of the state. At a cabinet meeting held on December 20, 1948, Interior Minister Yitzhak Gruenbaum reported: "Recently a committee from the university was organized, and it goes about after the army and gathers up books from the houses."[37]

Is state appropriation for the purposes of preservation a form of theft? In some cases, after all, the custodian of memory is the state itself. The National Library offers a case in point. On July 26, 1948, with West Jerusalem under Israeli control, a letter of unknown authorship was sent to Curt Wormann, director of the National Library: "I estimate that to date around 12,000 books or more have been collected. The best part of the libraries of the Arab writers and scholars is now in a safe place. We also have several bags of manuscripts, whose value has not yet been assessed. Most of the books come from Katamon, but we got to the German Colony, Baqa'a and Musrara as well. We found several wonderful Arabic libraries in Musrara." Shlomo Shunami, the librarian in charge of collecting the Palestinian books in 1948, had previously dedicated himself to salvaging the books of the European communities extinguished by the Holocaust. Shunami presented both projects as acts of rescue: "At the time of the War of Independence, the operation to salvage books in Jerusalem was carried out, and after that also in other places, in the abandoned Arab neighborhoods. The library staff together with the university's workers combed the territories, at risk to their lives. More than once bursts of Arab Legion bullets rained down on them, and [they] were miraculously saved."[38] But were they rescuing the books or looting them? Was this plunder or preservation?

Among the AP books we consulted at the National Library, we discovered one that had belonged to the Jerusalem educator Khalil al-Sakakini. It still bore the signature of his only son, Sari (AP 3249). Sakakini, a key figure in the shaping of Palestinian national identity, was born in Jerusalem into a prominent Greek Orthodox family in 1878. In 1908 he established a Muslim-Christian Association for mutual understanding, and in 1911 he founded the al-Dusturiyya school (*dusturiyya* means "national" or "constitutional" in Arabic). At the close of World War I, the Ottoman authorities arrested Sakakini for sheltering an American Jewish fugitive named Alter Levine. Both men were sent to Damascus to stand trial; they were freed when the Turkish forces withdrew from that city.[39]

Yet despite his efforts toward cross-cultural tolerance, Sakakini reserved a special scorn for the Zionists. In February 1914 he wrote in his diary: "If I hate the Zionist movement, I hate it because it endeavors to build its independent existence on the ruins of others." At the same time he appreciated the spirit of enterprise. "The Arab nation," he remarked, "needs someone like Rothschild to invest in its revival." In 1925, when Lord Balfour came to Jerusalem to attend the cornerstone-laying ceremony of the Hebrew University, Sakakini gave a fierce address from the *minbar* (pulpit) of al-Aqsa Mosque, condemning Lord Balfour, the British Mandate, and the Zionist movement.[40]

During the British Mandate, Sakakini headed the Arab Teachers College in Jerusalem and instructed British officers in Arabic. In 1937 he moved his family and his extensive library into a spacious house in the Katamon neighborhood (today Yordei Ha-Sira Street 8). As he recounts in the journal he kept between 1907 and his death in 1953, Sakakini named its rooms after Arab cities: Sana'a, Damascus, Baghdad, Cairo.

On April 30, 1948, Sakakini, age seventy, fled war-torn Jerusalem. He was forced to leave his cherished books behind. Exiled to Egypt, he agonized over their fate. "I clung to them day and night," he wrote in his diary. "Everyone who visited me . . . found me immersed in a book. . . . Farewell, my books! How much midnight oil did I burn with you. . . . Have you been plundered? Burned? Moved—with all due honor and respect—to some public or private library? Are you sitting on grocers' shelves, your pages used to wrap onions?"[41]

Sakakini's journals, at least, survived in the hands of his daughter, Hala, who remained in Jerusalem and who after the war dedicated herself to editing and publishing them. In 2007 they were published in the Hebrew translation of Gideon Shilo and made accessible to a new generation of Israeli readers. If his property was abandoned, his memory was not.

Our search for Jerusalem books awaiting return took us one afternoon to the grandest home of the Nashashibi quarter of Jerusalem's upscale Sheikh Jarrah neighborhood (named after the twelfth-century medic Hussam al-Din al-Jarrahi, personal physician to Saladin, who granted him the title *jarrah*, "healer"). Few of the patrons of the Gallery Café on the ground floor are aware of the storied library upstairs.

The stately house that became known as the Nashashibi Palace was built by the elusive Alexandria-born architect Spyro Houris (who may have been Arab, or perhaps Greek).[42] For the tiled facade, Houris commissioned a master ceramist from Armenia. David Ohannessian, a refugee of the Armenian Genocide, was invited to Jerusalem by Sir Ronald Storrs, the British military governor of Jerusalem, and Charles Ashbee, adviser on the urban development of Jerusalem, to retile the Dome of the Rock. The Islamic authorities rejected the Armenian Christian artist, choosing instead to import tiles from Muslim members of the Çinicioğlu family in Turkey. ("There is politics in every tile in this city," as the historian Simon Goldhill remarks.) Ohannessian opened a workshop to train orphans in the craft of Armenian ceramics and supplied his masterworks to the Rockefeller Museum, Saint Andrew's Church, Saint John's Eye Hospital (at its original Hebron Road location), and the Governor's House on the Hill of Evil Counsel. His signature facades also grace smaller buildings on Jaffa Road, Talbiyyeh, and the Greek Colony.[43]

The mansion in Sheikh Jarrah took the name of its wealthy owner, the Palestinian poet, writer, and teacher Isaaf Nashashibi. After graduating from Jerusalem's Collège des Frères, founded in 1876 inside the Old City's New Gate by the La Salle Brothers, a Catholic order, Nashashibi went to Beirut to study with Boutrus al-Bustani, known as "the master of the Arabic renaissance," and to immerse himself in the *nahda* (Arabic: "awakening," "renaissance") movement, the revival of Arab literature that emerged from Egypt and Lebanon in the late nineteenth century.

On returning to Jerusalem, Nashashibi made his home in Sheikh Jarrah into a salon for writers and artists from across the Levant, including his close friends Khalil al-Sakakini and the Egyptian "prince of poets" Ahmed Shawqi. Wasif Jawhariyyeh, a renowned collector and oud player, remembered "private gatherings at the Nashashibi palace," in the late 1920s, especially one occasion when the musician and performer Muhammad 'abd al-Wahhab stayed there when he came to Jerusalem and performed at the Zion Cinema on Jaffa Road.[44] Until the outbreak of the First World War, Nashashibi taught Arabic literature at the Salahiyya College just inside the Lion's Gate on the eastern side of the Old City.

He was even then fearful of what was to come. In November 1910, he complained of an event where "many people raised Zionist flags and marched singing the Zionist anthem. . . . Many more events [like this] will occur while the Palestinians sit and play." His students later remembered his words: "Awake, this is your homeland. Do not let it be sold to strangers."[45]

In the ensuing decades, Isaaf Nashashibi composed Arabic grammars, helped produce the modern translation of the Bible into Arabic (known as the Van Dyck Bible, popular among Arabic-speaking Protestants), and amassed a considerable library. According to his nephew Nasser Eddin Nashashibi, it amounted to some two hundred thousand volumes.[46]

Nashashibi fled the Israeli-Arab war of 1948, and died in Cairo. His library was dispersed. In her study *Till We Have Built Jerusalem*, the writer Adina Hoffman writes that "one eyewitness later reported that for months after Nashashibi's death and [the] wholesale pillaging of the house that Spyro Houris built, certain neighborhood grocers could be seen using pages of Nashashibi's most valuable books to wrap cones of sugar and salt." Yet it seems that at least some of those books have survived in the "abandoned property" shelves at the National Library, where we found several books that probably belonged to Nashashibi's collection.[47]

In 1982, after decades of neglect, the mansion was refitted into a research center bearing Nashashibi's name, complete with a new library. The new collection, gathered by Isḥaq al-Husseini, includes gifts from prominent Jerusalem figures. The library holds nearly five hundred Arabic manuscripts (put onto 16mm microfilm and later digitized), another five hundred rare books (including some thirty titles in Ottoman Turkish and Persian), and items from Wasif Jawhariyyeh's collection. The oldest manuscript dates to 1175. Most of the titles relate to Qur'anic studies, Sufism, and Arabic language and literature.[48]

When a full return proves impossible, a hope that cannot be fulfilled, can Jerusalemites reconcile themselves to the compromises of partial return?

Political Battlegrounds

The archives of the Orient House, with their fragmentary written remains of the Palestinian past, have vanished. Our inquiries as to their whereabouts with a colleague who works at the World Health Organization, the current occupant of this mansion in East Jerusalem, with the director of the Israel State Archives, and with the chief historian of the Israeli Police proved fruitless. What happens when an archive is ripped from the context that imbued it with meaning? What can the making and unmaking of an archive tell us about the fears that continue to divide Jerusalem?

The Orient House, a jewel of a building in the Sheikh Jarrah neighborhood, was completed in 1897 as a grand residence for the aristocratic Husseini family. Like Blair House in Washington, it served to host visiting heads of state. Kaiser Wilhelm II stayed there in 1898; Emperor Haile Selassie of Ethiopia came in 1936. After the 1948 war, it served as the headquarters of the United Nations Relief and Works Agency for Palestine Refugees (UNRWA) and then as a luxury hotel. Sinking into neglect after the Six-Day War of 1967, the building became a center of PLO activity in the 1980s under the leadership of Faisal Husseini, later appointed Palestinian Authority minister for Jerusalem affairs.

Husseini brought the Arab Studies Society to the Orient House in the early 1980s. Beginning with only two hundred volumes in 1980, the collection grew to some seventeen thousand books in both English and Arabic; a collection of Palestinian newspapers (including *al-Quds, al-Fajr,* and *al-Sha'ab*) from the 1970s to the Second Intifada; an oral history collection featuring interviews with Palestinians who lived through the Arab Revolt of 1936–1939; and the private library of Musa al-Alami, the Cambridge-educated chairman of the Arab Office in Jerusalem from 1947 to 1949. (Al-Alami was born in the Musrara neighborhood outside Damascus Gate to a prominent family; his father and grandfather both served as mayors of Jerusalem. As a young man, he studied under Khalil al-Sakakini.) The Orient House archives, meanwhile, also took in the personal books and papers of Faisal Husseini, documents relating to the Madrid Conference of 1991, and the Arab Studies Society photography collection.

Israeli authorities, suspicious of having PLO offices and representatives in Jerusalem, regarded the Orient House as a subversive center. It was, after all, the only official Palestinian political presence in the city. In 1988, after the outbreak of the First Intifada, the center was ordered shut down, but it reopened during the years of the Oslo Accords in the 1990s.

In August 2001, two days after the Sbarro restaurant suicide bombing in downtown Jerusalem, and a couple of months after the death of Faisal Husseini, the Israeli cabinet voted to close the Orient House for good. Israeli security forces staged an early-morning raid and impounded the building's archives. The city's Palestinian leaders regarded this as politically motivated looting—an erasure of a page of Palestinian history. They pointed to a precedent: in 1982, as the PLO was forced to evacuate Beirut, Israeli forces confiscated the Palestine Research Center's depository of Palestinian historical and political heritage. In that instance, Israel returned the archives. But the Orient House archives are nowhere to be found.

What is it about the Orient House archives that made them so threatening that they provoked the drastic measures of confiscation and concealment? We posed the question to Qasem abu Harb, director of the archives at the Arab Studies Society, member of the Palestine National Archives Committee, and Jerusalem's preeminent expert on Palestinian virtual archives and digitized collections. Abu Harb directed us to several Israeli historians who used to work in the archives. He found it ironic that more Israeli than Palestinian historians had used it. They in turn told us about their own findings before the raid: a collection of pamphlets from the First Intifada, newspaper clippings and records from the period of the 1993 Oslo Accords until the assassination of Prime Minister Yitzhak Rabin in November 1995, and material on Arab leaders in Haifa before 1948. Abu Harb lamented above all the lost personal archive of Faisal Husseini. If recovered, Husseini's personal papers promise to shed light on a history of Jerusalem's leading family from Sheikh Amin al-Husseini (the Grand Mufti who concluded agreements with the Nazis), to Faisal's father, 'Abd al-Qadr al Husseini, who commanded the Arab forces until his death in the Battle of the Castel (al-Qastal) in April 1948.

For all our prowling, we tried not to succumb to the tempting illusion that we were just around the corner from a fully recoverable past. Archival research is not necromancy. One day, however, perhaps we shall hear in the Orient House holdings the clamor of conversations past that have made Jerusalem the contentious place it is today—a place where Israelis and Palestinians ground their respective national identities.

The first of what would become known as the Dead Sea Scrolls were discovered near Qumran in the West Bank during the British Mandate in 1947. The rest were excavated between 1947 and 1956 by a joint expedition of the Department of Antiquities of Jordan and the École Biblique in Jerusalem and placed in the Palestine Archaeological Museum (today the Rockefeller Museum). An international committee governed the museum until the Jordanian government nationalized it in late 1966. To this day, the scrolls bear the catalogue numbers assigned to them by the experts who first pieced the fragments together.

Following the Six-Day War, Israel took control of the West Bank and its archaeological finds, as well as East Jerusalem, along with the Rockefeller and its scrolls. Unlike private and institutional property, which was deposited with the Custodian of Absentee Property and may still one day be returned to Palestinian hands, the museum was nationalized by Israel. Jordanians transferred the Copper Scroll, which describes the locations of sixty-one caches of gold, silver, and other treasures hidden near Jerusalem and Jericho in the first century CE, to Amman. But all the other Dead Sea Scrolls were brought to the Israel Museum and its Shrine of the Book and displayed as the greatest treasures of Jewish heritage. "The Dead Sea Scrolls were written by Jews and are part of the spiritual assets of the Jewish nation," said Uzi Dahari, deputy director of the Israel Antiquities Authority. "It is our right to possess the scrolls—it's not a legal but a moral issue."[49]

Palestinians saw things in a different light. In the words of Hamdan Taha, head of the archaeological department in the Palestinian Ministry of Tourism and Antiquities, "Hundreds of archaeological sites have been looted and plundered, and there has been an active illegal trade in cultural properties. . . . Official Israeli policy stimulates the looting of archaeological sites." In 2005, the scrolls were exhibited for the first time outside the Middle East, without incident. Several scrolls were displayed in Berlin's Martin Gropius-Bau Museum as part of an exhibit marking forty years of diplomatic relations between Germany and Israel. At the time, James Snyder, then director of the Israel Museum, called the scrolls "a kind of 'Mona Lisa' for us."[50]

But in 2009, Taha submitted a letter to the Canadian Museums Association (CMA) in advance of a temporary traveling exhibition of the Dead Sea Scrolls to Canada. Taha asked the CMA to adhere to the UNESCO Convention for the Protection of Cultural Property in the Event of Armed Conflict (1954). Article 2 of the first protocol of that convention requires a member state "to take into its custody cultural property imported into its territory either directly or indirectly from any occupied territory." Pro-Palestinian demonstrators rallied on the sidewalk opposite the Royal Ontario Museum in Toronto chanting that the ancient Hebrew scrolls were stolen property. The Canadian government issued a statement saying that "differences regarding ownership of the

Dead Sea scrolls should be addressed by Israel, Jordan and the Palestinian Authority. It would not be appropriate for Canada to intervene as a third party."[51]

In December 2017, Israel was forced to pull out of a planned exhibit of the Dead Sea Scrolls in Frankfurt because the German government would not guarantee their return if claimed by Palestinians. It seems that the German Foreign Ministry and federal commissioner for cultural affairs regarded the ownership of the scrolls as unclear.[52]

The question of rightful ownership of cultural assets lingers. Greece seeks the return of the marble friezes Lord Elgin took from the Parthenon to England, and Egypt demands the return of the Luxor obelisk from the place de la Concorde in Paris. The Palestinian Authority has repeatedly petitioned UNESCO to acknowledge World Heritage sites in the Occupied Palestinian Territories, including Qumran.

Many have remarked on the irony in the Palestinian claim to the Dead Sea Scrolls. Consider, for example, the Temple Scroll, the largest scroll discovered in the Qumran caves. Its eighteen sheets of parchment, dated to the first half of the first century CE, provide the details of divine instructions for the construction and operation of the very Temple that some Palestinians now deny existed. Although the Islamic Waqf afforded us exceptional access to the al-Aqsa libraries and manuscript restoration lab, the Temple remained a taboo subject for our Palestinian hosts on those visits. The most recent edition of the *Guide to the al-Aqsa Mosque* (published by the Waqf in 2015) makes no mention of the pre-Islamic history of the site. Palestinian guidebooks claim that the Jewish Temple was nothing but a fiction and advise visitors not to mention it.

In Jerusalem, when historical retrieval aims to legitimize origins, it always seems to require erasure.

The Memories of Others

What lessons can Jerusalem impart about the rescue and return of a literary legacy that is not one's own? Our visits to Jerusalem's libraries disclosed some telling examples not only of jealous possessiveness and erasure but also of one community preserving the cultural memory of another.

At the corner of the Via Dolorosa and al-Wad Street in the Old City, Israeli flags flutter over a yeshiva. In the eyes of many locals, the yeshiva stands as a symbol of provocative Jewish settlement in a predominantly Muslim neighborhood. Few know that it also exemplifies loyal friendship across religious and political divides.

Before our visit to the yeshiva, Yeshayahu Winograd, Jerusalem's most eminent bibliographer, showed us into his modest living room in the Rehavia neighborhood. A bookshelf displayed his life's work: an index of all incunabula published in Hebrew characters—in Hebrew, Ladino, and Judeo-Arabic—from 1469 to 1863. He calls this master index of some ninety-five thousand titles *Ozar Hasefer Haivri*, "Treasures of the Hebrew Book." He published it in 1980, though he continues to expand it in digital form. He made his living in the rare books business, but kept only two collections at home: a priceless collection of volumes by and about Elijah ben Solomon, the "Gaon [Genius] of Vilna," and the archive of his family's yeshiva.

His great-grandfather Yitzhak Winograd, a rabbi and one of the early Zionists drawn to Jerusalem by a dream of return, arrived in 1886. He bought a plot of land in the Old City and founded a yeshiva in 1894. As he leafed through the archive's albums, Yeshayahu described how Yitzhak Winograd's dream of return, briefly fulfilled, had been lost again. Plundered during the Arab riots of 1920, his yeshiva, called Torat Chaim, finally had to be abandoned during the Arab Revolt of 1936.[53] Torat Chaim was the only one of the Old City's eighty synagogues and yeshivas not destroyed by the Jordanians during the war of 1948. Its Arab caretaker hid the yeshiva's library behind a plastered wall.

Days after Israeli soldiers recaptured the Old City in 1967, Yeshayahu Winograd returned to al-Wad Street, accompanied by Major-General Chaim Herzog (later to serve as president of Israel). Winograd recognized the building but not its caretaker; as a child he remembered the man who used to bring monthly rent from the apartments attached to the yeshiva. This caretaker had died, and the man who greeted Winograd was the caretaker's brother. Much to his astonishment, Winograd discovered the library, dust-encrusted but intact. Herzog would recall the rediscovery of the library as one of the most moving moments of his visit to the Old City after the Six-Day War.[54]

When we visited him, Winograd could not remember the name of the savior of the books. But he did vividly recall finding in that room the archives and account books of the yeshiva from its founding, an invaluable window into the life of one of Jerusalem's leading religious academies. Besides the albums that Winograd showed us, we found parts of that archive in the National Library (ARC 4* 1609).

Some time after we visited Winograd, we went in search of the family that saved the Torat Chaim collection. It happened to be the first day of Ramadan and the morning after Jerusalem Day, in which thousands of flag-waving religious Israeli youth march down al-Wad Street escorted by policemen. The atmosphere in the Muslim Quarter was sluggish. We stopped in front of the yeshiva, today leased by Ateret Cohanim, an organization that acquires houses in the Muslim Quarter and transfers them to Jewish hands. We asked a shopkeeper about the former owners of the building. He sent us around the corner to 2 Barquq Street.

After some hesitation, Dina al-Basha welcomed us into her family's apartment just below the yeshiva. She gingerly placed a portrait of her late father, Ibrahim Basha ('Abdel Rani), as a young man next to her on the couch. She told us that Ibrahim's father, Jaudat Basha, came to Jerusalem from Turkey (hence the surname, Arabic for "pasha") after a tragic series of deaths of his children. Ibrahim became an educator admired by all people of Jerusalem, Dina recalled, and a man who instilled in her the imperatives of kindness. After 1948, the Jordanians allowed them to buy the house. They faithfully continued to safeguard the Winograd yeshiva and its three thousand books.

What makes some people treasure and preserve the memory of others, whose language they cannot read? "It was the right thing to do," Dina replied, with disarming simplicity.

EPILOGUE

THE CLOSED GATE

This gate shall be shut; it shall not be opened, and no man shall
enter by it, because the Lord God of Israel has entered by it;
therefore it shall be shut.
—*Ezekiel (44:2)*

In Jerusalem's Franciscan library, we came across an illuminated antiphonary made in Venice between 1401 and 1404 (MS 7). It depicted
the legend that when the Byzantine emperor Heraclius had rescued
the remains of the Holy Cross from the hands of the Persians (who
had seized Jerusalem in 614), he hastened to return it to Jerusalem. As
he approached, riding his horse in full regalia, the Golden Gate miraculously sealed itself. Only when he dismounted and walked with
humility—barefoot and in plain cotton clothes—did the gate reopen and
admit him.[1]

In the third century, the Christian theologian Origen said that to understand how the soul enters into divine things, it was necessary to read
about "the city of God, the heavenly Jerusalem, and of its foundations
and gates."[2] The beguiling gates of Jerusalem, so integral a part of the
city's topography, are thresholds of security and sanctity often invoked

in the city's texts, from the Psalms and the Gospels to pilgrim reports and guidebooks.

Jerusalem's libraries, too, can be seen as gates of knowledge—many of them closed. This closure begs for an explanation: What is the point of building a beautiful gate only to seal it again?

While writing this book we sought access to Jerusalem's diverse libraries as a way of understanding the city itself. Jerusalem's libraries, as we have seen, have seen their fair share of thefts and forgeries, aroused many jealousies. They have been party to calumny and cupidity. But of all the reasons offered for adhering to a policy of secrecy and closure, the sacredness of what they contain touches most deeply on what defines Jerusalem's libraries and is central to the trust Jerusalem's librarians seek to preserve.

The Sacred and the Secret

Father Mark Sheridan, born and raised in Washington, D.C., serves as a Benedictine monk at Dormition Abbey on Mount Zion, the site from which Mary was said to have been assumed body and soul into heaven. As a student of patristics and Coptic literature, he has thought deeply about concealment: "In the ancient world the idea was widespread, if not indeed universal, that sacred texts had hidden meaning," he argued.[3]

The hidden is pervasively embedded in Jerusalem, often in the form of signs that warn against trespassing on holy places. The sacred draws boundaries. So too with the more inaccessible and secretive of Jerusalem's libraries. Books are sometimes kept in sacristies that only ordained members of the priesthood may enter.

Libraries that inhabit sacred places are treated with special respect, as are objects that house sacred texts. Sacred verses require special performative gestures. Worshippers recite certain texts standing, kneeling, or in full prostration. Other sacred texts depend more on the performance than the words. Jews kiss the mezuzah on the doorposts of their homes, bind themselves head and hand with tefillin, and wear necklaced amulets inscribed in stone or metal. These objects' sacredness comes from the inscribed parchments hidden within.

What, then, do Jerusalem's texts teach about the symbiosis of the sacred and the secret? The philosopher Leo Strauss, who claimed to have rediscovered the art of esoteric writing, remarked on the two roots of Western tradition: Jerusalem and Athens, faith and philosophy. In Jerusalem, he said, "the one thing needful is obedient love"; in Athens, "the one thing needful is free inquiry."[4]

Obedient love involves a healthy respect for the role of the book as sacred—both in itself and for the knowledge it embodies. A Qur'an must never be left open on the table; it is *haram*—a word that denotes both "sacred" and "forbidden." It is haram to highlight passages or write in the margins of a sacred book, or to touch the Qur'an when in a state of impurity.

Torah scrolls are housed in a synagogue's Holy Ark (*Aron Ha-Kodesh*), a closed and curtained cabinet. The scrolls are mounted on wooden rods that allow reading the parchment from right to left. The reader uses a *yad* (a hand-shaped pointer) to avoid touching the scroll with bare hands. Commenting on a strange Talmudic text which suggests that touching the Holy Scriptures "makes the hands impure," the philosopher Emmanuel Levinas offered a modern midrash:

> Due to the fact that the hand touches the uncovered Torah scroll, the hands are declared impure. But why? Is it certain that the bareness of the scroll only means the absence of a covering over the parchment? I am not sure that that absence of covering does not already and especially symbolize a different bareness. . . . And is the hand just a hand and not a certain impudence of spirit as well, that seizes a text savagely, without preparation or teacher, approaching the verse as a thing or an allusion to history in the instrumental bareness of its vocables, without precautions, without mediation, without all that has been acquired through a long tradition strewn with contingencies?[5]

Levinas teaches that a sacred text is ungraspable by human hands. To attempt to de-sacralize the text is to de-sacralize oneself.

Levinas elsewhere calls Jerusalem "a city twinned with its ideal." That twinning teaches that if the sacred is that which is close to the divine, it poses a danger to mortals. God tells Moses in Exodus, "No man shall see Me and live." For our own protection, we must be screened off from the holy just as we must be kept from esoteric knowledge. Freud noted that many languages refer to the sacred and the forbidden with the same word. The sacred imposes distance.[6]

Of course touch poses a danger not just to the one who touches, but to the texts being touched. In Umberto Eco's *The Name of the Rose,* a novice Benedictine monk describes the vulnerability of the old pages:

> I saw Pacificus of Tivoli, leafing through an ancient volume whose pages had become stuck together because of the humidity. He moistened his thumb and forefinger with his tongue to leaf through his book, and at every touch of his saliva those pages lost vigor; opening them meant folding them, exposing them to the harsh action of air and dust, which would erode the subtle wrinkles of the parchment and would produce mildew where the saliva had softened but also weakened the corner of the page. As an excess of sweetness makes the warrior flaccid and inept, this excess of possessive and curious love would make the book vulnerable to the disease destined to kill it.

A book may perish, so to speak, by touch, and may in turn kill those who with moistened thumbs leaf through its lethal pages. If some books are kept out of reach because of their sacred status, others may be hidden away because of their contents. As Ibn 'Arabi noted, "For every knowledge there are people suitable for it."[7]

The author of *The Name of the Rose* speaks of a library as "an instrument not for distributing the truth but for delaying its appearance."[8] Jerusalem's libraries, with their secrets sacred and mundane, bear witness to truth delayed.

Opening the Gates

What might the opening of Jerusalem's libraries look like, and what might it mean for the city and its custodians of the written word?

Today the National Library of Israel is in the midst of a redesign that aims to let readers experience the library anew. After the Knesset passed the National Library Law in 2007, what used to be known as Beit Hasfarim, the House of the Books, would henceforth serve not only scholars of arcane subjects but "the nation." A new library building across from the Knesset, designed by the firm of Herzog de Meuron, is expected to be completed in 2022. "The core principle driving this transformative initiative, open access in all of its many forms," the library announced, "will be reflected in the new National Library home." The architectural brief for the new building emphasizes that the library will open "its physical and virtual doors to all potential users, academic and non-academic alike." David Blumberg, chairman of the board of the National Library, describes his vision in similar terms: "The democratization of knowledge is a central value that will guide and be promoted by the new library."[9] The new library will no longer act as a hushed storehouse of books, periodicals, card catalogues, and microfilms, but as a collaborative high-bandwidth information hub.

Does open access—a kind of digital-analog remix—represent the future of the book in Jerusalem? What can we expect of the transition from parchment to pixels?

Some of Jerusalem's collections are already being more or less successfully uploaded into the digital cloud. The al-Aqsa Mosque library has digitized more than 50,000 pages of its collection of Arabic newspapers and 119 of its manuscripts from the twelfth to the nineteenth centuries in the most immediate need of preservation (both are available online at the British Library's Endangered Archives Program website). To this collection, the National Library has recently added more than 100,000 pages of the Arabic Newspaper Archive of Ottoman and Mandatory Palestine through its project "Jrayed" (adding to over two million pages, already digitized, of Hebrew newspapers of the same period). Starting in 2011, the Syriac manuscripts Abuna Shimon Can showed us at Saint Mark's have been digitized by Benedictine friars at the Hill Museum and Manuscript Library in Minnesota, which is currently adding the Khalidi and Budeiri libraries to what is already the world's largest collection of images of manuscripts. (Father Columba Stewart, a Benedictine monk who has led the Hill since 2003, comes to Jerusalem once a year to check on progress.) Digitization is also under way at the American Colony archives, the Israel State Archives, Yad Vashem, and the Ben-Zvi Institute. In the courts and kollels of some of Jerusalem's ultra-Orthodox communities, we noticed young women busily bent over scanning machines.

Something is lost in digitization of a manuscript: the feel of the textures, the radiance of gold-leaf illumination, the concentrated richness of color. But as we saw firsthand in the imaging laboratories of the Israel Antiquities Authority and the École Biblique, something is gained too. A digital image, especially when taken in a spectrum of wavelengths, may reveal what is concealed to the naked eye.

The technologies and formats of Jerusalem's texts may be in flux, but as the Roman poet Horace said, "Littera scripta manet," the written word remains. We shall see what these new forms of rescue and "ingathering" will mean for the textured parchments, illuminated folios, and crumbling pages that have been digitized. Perhaps, in the end, the gap between physical archives and libraries and their "digital cloud" replicas will come to resemble the rift that separates the earthly and heavenly Jerusalems.

The City as Palimpsest

As befits the city's wealthiest and most powerful Christian institution, Jerusalem's Greek Orthodox library is a vast universe in itself. To describe its immensity, one of the elder archbishops told us, "day will be night and night will be day and you will grow old there."

After many months of patient anticipation, we heard that the patriarch had consented to show us the newly renovated manuscript library in person. Theophilos, sixty-five, was unanimously elected the 141st patriarch in 2005. His full title is His Most Godly Beatitude, the Patriarch of the Holy City of Jerusalem and all Palestine, Israel, Syria, Arabia, Beyond the Jordan River, Cana of Galilee, and Holy Zion. Born Ilias Giannopoulos in the Peloponnese in Greece, he studied theology at the University of Athens and completed a master's degree in Durham, England. In the 1990s, he served as a priest in Kafr Kanna (Cana) in Galilee, and then as Exarch of the Holy Sepulchre in Qatar.

Standing at a small desk in the center of the domed room with fitted windows that admitted soft light into the room (see plate 3), he gestured at the collections brought to the library for safekeeping, far from the hands of covetous manuscript hunters, 120 years ago by one of his predecessors, Nicodemus I (Greek Orthodox patriarch of Jerusalem, 1883–1890). On the far wall were seven hundred manuscripts in Syriac, Palestinian Aramaic, Greek, and Arabic brought from the desert monastery of Mar Saba. Before Nicodemus gathered them in Jerusalem, a number of manuscripts were stolen from the collection; today several can be found in the National Library of Russia and at the Walters Art Museum in Baltimore.

Theophilos swept his arm toward the right wall, whose heavy wooden bookcases contained the library of the former Georgian monastery of the Holy Cross, where Georgia's national poet Shota Rustaveli died in 1216. There were 161 manuscripts, written in Georgian between the eleventh and seventeenth centuries, including psalters, Gospels, lessons from Acts and Epistles, martyrologies, and collections of prayers called euchologies. Each bore the mark of the cross (Stavros). Some featured colophons that tell the stories of the pilgrims who carried them to Jerusalem. A treasured volume was a liturgical lectionary written in 1066 and presented to the Church of the Resurrection (the Holy Sepulchre) in Jerusalem by Anastasia, sister of one Nicholas Akimisdze. According to an outdated catalogue compiled in 1889 by Professor A. A. Tsagareli, some of the manuscripts are palimpsests with visible and much older texts underneath.[10] Theophilos had come under pressure to hand over these manuscripts into Georgian hands. In February 2012, Georgia's president announced that he would act to regain possession of the monastery of the Holy Cross in Jerusalem and revive Georgian culture there.

On the left wall stood a collection of 640 manuscripts that originated from the library of the Brotherhood of the Holy Sepulchre itself—each carrying the signature of Christ's tomb (Taphos)—and a smaller collection that used to be kept at the sacristy inside the Holy Sepulchre (called Anastasis). With the help of Archbishop Aristarchos, the patriarch had placed two remarkable manuscripts on the desk to show us. The first was a thirteenth-century manuscript of the book of Job in Greek Septuagint translation (Taphos 5), with 260 parchment folios and 117 exquisite illuminated miniatures (plate 11). The translation of Job into Greek, far from literal, is considered a poetic achievement. Orthodox worshippers in Jerusalem read from it throughout the Holy Week, seeing the suffering of Job as a prefiguration of the passion of Christ.

Many manuscripts of the book of Job were illustrated, but no single copy features more illustrations than the one that lay before us. The illuminations depict Job and his children, Christ and the Holy Spirit (but not God the Father), and Satan.[11] "God is present in his absence," Aristarchos remarked, "but the Devil is always there." The miniatures bore stylistic similarity to frescoes painted at the Church of Saint Euphemia in Constantinople in 1280. In the early eighteenth century, the volume was sent to Jerusalem from

Constantinople by Patriarch Dositheos II Notaras. He wrote at the back of the manuscript that he was sending it to Jerusalem, "away from the ignorant people." The Septuagint "is how we, pagans, were given the revelation," noted the learned archbishop with a twinkle in his eye. Another absence marks this manuscript: a missing folio with a miniature. Stolen by Porphyri Uspensky, it is now in the National Library of Russia.[12]

The second volume Theophilos had chosen for us was smaller but no less dazzling: a thirteenth-century psalter (Taphos 51). He opened the manuscript to folio 108, a full-page illumination depicting King David in prostration, repenting his sin before God (see plate 4). It used to be a requirement for Greek Orthodox novices to know Psalms by heart. Today it is rare. Both Patriarch Theophilos and Aristarchos admitted that their favorite psalm was number 50 (51), in which the Psalmist begs, "Have mercy upon me, O God, according to thy lovingkindness: according unto the multitude of thy tender mercies blot out my transgressions."

Thousands of property deeds, stored in a windowless room in the Patriarchate's archives, adjacent to the library, testify to the Greek Orthodox Patriarchate's power as the largest nongovernmental landowner in the city today. We were shown some of these treasures by Agamemnon Tselikas, the most eminent Greek paleographer in the world, honored with the Cross of the Holy Sepulchre for his work in the archives. "These archives hold the history of the Patriarchate," he explained, "which is the same as the history of the city itself." One contract for the purchase of property dates back to the twelfth century. Tselikas was the first to use infrared light to read palimpsests. He adapted the technology, he said, from its original application: the detection of uterine cancer.[13]

Two of the Greek Orthodox library's best-known manuscripts were palimpsests. The first was no longer in the library's possession. The sheepskin vellum of the Archimedes Palimpsest, a tenth-century manuscript containing a copy of writings of the ancient Greek mathematician Archimedes, was overwritten two hundred years later by a Greek liturgical text. It was brought from Mar Saba to the Patriarchate in Jerusalem in the nineteenth century and sold under mysterious circumstances to a French collector, Marie Louis Sirieix, in the 1920s. His daughter decided to sell it on consignment to Christie's New York in 1998. The Patriarchate

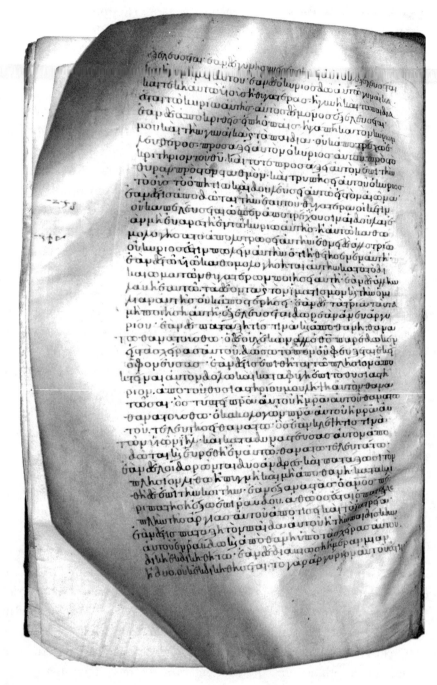

Palimpsest from a ninth-century manuscript of the Septuagint (the text underneath is fifth century), Greek Orthodox manuscript library (Taphos 2, fol. 56). (Photo by Frédéric Brenner, 2017; courtesy of the photographer / Howard Greenberg Gallery.)

ρίζαικη φόρμικ φόρμιφ ἀυτὴ ὥσπ ὁ γραμμω ὅταν
γραμμένη. λοιπὴ ὡς κτ τοῖς ὥ πραικῶ
μωπῶν
ἀιρηφ
ἡ τῶ ἀμὴ

ἐὰν δὲ μάχωνται δύο τινὲς ἀνδρες καὶ πατάξ... ωσι γυναῖκα ἐν γαστρὶ ἔχουσα
καὶ ἐξέλθη τὸ παιδίον αὐτῆς ... γραμμῖ ἐζημιωμοσλεε νόμω. ἐὰν ἢ γὴ ἐξέλθον ζημιωθήσε
ται. καθότι ἂν ... ἐπιβάλη ὁ ἀνὴρ τῆς γυναικός. καὶ δύσει μετὰ ἀξιώ
ματος. ἐὰν δὲ ... ἐξεικονισμένον ἢ, δύσει ψυχὴν ἀντὶ ψυχῆς. ὀφθαλ
μὸν ἀντ ὀφθαλμοῦ. ὀδόντα ἀντὶ ὀδόντος. χεῖρα ἀντὶ χειρός. πόδα
ἀντὶ ποδὸς. κατάκαυμα ἀντὶ κατακαύματος. τραῦμα ἀντὶ τραύματος
μώλωπα ἀντὶ μώλωπος. ἐὰν δέ τις πατάξῃ τὸν ὀφθαλ
μὸν τοῦ οἰκέτου αὐτοῦ ἢ τὸν ὀφθαλμὸν τῆς θεραπαίνης καὶ ἀπ...
καὶ ἐκτυφλώσῃ. ἐλευθέρους ἐξαποστελεῖ αὐτοὺς ἀντὶ τοῦ ὀφθαλ
μοῦ αὐτῶν. ἐὰν δὲ τὸν ὀδόντα τοῦ οἰκέτου ἢ τὸν ὀδόντα τῆς θε
ραπαίνης αὐτοῦ ἐκκόψῃ. ἐλευθέρους ἐξαποστελεῖ αὐτοὺς ἀντὶ τοῦ
ὀδόντος αὐτῶν. ἐὰν δὲ κερατίσῃ ταῦρος ἄνδρα ἢ γυναῖκα καὶ ἀπο
θάνῃ. λίθοις λιθοβοληθήσεται ὁ ταῦρος. καὶ οὐ βρωθήσεται τὰ κρέα
αὐτοῦ. ὁ δὲ κύριος τοῦ ταύρου ἀθῶος ἔσται. ἐὰν δὲ ὁ ταῦ
ρος κερατιστὴς ἦν πρὸ τῆς χθὲς, καὶ πρὸ τῆς τρίτης. καὶ διαμαρτύ
ρωνται τῷ κυρίῳ αὐτοῦ καὶ μὴ ἀφανίσῃ αὐτὸν. ἀνέλῃ δὲ ἄνδρα ἢ
γυναῖκα. ὁ ταῦρος λιθοβοληθήσεται. καὶ ὁ κύριος αὐτοῦ προσαποθα
νεῖται. ἐὰν δὲ λύτρα ἐπιβληθῇ αὐτῷ. δώσει λύτρα τῆς ψυχῆς αὐτοῦ ὅσ
ἐὰν ἐπιβάλωσιν αὐτῷ κράτι... ἐὰν δὲ ὑιὸν ἢ θυγατέρα κερατίσῃ. κ...
τὸ δικαίωμα τοῦτο ποιήσωσιν αὐτῷ. ἐὰν δὲ παῖδα κεράσῃ ὁ ταῦρος ...
ἢ παιδίσκην. ἀργυρίου τριάκοντα δίδραχμα δώσει τῷ κυρίῳ αὐτῶν.
ὁ δὲ ταῦρος λιθοβοληθήσεται. ἐὰν δέ τις ἀνοίξῃ λάκκον ἢ λατομῇ λ...
λάκκον καὶ μὴ καλύψῃ αὐτὸν. καὶ ἐμπέσῃ ἐκεῖ μόσχος ἢ ὄνος. ὁ κύρι
τοῦ λάκκου ἀποτίσει. ἀργύριον δώσει τῷ κυρίῳ αὐτῶν. τὸ δὲ τετελευτη
αὐτῷ ἔσται. ἐὰν δὲ κερατίσῃ τις ταῦρος τὸν ταῦρον τοῦ πλησίον καὶ τε
λευτήσῃ. ἀποδώσονται τὸν ταῦρον τὸν ζῶντα. καὶ διελοῦνται τὸ ἀργύρι
αὐτοῦ. ὁ δὲ ταῦρος τὸν τεθνηκότα διελοῦνται. ἐὰν δὲ γνωρίζηται
ὁ ταῦρος ὅτι κερατιστής ἐστι πρὸ τῆς χθὲς. καὶ πρὸ τῆς τρίτης ἡμέρας. καὶ δια
μεμαρτυρημένοι ὦσι τῷ κυρίῳ αὐτοῦ. καὶ μὴ ἀφανίσῃ αὐτὸν. ἀποτίσῃ
ταῦρον ἀντὶ ταύρου. τὸ δὲ τετελευτηκὸς αὐτῷ ἔσται. ἐὰν δέ τις
κλέψῃ μόσχον ἢ πρόβατον. καὶ σφάξῃ αὐτὸ ἢ ἀποδῶται. πέντε μόσχους
ἀποτίσει ἀντὶ τοῦ μόσχου. καὶ τέσσαρα πρόβατα ἀντὶ τοῦ προβάτου.

γράφεται ἄλλα τοσὸ

in Jerusalem had not announced it had gone missing until it went up for auction. Claiming to be the rightful owner, a day before the auction the Patriarchate sought a temporary restraining order. A New York court denied the request, and the palimpsest was sold at auction for two million dollars. The Patriarchate then filed suit in the Southern District of New York, seeking the return of the palimpsest. The Sirieix family could produce no receipt, contract, or bill of sale. Christie's asked for a motion of summary judgment, which the court granted and ruled that the sale was valid. The anonymous purchaser lent the palimpsest to the Walters Art Museum, in Baltimore, and there it remains, still exiled from Jerusalem.

The library of the Greek Orthodox Patriarchate guards another famous palimpsest: the so-called Jerusalem Palimpsest of Euripides (Cod. Hierosolymitanus Sancti Sepulcri 36). The top layer is a 556-page (278-sheet) text of the sixteen prophets in the Septuagint version from about 1300. Beneath are 68 pages of a lost play by the Greek tragedian

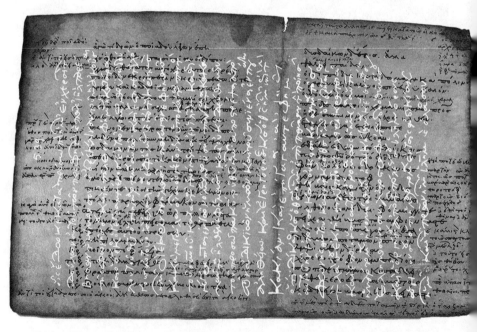

Codex Hierosolymitanus Sancti Sepulcri 36, p. 539. (Reproduced with gratis permission of the Greek Orthodox Patriarchate of Jerusalem and PALAMEDES © PALAMEDES 2018 www.palamedes.online.)

Euripides from almost four centuries earlier, and Cyril of Alexandria's Commentary on Luke, probably from the eighth century.[14]

Palimpsests like this one do not eradicate memory so much as they appropriate and recycle earlier memories. We have attempted to read Jerusalem as a kind of conversation among languages, a palimpsest in which writers reached for one other across the centuries. Much as the three Abrahamic faiths inscribed themselves on earlier faiths, erasing some features and embellishing others, so too can Jerusalem be seen as layer upon layer of its words, a physical record of longings for a redemptive future and mourning for destructions past.

As suggested in the Prologue, to experience Jerusalem like a Jerusalemite is not at all the same as approaching it through a prescribed chronological scheme. That experience involves discovering the ways that overlapping layers of memory, joined and jumbled with imagination, no sooner formed than dissolved, often overwhelm the present. T. E. Lawrence, who as a young major witnessed the British capture of Jerusalem in 1917, wrote, "These united forces of the past and the future were so strong that the city almost failed to have a present."[15] Jerusalem is as text-obsessed as any city ever has been, and if nothing else those who live here have its texts in common. But each of its libraries, taken alone, is necessarily incomplete.

In Jerusalem's characteristic tensions between secrecy and sharing, the former does not always prevail. Our forays into the city's libraries offered us models not only of exclusion, secrecy, and possessiveness, but also of their opposites: translation, dialogue, and the commingling of cultures and languages. If we read Jerusalem as a polyglot palimpsest, perhaps we could understand the many languages in which it expresses itself as what Walter Benjamin calls "fragments of a greater language, just as fragments are part of a vessel."[16]

The sin of the Tower of Babel culminates in collective punishment, the fragmentation of a single language into a cacophony of languages that are all but unintelligible to one another. Its impact still defines the city and its estrangements. For all of Jerusalem's dragomans and custodians of literary heritage—and their noble attempts at translation and cross-cultural confluence—those vessels remain broken.

NOTES

Unless otherwise indicated, translations are our own. Quotations from the Bible are taken from the New King James Version.

Introduction. The Hidden

1. Candida Höfer, with an essay by Umberto Eco, *Libraries* (London: Thames and Hudson, 2005), 9.

2. Diane Asséo Griliches, *Library: The Drama Within* (Albuquerque: University of New Mexico Press, 1996), vii.

3. Andrew Palmer, "The History of the Syrian Orthodox in Jerusalem," *Oriens Christianus* 75 (1991): 16–43.

4. Palmer, "History of the Syrian Orthodox in Jerusalem," 17.

5. Jorge Luis Borges, *The Book of Sand,* trans. Andrew Hurley (London: Penguin Classics, 1989), 93.

6. The manuscript is catalogued as number 1 at Saint Mark Monastery, Jerusalem (SMMJ 001). William Henry Paine Hatch, granted access to the Syriac collection in the 1940s, made facsimile reproductions of some of its illuminated manuscripts. See William Henry Paine Hatch, *An Album of Dated Syriac Manuscripts* (Boston: American Academy of Arts and Sciences, 1946), 127; Hatch, *Greek and Syrian Miniatures in Jerusalem* (Cambridge, Mass.: Medieval Academy of America, 1931).

7. SMMJ 235, fol. 491v. See John W. Watt, "The Recovery of an Old Text: Scribes, Scholars, Collectors and the Rhetoric of Antony of Tagrit," *Harp* 16 (2003): 285–95.

8. SMMJ 162, fol. 181r. See the posting by Adam C. Collum, "A Self-Deprecating Scribe, One Among Many," September 24, 2013, at https://hmmlorientalia.wordpress.com/category/jacob-of-sarug/ (accessed September 19, 2018).

Chapter One. Creating a Canon

Epigraph: Siken borrowed this line from Carl Gustav Jung's opening of *The Seven Sermons to the Dead—Septem Sermones ad Mortuos* (1916).

1. See Lauren A. S. Monroe, *Josiah's Reform and the Dynamics of Defilement: Israelite Rites of Violence and the Making of a Biblical Text* (Oxford: Oxford University Press, 2011).

2. Hans H. Wellisch, "Ebla: The World's Oldest Library," *Journal of Library History* 16 (1981): 488.

3. We thank Professor Nathan Wasserman for this translation. See also Jeanette C. Fincke, "The Babylonian Text of Nineveh: Report on the British Museum's Ashurbanipal Library Project," *Archiv für Orientforschung* 50 (2003–2004): 122. According to some Persian and Armenian traditions, the library of Nineveh inspired Alexander the Great to found his own library. His successor in Egypt, Ptolemy I, oversaw the founding of Alexander's library—the renowned Library of Alexandria. The third-century BCE astronomer and geographer Ptolemy II vastly expanded its collections, aiming at nothing short of gathering together "all the books in the world." (One of these volumes was the Septuagint.) In expanding from political and commercial records to poetic and cultic texts, the Alexandria collection marks the threshold that divides archive from library. Alexandria's library was not just comprehensive; it was public, the first step in the evolution of what we now call open access. The Roman historian Livy (who died in 17 CE) called the Alexandria library "the most distinguished achievement of the good taste and solicitude of kings."

In the first century CE, the Stoic philosopher and Roman statesman Seneca the Younger regarded the library as an extravagance. Citing Livy's praise, he went on, "There was no 'good taste' or 'solicitude' about it, but only learned luxury [*studiosa luxuria*]—no, not even learned, since they had collected the books not for the sake of learning but to make a show, just as many who lack even a child's knowledge of letters use books, not as the tools of learning, but as decorations for the dining room." Indeed the very idea of a library was wrongheaded in his view: "What is the use of having countless books and libraries, whose titles their owners can scarcely read through in a whole lifetime? The learner is not instructed, but burdened by the mass of them, and it is much better to surrender yourself to a few authors than to wander through many." Remarking on the great fire that consumed the library, Seneca writes: "Forty thousand books were burned at Alexandria; let someone else praise this library as the most noble monument to the wealth of kings" (Seneca, *Moral Essays*, vol. 2: *De tranquillitate animi*, 9, 4, trans. John W. Basore [Cambridge: Harvard University Press, 1932]).

The thirteenth-century Egyptian writer Ibn al-Qifti, among others, reported that the destruction of the Library of Alexandria resulted not from Julius Caesar's conquest, nor from a decree of the Coptic pope Theophilus of Alexandria, as others had suggested, but from a direct order of Caliph 'Umar Ibn al-Khaṭṭāb after the Muslim conquest of Egypt in the seventh century. (Qifti lived for many years in Saladin's Jerusalem, where he must have heard many stories about Caliph 'Umar as he gathered material for his book *Ta'rikh al-hukama,* "The History of Learned Men.") In the caliph's judgment, the divine Qur'an rendered other books superfluous. "If there is in it what complies with the Book of God," he said, "then it is already there and is not needed, and if what is in these books contradict the Book of God there is no need for it. And you can then proceed in destroying them" (*Ta'rikh al-hukama,* ed. and trans. August Müller and Julius Lippert [Leipzig: Dieterich, 1903]). The library's scrolls fed the furnaces of Alexandria's bathhouses for many months.

4. See Lionel Casson, *Libraries in the Ancient World* (New Haven: Yale University Press, 2001); Ernst Posner, *Archives in the Ancient World* (Cambridge: Harvard University Press, 1972).

5. Ephraim Isaac, "Shelf List of Ethiopian Manuscripts in the Monasteries of the Ethiopian Patriarchate of Jerusalem," *Rassegna di Studi Etiopici* 30 (1984): 53–80.

6. The first book of Maccabees was probably written in Hebrew. Jerome used it in his Latin translation. Although it survives in Greek translation, the original has been lost.

7. James Wood, "Desert Storm," *New Yorker,* October 1, 2007.

8. Stella Panayotova, "The Illustrated Psalter: Luxury and Practical Use," in *The Practice of the Bible in the Middle Ages: Production, Reception, and Performance in Western Christianity,* ed. Susan Boynton and Diane J. Reilly (New York: Columbia University Press, 2011), 247.

9. Martin Luther, *An Open Letter on Translating,* trans. Howard Jones (Oxford: Taylor Institution Library, 2017).

10. *Saint Augustine: Select Letters,* trans. J. H. Baxter (Cambridge: Harvard University Press, 1930), Epistle 108. See also Ora Limor, "Reading Sacred Space: Egeria, Paula, and the Christian Holy Land," in *De Sion Exibit Lex et Verbum Domini de Hierusalem,* ed. Yitzhak Hen (Turnhout: Brepols, 2001), 1–15.

11. Saint Possidius, *The Life of Saint Augustine* (Merchantville, N.J.: Arx, 2008), 57; Clare Costley King'oo, *Miserere Mei: The Penitential Psalms in Late Medieval and Early Modern England* (Notre Dame, Ind.: University of Notre Dame Press, 2012), 4.

12. Patriarch Timothy I, Letter 47, in Sebastian P. Brock, "A Brief Outline of Syriac Literature," *Moran Etho* 9 (Kottayam: SEERI, 1997), 248. See also Floyd V. Filson, "Some Recent Studies of the Dead Sea Scrolls," *Biblical Archaeologist* 13, no. 4 (December 1950): 96.

13. Saint Jerome, "Ad Cyprianum," Epistle 140, 4, in Walter Drum, "Psalms," in *The Catholic Encyclopedia,* vol. 12 (New York: Appleton, 1911). Only 73 psalms of the 150 name David as their author. The psalms of Asaph, for example, are commonly thought to be dated nearly three centuries after David, the time of the Assyrian invasion (737 BCE). Psalm 74 (73), a plea of relief, was probably composed even later, during the Babylonian Exile (i.e., sometime after 586 BCE).

14. Quoted in *Eusebius, Bishop of Caesarea: "The Ecclesiastical History" and "The Martyrs of Palestine,"* 2 vols., ed. and trans. Hugh J. Lawlor and John E. L. Oulton (London: Society for Promoting Christian Knowledge; New York: Macmillan, 1927), 1:190; Patriarch Timothy I, Letter 47, in Brock, "A Brief Outline of Syriac Literature."

15. See Rachel Elior, *Memory and Oblivion: The Mystery of the Dead Sea Scrolls* (Berlin: De Gruyter, forthcoming in 2019); Norman Golb, *Who Wrote the Dead Sea Scrolls? The Search for the Secret of Qumran* (New York: Touchstone, 1996).

16. Sidnie White Crawford, "The Qumran Collection as a Scribal Library," in *The Dead Sea Scrolls at Qumran and the Concept of a Library,* ed. Cecilia Wassen and Sidnie White Crawford (Leiden: Brill, 2015), 109–31; *Flavius Josephus: Translation and Commentary 10, Against Apion,* ed. Steve Mason, trans. John M. G. Barclay (Leiden: Brill, 2007), 1.29. The eyewitness chronicles of Josephus became the greatest source of knowledge of Jerusalem "between the Testaments." His *Antiquities of the Jews* circulated throughout the Christian world in the Middle Ages, first in Greek then in Latin, and later in numerous colloquial translations. Its images of Jerusalem, especially in the scenes of destruction, inspired an abundance of illustrated manuscripts and guidebooks. In many a Victorian home and American Sunday School library, a copy of William Whiston's translation of Josephus's works, first published in 1737 and reprinted more than two hundred times since, held pride of place next to the Scriptures.

17. *Flavius Josephus: Translation and Commentary 9, Life of Josephus,* ed. and trans. Steve Mason (Leiden: Brill, 2001), 17.

18. Ibid., 416.

19. Ibid., 165–66, 418.

20. The Qumran discoveries included one manuscript of Genesis, two of Leviticus, one of Deuteronomy, two of Psalms, and one of Ezekiel, as well as one apocryphal Genesis work, a copy of Ben Sira, a Joshua Apocryphon, and a copy of Songs of the Sabbath Sacrifice. See Crawford, "The Qumran Collection as a Scribal Library," 119.

21. Athanasius Yeshue Samuel, *Treasure of Qumran: My Story of the Dead Sea Scrolls* (Philadelphia: Westminster, 1966), 25.

22. Edmund Wilson, *The Scrolls from the Dead Sea* (Oxford: Oxford University Press, 1955), 7; Samuel, *Treasure of Qumran,* 51.

23. Samuel, *Treasure of Qumran,* 55–56.

24. Ibid., 149.

25. Edmund Wilson, *Israel and the Dead Sea Scrolls* (London: Routledge, 2017), 118.

26. Yigael Yadin, *The Message of the Scrolls* (New York: Simon and Schuster, 1957), 14.

27. John C. Trever, "The Discovery of the Scrolls," *Biblical Archaeologist* 11, no. 3 (1948): 55.

28. Classified advertisement, *Wall Street Journal,* June 1, 1954.

29. Hershel Shanks, "The Dead Sea Scroll Monopoly," *Washington Post,* October 8, 1991.

30. Hershel Shanks, *Understanding the Dead Sea Scrolls: A Reader from the Biblical Archaeology Review* (New York: Vintage, 1993), 120–21; Yigael Yadin, *The Temple Scroll: The Hidden Law of the Dead Sea Sect* (New York: Random House, 1985).

31. Martin Schøyen, "Acquisition and Ownership History: A Personal Reflection," in *Gleanings from the Caves: Dead Sea Scrolls and Artefacts from the Schøyen Collection,* ed. Torleif Elgvin, Michael Langlois, and Kipp Davis (London: Bloomsbury, 2016), 27.

32. Robert Deutsch, Shlomo Moussaieff, and André Lemaire, *Biblical Period Personal Seals in the Shlomo Moussaieff Collection* (Tel Aviv: Archaeological Center Publications, 2000), 3; Mark Prigg, "Dead Sea Scrolls Go Up for Sale as Family Sells Off Fragments It Secretly Stashed in a Swiss Safety Deposit Box," *Daily Mail,* May 27, 2013.

33. Jonathan Lis, "Archaeologist Held for Allegedly Purchasing Stolen Ancient Scroll," *Haaretz,* November 2, 2005.

34. Daniel Estrin, "Dead Sea Scroll Fragments to Hit the Auction Block," Associated Press, May 25, 2013.

35. Arieh O'Sullivan, "Palestinians Claim Dead Sea Scrolls," *Jerusalem Post,* January 3, 2010; ToI Staff, "Israel Says Palestinians May Try to Claim Dead Sea Scrolls," *Times of Israel,* November 6, 2016.

36. Amos Elon, "Politics and Archaeology," in *The Archaeology of Israel: Constructing the Past, Interpreting the Present,* ed. Neil Asher Silberman and David B. Small (Sheffield: Sheffield Academic Press, 1997), 43.

37. See also Midrash Tadsha (Baraita Phinehas ben Jair) 10; Midrash Zuta, Song of Songs 3:1; Midrash ha-Gadol, Genesis 46:8.

38. L. W. Hurtado, "The Origin of the Nomina Sacra: A Proposal," *Journal of Biblical Literature* 117 (1998): 657; Bruce M. Metzger, *Manuscripts of the Greek Bible: An Introduction to Palaeography* (New York: Oxford University Press, 1981), 36–37.

39. "Quid ergo Athenis et Hierosolymis?" Tertullian, *De praescriptione haereticorum* (On the Prescriptions Against Heretics), 7:9.

40. Flavius Josephus, *Judean Antiquities* 12:2, in *Judean Antiquities 12–13,* ed. and trans. Ralph Marcus (Cambridge: Harvard University Press, 1943); Philo, *On the Life of Moses* 2:7, in *On the Life of Moses,* trans. F. H. Colson (Cambridge: Harvard University Press, 1960). The Jewish sources include the Talmud (Tractate Megillah 9) and the apocryphal Tractate Sofrim (Tractate of the Scribes) 1:8–9. The story is also discussed in the "Letter of Aristeas": *Aristeas to Philocrates (Letter of Aristeas),* ed. and trans. Moses Hadas (Eugene, Ore.: Wipf and Stock, 2007). For a modern approach to comparing the Hebrew and Greek texts of the Bible, see the Jerusalem-based CATSS (Computer Assisted Tools for Septuagint Studies) project, launched by Professor Emanuel Tov of the Hebrew University and Professor R. A. Kraft of the University of Pennsylvania. See also Tov's *The Text-Critical Use of the Septuagint in Biblical Research* (Winona Lake, Ind.: Eisenbrauns, 2015).

41. Walter Benjamin, "The Task of the Translator," in *Walter Benjamin: Selected Writings,* vol. 1: *1913–1926,* ed. Marcus Bullock and Michael W. Jennings (Cambridge, Mass: Belknap, 1996), 254. Israel's National Library has a parchment-bound notebook, sewn with red thread, that Benjamin filled with his compact scrawled drafts and journal entries.

42. Azariah de' Rossi, *Imre Binah* 1:6, in *Me'or 'Eynayim,* vol. 1, ed. David Cassel (Vilnius: Rozenkrantz, 1863), 103. Philo referred to Jerusalem as Hierapolis, Greek for "holy city."

43. Anthony Grafton and Megan Hale Williams, *Christianity and the Transformation of the Book* (Cambridge: Harvard University Press, 2008), 20. Julius Africanus, *Kestoi* 5.1.50–54, in Sextus Julius Africanus, *Les Cestes*, ed. R. Vieillefond (Florence: Sansoni; Paris: Didier, 1971).

44. *Eusebius, Bishop of Caesarea: "The Ecclesiastical History" and "The Martyrs of Palestine,"* 1:329.

45. Ibid., 1:194.

46. Ibid., 1:190–94. See also Grafton and Williams, *Christianity and the Transformation of the Book*, 56–62. A collection of previously unknown homilies of Origen on David's Psalms was discovered in 2012 in the Bayerische Staatsbibliothek in Munich and published by Lorenzo Perrone, professor of early Christian literature at the University of Bologna. In one of them, Origen remarks, "We know very well that Jerusalem has no river, since we are near to it" (Hom. 77 Ps VII). Although this sermon was not given in Jerusalem, Origen and his audience clearly knew the city. We are grateful to Lorenzo Perrone for his guidance. See *Origenes: Werke: Die neuen Psalmenhomilien: Eine kritische Edition des Codex Monacensis Graecus 314,* ed. Lorenzo Perrone (Berlin: De Gruyter, 2015).

47. Grafton and Williams, *Christianity and the Transformation of the Book,* 131, 69. Eusebius (260/265–339/340) wrote: "There is no better way than to hear the epistles themselves which we have taken from the archives and have literally translated from the Syriac language" (*Ecclesiastical History* 1:13, 5). His documents included an exchange of letters in Syriac between Jesus and King Abgar of Edessa, the importance of which compelled him to translate them for his readers into Greek. To reach a Christian audience in Europe, Byzantium, and Hellenized Egypt, Eusebius wrote all his books in Greek.

48. Grafton and Williams, *Christianity and the Transformation of the Book,* 91. A Syriac copy of the Hexapla was made at the court of the patriarch in the Church of the East (Nestorians) in Baghdad in the ninth century. Patriarch Timothy I describes it in a letter to the metropolitan of Elam (the pre-Iranian civilization centered in the far west of present-day Iran): "On the subject of the book of the Hexapla about which your reverence wrote, we have already written and informed you last year that a copy of the Hexapla, written on sheets using the Nisibene format, was sent to us through the diligence of our brother Gabriel, synkellos of the resplendent caliph [lit., "king"]. We hired six scribes and two people to dictate, who dictated to the scribes from the text of the exemplar. We wrote out the entire Old Testament, with Chronicles, Ezra, Susanna, Esther and Judith, producing three manuscripts, one for us and two for the resplendent Gabriel; of those two, one was for Gabriel himself, and the other for Beth Lapat, for this is what Gabriel had instructed in writing. The manuscripts have now been written out with much diligence and care, at the expense of great trouble and much labor, over six months more or less; for no text is so difficult to copy out or to read as this, seeing that there are so many things in the margin, I mean readings of Aquila, Theodotion, Symmachus and others, taking up almost as much space as the text of the Septuagint in the body of the manuscript. There are also a large number of different signs above them—how many, it is not possible for anyone to say. But we had bad and greedy scribes, eight men for just under six months. The copying was

done as far as possible using correction, seeing that it had been made from dictation; the copies were gone over a second time and read out. As a result of the excessive labour and work of correction my eyes were harmed and I nearly lost my sight—you can get an idea of the weakness of our vision from these shapeless letters that we are writing now. . . . At the end of every biblical book the following was written: 'This was written, collated and compared with the exemplar of Eusebius, Pamphilus, and Origen.'" Patriarch Timothy I, Letter 47, in Brock, "A Brief Outline of Syriac Literature," 245–47.

49. Saint Jerome, "Letter 45 to Arsella," in *The Letters of Saint Jerome*, trans. W. H. Fremantle, G. Lewis, and W. G. Martley (London: Aeterna Press, 2016).

50. In preparing his Latin translation, Jerome also consulted a copy of the third-century Hexapla of Origen. This polyglot version of the Hebrew Bible aimed to correct the Septuagint and bring it into literal agreement with the Hebrew source.

51. *Letters of Augustine*, nos. 28, 71, 82, and *Letters of Jerome*, no. 112 in *A Select Library of Nicene and Post-Nicene Fathers of the Christian Church, Translated into English with Prolegomena and Explanatory Notes under the Editorial Supervision of Henry Wace and Philip Schaff* (Oxford: Christian Literature Company, 1890–1900).

52. John Wilkinson, *Egeria's Travels* (London: Society for the Promotion of Christian Knowledge, 1971), 13:1, 17:1; Limor, "Reading Sacred Space: Egeria, Paula, and the Christian Holy Land," 8.

53. Francis X. Murphy, "Melania the Elder: A Biographical Note," *Traditio* 5 (1947): 71.

54. Saint Jerome, Letter 133 to Ctesiphon, *Saint Jerome Collection* (New York: Aeterna, 2016), 774. When Origen died he was a celebrated figure in the church. But in the fifth ecumenical council in 553 CE, Origen's teaching was condemned, his writings destroyed, and his name added to the list of heretics. See Daniel Hombergen, "Barsanuphius and John of Gaza and the Origenist Controversy," in *Christian Gaza in Late Antiquity*, ed. Brouria Bitton Ashkelony and Arieh Kofsky (Leiden: Brill, 2004), 174.

55. Consider the apocryphal texts expelled from the rabbinic canon but preserved and adopted by Christians. In his introduction to the book of Judith, Jerome notes that since he was unable to find the Hebrew original he relied on an old Aramaic translation that one of his Jewish colleagues translated for him into Hebrew. See Avraham Kahana, *Hasfarim Hachitsoniim* (The Apocryphal Books) (Jerusalem: Makor, 1969), 1:9.

56. Another book intended for the elect, *The Vision of Ezra* (or *Esdras*), was written in Hebrew by a Jerusalemite, an eyewitness to the destruction of the Temple in 70 CE. Though the Hebrew original was lost, the text survived in Latin as an appendix to the Vulgate (and in later translations into Ge'ez, Arabic, and Syriac). Like many other Jerusalem texts, the book survived thanks to its translation into another language and adoption by another faith. *Esdras* was translated back into Hebrew only in 1956. Kahana, *Hasfarim Hachitsoniim*, 2:709.

57. The Saint James liturgy, named after Jerusalem's first bishop, is still in use by some of the oriental churches in Jerusalem. See Derek Krueger, *Liturgical Subjects: Christian Ritual,*

Biblical Narrative, and the Formation of the Self in Byzantium (Philadelphia: University of Pennsylvania Press, 2014), 25.

58. Some believe the room was originally a funerary chapel, others that it was part of a monastery. See F. J. Bliss, *Excavations in Jerusalem, 1894–1897* (London: Palestine Exploration Fund, 1898), 253–59. Kevork (George) Hintlian writes: "This is the funerary chapel of St. Polyeucte, an officer of the twelfth legion, a soldier martyr of the third century, who along with many of his soldiers lies buried under the cave-tomb below the mosaic floor": Kevork (George) Hintlian, *History of the Armenians in the Holy Land* (Jerusalem: St. James Press, 1976), 15. An Armenian mosaic inscription in Saint John's Chapel inside the Russian Convent of the Ascension at the Mount of Olives may be even older. Its inscription reads: "This is the tomb of the blessed Susanna, Mother of Atravan."

59. M. Tarchnisvili, "Le iscrizioni musive del monastero di Bir el-Qutt," in *Gli scavi di Khirbet Siyar el-Ghanam (Campo dei Pastori) e i monasteri dei dintorni*, ed. Virgilio Corbo (Jerusalem: SBF, 1955), 135–39.

Chapter Two. The Arabic Era

1. Stephen J. Shoemaker, *The Death of a Prophet: The End of Muhammad's Life and the Beginnings of Islam* (Philadelphia: University of Pennsylvania Press, 2012). In the Hebrew Bible, Gabriel is the archangel who announces to the prophet Daniel the time of the end and the destruction of Jerusalem, whereupon Daniel breaks into a song of atonement. As reward for Daniel's contrition, Gabriel appears to him again and proclaims the tidings of the future reconstruction of Jerusalem (Daniel 8–9).

2. Mark Sheridan, "'The Desert was Made a City': The Role of the Desert in Early Egyptian Monasticism and Christian Hagiography," unpublished paper, available at Academia.edu, http://www.academia.edu/19952744/_The_Desert_was_made_a_city._The_Role_of_the_Desert_in_early_Egyptian_Monasticism_and_Christian_Hagiography (accessed September 24, 2018).

3. For example, Bibliothèque Nationale et Universitaire de Strasbourg MS 4226, and Biblioteca Apostolica Vaticana MS Ar. 71.

4. One of the earliest fragments discovered is a ninth-century trilingual Psalter (Greek-Syriac-Arabic). Originally kept in Mar Saba, it is now in Saint Petersburg. One of the latest, also in Saint Petersburg, is a seventeenth-century psalter with 33 miniatures (MS Arabic 187). See Ioana Feodorov, "The Arabic Psalter, Facsimile Edition of Manuscript A 187, the Petersburg Arabic Illuminated Psalter from the Collections of the Institute of Oriental Studies of the Russian Academy of Sciences," *Revue des études sud-est européennes* 46 (2008): 481–84.

5. Seven Targums, or Aramaic translations of the Torah, are extant from the fourth and fifth centuries. These were based on earlier Targums, from before 200 CE. Saint Mark's monastery in Jerusalem holds early copies of the Peshitta, the second-century Syriac Bible, probably directly translated from the Hebrew in Edessa. See M. P. Weitzman, *The Syriac Version of the Old Testament* (Cambridge: Cambridge University Press,

2005), 1. The National Library of Israel holds one of the oldest extant copies of the Peshitta, written in the ninth century and donated by the Vienna-born philanthropist and Judaica collector Erica Jesselson in 1995 (MS Or. 63). Much like Jerome's Vulgate, the Peshitta was designed to make the Bible accessible to readers in their own vernacular. Its name derives from the word "simple" or "made straight." One Syriac tradition ascribes the translation of the Peshitta to King Solomon, who composed it for King Hiram of Tyre.

6. Daniel J. Sahas, *John of Damascus on Islam: The "Heresy of the Ishmaelites"* (Leiden: Brill, 1972), 39–40. See also Sidney H. Griffith, "Anthony David of Baghdad, Scribe and Monk of Mar Sabas: Arabic in the Monasteries of Palestine," *Church History* 58, no. 1 (1989): 7–19.

7. C. Mango, "Greek Culture in Palestine after the Arab Conquest," in *Scritture, libri e testi nelle aree provinciali di Bisanzio,* ed. G. Cavallo et al. (Spoleto: Fondazione CISAM, 1991), 1:149–50; Sidney H. Griffith, "From Aramaic to Arabic: The Languages of the Monasteries of Palestine in the Byzantine and Early Islamic Periods," *Dumbarton Oaks Papers* 51 (1997): 11.

8. Translation available at Greek Orthodox Archdiocese of America website, "Liturgical Texts of the Orthodox Church: Funeral Service," https://www.goarch.org/-/funeral-service. These works of John of Damascus in the Greek Orthodox library in Jerusalem include Taphos manuscripts 15 (eleventh century), 151 (sixteenth century), 175 (sixteenth century), 240 (eighteenth century), 266 (eighteenth century), 350 (eighteenth century), 412 (eighteenth century), 591 (eighteenth century), 614 (fifteenth century), and 672 (sixteenth century), and Stavros manuscripts 61 (seventeenth century) and 87 (sixteenth century).

9. S. H. Griffith, "Stephen of Ramlah and the Christian Kerygma in Arabic in Ninth-Century Palestine," *Journal of Ecclesiastical History* 36, no. 1 (1985): 41. See also Sidney H. Griffith, *The Church in the Shadow of the Mosque: Christians and Muslims in the World of Islam* (Princeton: Princeton University Press, 2012), 52–53. Stephen of Ramlah completed the manuscript at the monastery of Mar Chariton in 897.

10. The first, now in the Vatican (Arabic MS 171), includes a life of Epiphanius of Salamis by John of Constantinople, lives of Saint Euthymius and Saint Sabbas by Cyril of Schythopolis, a homily on psalm 6 by Anastasius of Sinai, and a life of Saint Xenophon. The other manuscript, now in Strasbourg (Oriental MS 4226), includes a homily on Jesus's victory over death and the devil, a homily against laughing (both attributed to Saint Ephraem), an account of the miracles of Saint Nicholas, excerpts from Gregory of Nyssa's history of Gregory the Wonder Worker, questions and answers attributed to Saint Athanasius, and a homily in praise of the Virgin Mary by John of Damascus.

11. Sidney H. Griffith, "Anthony David of Baghdad, Scribe and Monk of Mar Sabas: Arabic in the Monasteries of Palestine," *Church History* 58, no. 1 (1989): 9. Reprinted with permission of Cambridge University Press.

12. Robert Curzon, *Visits to Monasteries in the Levant* (New York: Cosimo Classics, 2007), 225.

13. The colophon of this lectionary, Add MS 39604, can be viewed at the British Library website: http://www.bl.uk/manuscripts/Viewer.aspx?order=b&ref=add_ms_39604.

14. Oleg Grabar, *The Shape of the Holy: Early Islamic Jerusalem* (Princeton: Princeton University Press, 1996), 62–63.

15. Oleg Grabar, "Space and Holiness in Medieval Jerusalem," *Islamic Studies* 40, no. 3 (2001): 681.

16. Griffith, *The Church in the Shadow of the Mosque*, 33. The building's polemics included the erasure of earlier texts. Two twelfth-century pilgrims to Jerusalem, John of Würzburg (ca. 1165) and Theodoric (1172), mentioned Latin inscriptions both inside and outside the dome, texts which have since been erased or overwritten. See Denys Pringle, *The Churches of the Crusader Kingdom of Jerusalem: A Corpus*, 3 vols. (Cambridge: Cambridge University Press, 1993–2007), 3:414.

17. The Persian traveler Nasir-i Khusraw described it in 1047 as the chain which "David—peace be upon him!—hung up, and it was so that none who spoke not the truth could grasp it, the unjust and the wicked man could not lay hand on it." Cited in *Collected Works of Guy Le Strange: The Medieval Islamic World*, ed. Hugh Kennedy (London: I. B. Tauris, 2014), 152.

18. Nabil Matar, "The Cradle of Jesus and the Oratory of Mary on Jerusalem's Haram al-Sharif," in *Jerusalem, 1000–1400: Every People Under Heaven*, ed. Barbara Drake Boehm and Melanie Holcomb (New York and New Haven: Metropolitan Museum of Art and Yale University Press, 2016), 138–40.

19. Quoted in Oleg Grabar, *The Formation of Islamic Art* (New Haven: Yale University Press, 1987), 64–65.

20. 'Abd al-Raḥman Ibn Khaldūn, *Tārikh Ibn Khaldūn*, part 7 (Beirut: Mu'assassat Jamāl, 1979). See Khader Salameh, *The Qur'an Manuscripts in the al-Haram al-Sharif Islamic Museum, Jerusalem* (Reading: Ithaca Press, 2001), 67.

21. Al-Hasan al-Basri, quoted in Thomas H. Weir and Aaron Zysow, eds., *Encyclopaedia of Islam* (Leiden: Brill, 1999), s.v. "Sadaka."

22. A copy dated 1233–34 is now kept at the Museum of Islamic Art in Doha (MS 788-03). The epigraph to this section is from Nizar Qabbani, *On Entering the Sea: The Erotic and Other Poetry of Nizar Qabbani*, trans. Lena Jayyusi (Northampton, Mass.: Interlink Books, 1996), 148.

23. Mujir al-Din al-Hanbali, *Al-'Uns al-Jalil fi Tarikh al-Quds wa al-Khalil* (The Significant Ambiance in the History of Jerusalem and Hebron) (Amman: Maktabat al-Muhtasib, 1973).

24. Al-Ghazali, *Deliverance from Error and the Beginning of Guidance*, trans. W. Montgomery Watt (Kuala Lumpur: Islamic Book Trust, 2005), 52.

25. Daniella J. Talmon-Heller, *Islamic Piety in Medieval Syria: Mosques, Cemeteries and Sermons Under the Zangids and Ayyubids (1146–1260)* (Leiden: Brill, 2007), 63.

26. Al-Ghazali, *The Mysteries of Worship in Islam: Translation with Commentary and Introduction of al-Ghazzali's Book of the Ihyā' on the Worship*, trans. Edwin Elliot Calverley (Lahore: Sh. M.

Ashraf, 1925), 142, 50. Al-Ghazali, "Ayyuhal Walad" (Oh My Beloved Son), trans. Shaykh Seraj Hendricks, at https://shadowofpurelight.wordpress.com/2010/10/22/of-grace-its-perfection-by-imam-ghazali/.

27. Salman H. Bashier, *Ibn Al-'Arabi's Barzakh: The Concept of the Limit and the Relationship Between God and the World* (New York: State University of New York Press, 2012), 60–66.

28. Ibid., 61. A century and a half later, a scribe named Ahmad b. Muhammad b. Muthabbit discovered seventeen complete autograph manuscripts of Ibn 'Arabi's work and spent two years at al-Aqsa Mosque copying them. Those copies are today housed in the Beyazit Library in Istanbul (Veliyuddin 51). See Jane Clark and Denis McAuley, "Some Notes on the Manuscript Veliyuddin 51," *Journal of the Muhyiddin Ibn 'Arabi Society* 40 (2006). One manuscript of Ibn 'Arabi's *Book of Unity* bears an author's note copied by a scribe: "I composed it in Jerusalem (*Bayt al-Muqaddas*) in an hour in the daytime."

29. Maimonides, *Mishneh Torah*, Laws of the Foundations of the Torah, 4:13, in *Sefer Hamadah—Book of Knowledge* (Mishneh Torah Series), trans. Rabbi Eliyahu Touger (New York: Moznaim, 2010). On concealment see *Hekhalot Zutarty: The Lesser Book of the Heavenly Palaces*, in James Davila, *Hekhalot Literature in Translation: Major Texts of Merkavah Mysticism* (Leiden: Brill, 2013), 199–244.

30. See, for example, Ibn Taymiyya's critiques of Ibn 'Arabi in the fourteenth century: Alexander D. Knysh, *Ibn 'Arabi in the Later Islamic Tradition: The Making of a Polemical Image in Medieval Islam* (New York: State University of New York Press, 1999), 84–112.

31. Mujir al-Din, al-'Uns, 2:329, in Daphna Ephrat, *Spiritual Wayfarers, Leaders in Piety: Sufis and the Dissemination of Islam in Medieval Palestine* (Cambridge: Harvard University Press, 2008), 136. For Mujir al-Din's description of Badr al-Din and the Wafa'iyyah, see Ephrat, *Spiritual Wayfarers,* 158–59. See also Donald P. Little, "Mujīr al-Dīn al-'Ulaymī's Vision of Jerusalem in the Ninth/Fifteenth Century," *Journal of the American Oriental Society* 115, no. 2 (1995): 246.

32. For early hadith on the Night Journey see Mustafa Abu Sway, "The Holy Land, Jerusalem and Al-Aqsa Mosque in the Islamic Sources," *Journal of the Central Conference of American Rabbis* (2000): 60–62.

33. See Navtej Sarna, *Indians at Herod's Gate: A Jerusalem Tale* (Delhi: Rupa Publications, 2014). Until the sixteenth century, this gate was called Bab al-Sahara (Gate of the Vigil) and took its name from the nearby cemetery. Bab al-Zahra (Flower Gate) seems to be a distortion of the earlier name.

34. Shamsuddin al-Kilani, "The Muslim Fascination with Jerusalem: The Case of the Sufis," *Islamic Studies* 40, nos. 3/4 (2001): 626.

35. These include Al-Qadiriyya (also known as al-Afghaniyya), al-Naqshabandiyya (established in the fourteenth century and rebuilt in 1625), al-Hedamiyya, and al-Asaadiyya on the Mount of Olives. *Naqsh* (engraving) suggests engraving the name of God in the believer's heart. Ibid., 622.

36. Ali Qleibo, "The Jerusalem Blues," *This Week in Palestine* 202.5 (February 2015), http://thisweekinpalestine.com/the-jerusalem-blues/.

37. Margaret Smith, *Rabi'a the Mystic and Her Fellow-Saints in Islam* (Cambridge: Cambridge University Press, 2010), 184.

38. Camille Adams Helminski, *Women of Sufism: A Hidden Treasure* (Boston: Shambhala, 2013), xx.

39. Some scholars point to parallels in terminology and imagery between the Dead Sea Scrolls and early Karaite literature. In the early Middle Ages, part of the Qumran library apparently came into the hands of Jerusalem's Karaites. This included the Damascus Document, the only Qumran sectarian work that was known before the discovery of the Dead Sea Scrolls. A medieval copy was found by Solomon Schechter in the Cairo Genizah.

40. Jacob Mann, "A Tract by an Early Karaite Settler in Jerusalem," *Jewish Quarterly Review* 12, no. 3 (1922): 257.

41. Ibid., 263. For a different view see Leon Nemoy, "The Pseudo-Qūmisīan Sermon to the Karaites," *Proceedings of the American Academy for Jewish Research* 43 (1976): 49–105. A tenth-century manuscript of al-Qumisi's commentary on Psalms is housed at the library of the Jewish Theological Seminary in New York (ENA 2778.1).

42. James T. Robinson, *Asceticism, Eschatology, Opposition to Philosophy: The Arabic Translation and Commentary of Salmon Ben Yeroham on Qohelet (Ecclesiastes)*, Karaite Texts and Studies (Leiden: Brill, 2012), 30. See also Leon Nemoy, "The Epistle of Sahl Ben Maṣlīaḥ," *Proceedings of the American Academy for Jewish Research* 38–39 (1970): 145–77.

43. He quoted Anan ben David's principle: "Search thoroughly in Scripture and do not rely upon my opinion." Mann, "A Tract by an Early Karaite Settler in Jerusalem," 264.

44. Zeev Elkin and Menahem Ben Sasson, "Abraham Firkovich and the Cairo Genizah," *Peamim* 90 (2002): 51–95 [Hebrew].

Chapter Three. Medieval Mingling

1. The Holy Sepulchre became the most copied building in medieval Europe and western Asia. Examples include Neuvy-Saint-Sépulchre in France; the Jerusalem Chapel and Adornes Domain in Bruges; the tiny cemetery chapel of Saint Michael at Fulda; almshouses in North Yorkshire; the Temple Church in London; the tenth-century church on Mount Van in Armenia; the twelfth-century Holy Sepulchres at Cambridge and Northampton, England; the Sacri Monti of Piedmont; a fifteenth-century chapel in the cathedral of Mtskheta, the ancient capital of Georgia, also called "the Second Jerusalem"; the Heiliges Grab of Görlitz, constructed between 1481 and 1504; and the Nuova Gerusalemme at the church of Santo Stefano in Bologna (based on the precise dimensions of the Holy Sepulchre as the Crusaders found it). Each of these became pilgrimage sites in their own right. They were not intended as exact replicas, but as cues for meditating on the meaning of Jerusalem. Mount Saint Sepulchre Franciscan Monastery in Washington, D.C., designed by the architect Aristide Leonori and completed in 1899, is a later copy of the Holy Sepulchre.

2. William of Tyre [Willelmus Tyrensus], *Chronicon* 8, 20, ed. R. B. C. Huygens (Turnhout: Brepols, 2014), *A History of Deeds Done Beyond the Sea*, trans. Emily Atwater Babcock and A. C. Krey, 2 vols. (New York: Columbia University Press, 1943), 1:372.

3. John of Würzburg, *Description of the Holy Land* 27, trans. Aubrey Stewart (London: Palestine Pilgrims Text Society, 1890), 69. For a recent edition of the Latin text see *Peregrinationes Tres: Saewulf, John of Würzburg, Theodoricus*, ed. R. B. C. Huygens (Turnhout: Brepols, 1994). Latin still makes occasional appearances in Jerusalem. In 2014, for instance, excavators from the Israel Antiquities Authority found a large Latin inscription around the opening of a deep cistern north of Damascus Gate. It was dedicated by Legio X Fretensis to the emperor Hadrian in the year 129–130 CE.

4. Daniel Galadza, "Greek Liturgy in Crusader Jerusalem: Witnesses of Liturgical Life at the Holy Sepulchre and St. Sabas Lavra," *Journal of Medieval History* 43, no. 4 (2017): 429.

5. Edward Peters, *The First Crusade: "The Chronicle of Fulcher of Chartres" and Other Source Materials* (Philadelphia: University of Pennsylvania Press, 2011), 281–82.

6. Jaroslav Folda, "Melisende of Jerusalem: Queen and Patron of Art and Architecture in the Crusader Kingdom," in *Reassessing the Roles of Women as Makers of Medieval Art and Architecture*, ed. Therese Martin (Leiden: Brill, 2012), 452. Another missal of the Holy Sepulchre mixes Italian with northern European influences. The Bibliothèque Nationale in Paris holds a copy of the Gospel of John which due to its mixed Byzantine-Frankish style is also believed to have been produced in Jerusalem.

7. *The Letters of St. Bernard of Clairvaux*, ed. Beverly Kienzle, trans. Bruno Scott James (Kalamazoo, Mich.: Sutton, 1998), 346.

8. Ibid., 121.

9. William of Tyre, *Chronicon* 16, 3, *History of Deeds Done Beyond the Sea*, 2:139–40.

10. William of Tyre, *Chronicon* 15, 27, *History of Deeds Done Beyond the Sea*, 2:135.

11. William Caxton, who introduced the printing press to England, translated William's history of the First Crusade from the French and published it in 1481 under the title *Godeffroy of Boloyne; or, The Siege and Conqueste of Jerusalem*. William's first book, *Gesta orientalium principum* (Deeds of the Eastern Rulers), a history of the Arab East, has been lost, though fragments have been preserved in the *Historia orientalis* of Jacques de Vitry, a history of the Holy Land that survived in at least 124 manuscripts. See Jacques de Vitry, *Histoire orientale/Historia orientalis*, ed. and trans. J. Donnadieu (Turnhout: Brepols, 2008).

12. William of Tyre, *Chronicon* 15, 26, *History of Deeds Done Beyond the Sea*, 2:133–34.

13. See Jaroslav Folda, *The Art of the Crusaders in the Holy Land, 1098–1187* (Cambridge: Cambridge University Press, 1995), 119–328; Folda, "Melisende of Jerusalem"; Barbara Zeitler, "The Distorting Mirror: Reflections on the Queen Melisende Psalter," in *Through the Looking Glass: Byzantium Through British Eyes—Papers from the Twenty-Ninth Spring Symposium of Byzantine Studies*, ed. Robin Cormack and Elizabeth Jeffreys (Aldershot: Ashgate Variorum, 2000); Therese Martin, "The Art of a Reigning Queen as Dynastic Propaganda in Twelfth-Century Spain," *Speculum* 80, no. 4 (October 2005): 1134–71.

14. Folda, "Melisende of Jerusalem," 470. See also Nurith Kenaan-Kedar, "Armenian Architecture in Twelfth-Century Crusader Jerusalem," *Studies in Art History* 3 (1998): 80–86.

15. Folda, "Melisende of Jerusalem," 459. See also Helen Gaudette, "The Piety, Power, and Patronage of the Latin Kingdom of Jerusalem's Queen Melisende" (Ph.D. diss., City University of New York, 2005).

16. See Denys Pringle, *The Churches of the Crusader Kingdom of Jerusalem: A Corpus* (Cambridge: Cambridge University Press, 1993–2007), 3:385.

17. See Michael E. Stone, *The Manuscript Library of the Armenian Patriarchate in Jerusalem* (Jerusalem: Saint James Press, 1969).

18. See Dickran Kouymjian, "The Evolution of Armenian Gospel Illumination: The Formative Period (9th–11th Centuries)," in *Armenia and the Bible*, ed. Christoph Burchard (Atlanta: Scholars' Press, 1993), 125–42.

19. Kevork (George) Hintlian, *History of the Armenians in the Holy Land* (Jerusalem: St. James Press, 1976), 49; Sirarpie Der Nersessian, *Miniature Painting in the Armenian Kingdom of Cilicia from the Twelfth to the Fourteenth Century*, jointly prepared for publication with Sylvia Agemian, 2 vols. (Washington, D.C.: Dumbarton Oaks, 1993), 1:65.

20. Jerome to Eustochium, Letter 22:32 (dated 384), in *The Letters of Saint Jerome*, trans. W. H. Fremantle, G. Lewis, and W. G. Martley (London: Aeterna Press, 2016), 59.

21. See D. S. Richards, "Arabic Documents from the Monastery of St. James in Jerusalem Including a Mamluk Report on the Ownership of Calvary," *Revue des études arméniens* 21 (1988–89): 455–69.

22. Arthur Hagopian, "Queen Keran Gets Back Her Royal Train," Armenian News Network / Groong, November 27, 2011.

23. Vrej Nersessian, *The Repatriation of an Armenian Cultural Treasure: The Gospel of Queen Keran, Sis, Cilicia, 1272 AD* (London: Armenian Community and Church Council of Great Britain, 2011).

24. Hagopian, "Queen Keran Gets Back Her Royal Train."

25. Maimonides, *Mishneh Torah*, Laws of Theft 5:1, in Hyman Klein, trans., *The Code of Maimonides (Mishneh Torah): Book 11, The Book of Torts* (New Haven: Yale University Press, 1954).

26. The letter was among several discovered by the historian S. D. Goitein, professor at the Hebrew University, in 1952. See S. D. Goitein, *A Mediterranean Society: The Jewish Communities of the Arab World as Portrayed in the Documents of the Cairo Geniza*, 6 vols. (Berkeley: University of California Press, 1967–1993), 5:372–79. On the Aleppo Codex and its recent fate, see Chapter 5.

27. Vrej Nersessian, "13th Cent Armenian Miniatures Returned to Jerusalem Patriarchate," November 23, 2011, http://theorthodoxchurch.info/blog/news/13th-cent-armenian-miniatures-returned-to-jerusalem-patriarchate (accessed September 21, 2018). The full story is also told in Nersessian, *The Repatriation of an Armenian Cultural Treasure.*

28. "Nazi Germany's Road to War," *Times* (London), November 24, 1945, 4; see Victor Azarya, *The Armenian Quarter of Jerusalem: Urban Life Behind Monastery Walls* (Berkeley: University of California Press, 1984).

29. B. T. A. Evetts, ed., *The Churches and Monasteries of Egypt* (Oxford: Clarendon, 1895), 5-6.

30. Medieval liturgical books added Psalm 79 (78 in the Septuagint) to the daily mass between the Lord's Prayer and Agnus Dei: "O God, the nations have invaded your inheritance." See Amnon Linder, "The Loss of Christian Jerusalem in Late Medieval Liturgy," in *The Real and Ideal Jerusalem in Jewish, Christian and Islamic Art: Studies in Honor of Bezalel Narkiss on the Occasion of His Seventieth Birthday*, ed. Bianca Kühnel (Jerusalem: Center for Jewish Art, Hebrew University of Jerusalem, 1998), 167.

31. Donald P. Little, "Jerusalem Under the Ayyubids and the Mamluks, 1187–1516 AD," in *Jerusalem in History*, ed. K. J. Asali (New York: Olive Branch, 1990), 183; David Abulafia, *Frederick II: A Medieval Emperor* (Oxford: Oxford University Press, 1992), 182.

32. Abulafia, *Frederick II*, 187.

33. Ibid., 185.

34. Ibid.

35. Ibid., 187–88.

36. Two lesser manuscripts identified as possible products of the scriptorium in thirteenth-century Jerusalem are the Egerton Sacramentary (British Library, MS Egerton 2902) and the Pontifical of Apamea (British Library, MS App. 57528).

37. See Jaroslav Folda, *Crusader Art in the Holy Land, From the Third Crusade to the Fall of Acre* (Cambridge: Cambridge University Press, 2005), 212–17.

38. See Kenaan-Kedar, "Armenian Architecture in Twelfth-Century Crusader Jerusalem"; Cyril Aslanov, "Languages in Contact in the Latin East: Acre and Cyprus," *Crusades* 1 (2002): 155–81; *Jerusalem, 1000–1400: Every People Under Heaven*, ed. Barbara Drake Boehm and Melanie Holcomb (New York: Metropolitan Museum, 2016), 68.

39. The Franciscan brothers at Saint Savior Monastery ran a pharmacy and an infirmary for pilgrims and the needy, as described by the Polish nobleman Prince Mikołaj Krzysztof Radziwiłł, who visited Jerusalem in 1583. The monastery included a small garden for medicinal herbs and a medical library. See Olivier Lafon, "The Library of the Franciscan Pharmacy in Jerusalem," *Revue d'histoire de la pharmacie* (March 2015): 7–19, and Narcys Klimas, "Franciscan Medicine in Jerusalem," in *Jerusalem: A Medical Diagnosis; The History of Jerusalem Reflected in Medicine and Beliefs*, ed. Nirit Shalev-Khalifa and Eilat Lieber (Jerusalem: Ben-Zvi Institute, 2014), 36–38.

40. Michele Campopiano, "Islam, Jews and Eastern Christianity in Late Medieval Pilgrims' Guidebooks," *Al Masaq* 24 (2012): 75–89.

41. Ibid. The latter were digitized by Ardon Bar-Hama, who also photographed the Dead Sea Scrolls, the tenth-century Aleppo Codex, the oldest-known Talmudic fragment in existence, and parts of the Shlomo Moussaieff manuscript collection. Prof.

Bartolomeo Pirone, an Italian scholar who has been researching the archives of the Custody of the Holy Land since 1980, has extensively studied the titles of ownership. "These documents are the legitimacy of the right of property of the Franciscans on different sanctuaries," Pirone told the journalist Beatrice Guarrera. "Some are from the Arab period and some are written in the Ottoman language." Guarrera, "40 Years of Research for the Custody: A Conversation with Prof. Pirone," *Custodia Terrae Sanctae,* February 7, 2018.

Chapter Four. From Mamluk Patronage to Ottoman Occupation

1. See Malachi Beit Aryeh, "Hebrew Manuscripts That Were Copied in Jerusalem or by Former Jerusalemites Until the Ottoman Conquest," in *Chapters in the History of Medieval Jerusalem,* ed. Benjamin Z. Kedar (Jerusalem: Ben-Zvi Institute, 1979), 244–78; Meir Benayahu, "The Edict Against Removing Books from Jerusalem," in *Mincha Leyehuda,* ed. Simha Assaf et al. (Jerusalem: Mossad Harav Kook, 1949), 226–34 [Hebrew].

2. Matt Goldish, "Meir Benayahu (1924–2009): In Memoriam," *Jewish Quarterly Review* 100, no. 4 (Fall 2010).

3. Jonathan Garb, "The Kabbalah of Rabbi Joseph Ibn Sayyah as a Source for the Understanding of Safedian Kabbalah," *Kabbalah: Journal for the Study of Jewish Mystical Texts* 4 (1999): 213–55.

4. Jonathan Garb, *Shamanic Trance in Modern Kabbalah* (Chicago: University of Chicago Press, 2011), 63.

5. "The Khâlidiyya Library in Jerusalem, 1900–2000," at http://www.khalidilibrary.org/rymondarticlee.html (accessed August 9, 2018).

6. For more on the village before and after the 1948 war, see Walid al-Khalidi, ed., *All That Remains: The Palestinian Villages Occupied and Depopulated by Israel in 1948* (Washington, D.C.: Institute for Palestine Studies, 1992).

7. Donald P. Little, "Mujīr al-Dīn al-'Ulaymī's Vision of Jerusalem in the Ninth/Fifteenth Century," *Journal of the American Oriental Society* 115, no. 2 (1995): 239.

8. Ibn Sayyah may have acquired some of these practices from Muslim Sufis. See Jonathan Garb, "Trance Techniques in the Kabbalah of Jerusalem," *Peamim* 70 (1996): 47–67.

9. Newton's nonscientific writings were auctioned at Sotheby's in London in 1936. Some were acquired by British economist John Maynard Keynes, and others by Abraham Shalom Yahuda, who bequeathed them to the State of Israel. The National Library in Jerusalem exhibited them in 2007. See, for example, Newton's "Notes on the Jewish Temple," which includes Newton's use of Hebrew and Aramaic phrases (Yah. Ms. 28e).

10. Raquel Ukeles, "Abraham Shalom Yahuda: The Scholar, the Collector and the Collection," in Efraim Wust, *Catalogue of the Arabic, Persian, and Turkish Manuscripts of the Yahuda Collection of the National Library of Israel,* vol. 1 (Leiden: Brill, 2016), 1–12.

11. See Rehav Rubin, "Proskynetarion: One Term for Two Kinds of Jerusalemite Pilgrimage Souvenirs," *Eastern Christian Art* 10 (2016): 97–111.

12. See Denys Pringle, *The Churches of the Crusader Kingdom of Jerusalem: A Corpus*, 3 vols. (Cambridge: Cambridge University Press, 1993–2007), 3:211–12, church no. 326; Joseph Patrich, *The Sabaite Heritage in the Orthodox Church from the Fifth Century to the Present* (Leuven: Peeters, 2001), 16.

13. Ephraim Isaac, "Shelf List of Ethiopian Manuscripts in the Monasteries of the Ethiopian Patriarchate of Jerusalem," *Rassegna di studi etiopici* 30 (1984): 56.

14. The conversion is recorded by the Latin historian Rufinus in his *Historia Ecclesiastica* 1:9.

15. Listed in Isaac, "Shelf List of Ethiopian Manuscripts," as JE 958E.

16. Robert Schick, "Who Came on Pilgrimage to Jerusalem in the Mamluk and Ottoman Periods? An Interreligious Comparison," in *Für Seelenheil und Lebensglück: Das byzantinische Pilgerwesen und seine Wurzeln*, ed. Despoina Ariantzi and Ina Eichner (Mainz: Verlag des Römisch-Germanischen Zentralmuseums, 2018), 243–60.

17. Efraim Halevi, "My Mashhad Family," *Kyria Neemana* 3 (2013): 22–23 (Hebrew); Halevi, "The Cogen-Aharonof," *Leveit Avota: Studies and Sources in Family Research* (1992): 5–6 (Hebrew). The prayer book, in two volumes, was translated by Mordechai Ben Rafael Ekeler (or Mulla Morad); a copy can be found at the National Library, shelfmark A=583=0=R89.

18. See Yali Hashash, "Shifting Social Attitudes and Economic Change in the Sephardic Community in Palestine, 1841–1880" (Ph.D. diss., Hebrew University, 2011).

19. See Yaron Ben-Naeh, "Religious Life of the Jews in Nineteenth-Century Jerusalem," in *The History of Jerusalem: The Late Ottoman Period*, ed. Israel Bartal and Haim Goren (Jerusalem: Yad Ben-Zvi, 2010), 315–28 (Hebrew).

20. Mehmet Tütüncü, *Turkish Jerusalem (1516–1917)* (Haarlem: Turkestan and Azerbaijan Research Centre, 2006), 38.

Chapter Five. Dragomans and Thieves

1. The Akkadian term *targumannu* first appears in the nineteenth century BCE. See Giulio Lepschy, *History of Linguistics*, vol. 1: *The Eastern Traditions of Linguistics* (Oxford: Routledge, 2014), 93.

2. Charles Clermont-Ganneau, "The Arabs in Palestine," *Macmillan's Magazine*, August 1875, 363.

3. Robert Curzon, *Visits to the Monasteries in the Levant* (New York: Cosimo Classics, 2007), 66; "Notes and News," *Palestine Exploration Fund Quarterly* 27, no. 4 (1895): 298.

4. Jane Fletcher Geniesse, *American Priestess: The Extraordinary Story of Anna Spafford and the American Colony in Jerusalem* (New York: Knopf Doubleday, 2008), 126.

5. Eliezer Ben-Yehuda, *The Dream and Its Realization* [*Hachalom Veshivro*] (Jerusalem: Bialik, 1978), 125 (Hebrew).

6. Patrick J. Geary, *Furta Sacra: Thefts of Relics in the Central Middle Ages* (Princeton: Princeton University Press, 2011), xii.

7. Curzon, *Visits to the Monasteries in the Levant*, 268.

8. "Bishop Porphyrius (Uspensky) and His Collection," National Library of Russia website, available at http://www.nlr.ru/eng/exib/CodexSinaiticus/porf.html (accessed May 20, 2018). Cited with kind permission of the National Library of Russia. We recount the story of our visit to the library of the Greek Orthodox Patriarchate in the Epilogue.

9. Derek Hopwood, *The Russian Presence in Syria and Palestine, 1843–1914: Church and Politics in the Near East* (Oxford: Clarendon, 1969), 35.

10. Ibid., 36.

11. Ibid., 39–40. Indeed, when Patriarch Athanasios of Jerusalem died in 1845, Uspensky supported the election of his friend Cyril, the bishop of Lydda, who settled in Jerusalem in 1845.

12. Porphyrius Uspensky, *The Book of My Existence*, 7 vols. (Saint Petersburg: Imperial Academy of Science, 1894), 7:169, 173 (March 19, 1858). We thank Anastasia Keshman for the translation.

13. Ibid., 7:261 (March 30, 1860); see Patricia Kennedy Grimsted, *Archives in Russia: A Directory and Bibliographic Guide to Holdings in Moscow and St. Petersburg* (New York: Routledge, 2016).

14. Illuminated folios Uspensky took from the Greek Orthodox Patriarchate in Jerusalem to Saint Petersburg include Taphos 53, Psalter, four folios and three miniatures (Gr. 266); Taphos 51, Psalter, one folio with full-page miniatures on both sides; Taphos 5, book of Job, one folio with miniature (Gr. 382); Taphos 14, Liturgical homilies of Saint Gregory of Nazianzos, one folio with four miniatures (Gr. 334); Saint Sabas 63, Synaxarion, two folios (Gr. 352) (of thirteen miniatures, seven are missing); Stavros 42, two miniatures on four folios (Gr. 379).

15. "Bishop Porphyrius (Uspensky) and His Collection," National Library of Russia website (accessed May 20, 2018).

16. The scholar Athanasios Papadopoulos Kerameus, invited to become secretary to Nicodemus in 1883, spent years cataloguing the Greek codices and manuscripts belonging to the Patriarchate. The result was his four-volume *Hierosolimitike Bibliotheke* (St. Petersburg: Kirspaoum, 1891–1899).

17. Zeev Elkin and Menahem Ben-Sasson, "Abraham Firkovitch and the Cairo Genizah," *Peamim* 90 (2002): 51 (Hebrew).

18. Ibid., 55.

19. See Dan Shapira, *Avraham Firkowicz in Istanbul, 1830–1832* (Ankara: Karam Press, 2003).

20. Abraham Firkovich, *Chotam Tokhnit* (Eupatoria: Firkovich, 1835), 54a. The accusation was not included in the edition published in Israel (Ramlah: Hizuk Emuna, 1835). See Golda Akhiezer, "Abraham Firkovich's Research Project," in *Studies in Caucasian, Georgian, and Bukharan Jewry: Historical, Sociological, and Cultural Aspects*, ed. G. Akhiezer, R. Enoch, and S. Weinstein (Ariel: Ariel University Institute for Research of Jewish Communities of the Caucasus and Central Asia, 2014). Citing Matthew 5:18, in which Jesus insists he intends to change "not one jot or tittle" of the law, Firkovich considered Jesus to have been himself a Karaite.

21. "Oriental Manuscripts," National Library of Russia website, http://nlr.ru/eng/coll/manuscripts/eastscripts.html (accessed May 20, 2018).

22. Reuven Gafni, Aryeh Morgenstern, and David Kasuto, *Ha-Hurva* (Jerusalem: Yad Ben Zvi, 2010) (Hebrew).

23. Among the manuscripts Saphir brought back to Jerusalem were a fourteenth-century Yemenite *Kitab al-Haya* (Book of Astronomy) that includes an abbreviated version of Ptolemy's *Almagest* (now in Cambridge University Library, Add. 1191). The most comprehensive study of Saphir is by Y. Y. Rivlin, "R. Yaaqov Sapir," *Moznaim* 11 (1940): 74–81; 385–99 (Hebrew).

24. Yosef Ofer, "Abraham Firkovich and the Dedication Inscription of the Aleppo Codex," *Hebrew Union College Annual* 76 (2005): 259–72.

25. Ephraim Deinard, *Masa' Krim* (Travels in Crimea) (Warsaw: Y. Goldman, 1878), p. 1 (Hebrew). Deinard founded the great Hebrew collections at Harvard and Hebrew Union College in Cincinnati. The Hebraic Section of the Library of Congress was established in 1914 with ten thousand books and pamphlets from Deinard's private collection (purchased with funds donated by Jacob H. Schiff). He sold manuscripts to the libraries of Oxford and Cambridge. He attacked Kabbalists and the *Zohar* (a forgery, he argued), the followers of the Baal Shem Tov (he regarded Hasidism as Catholicism in disguise), and Jewish converts to Christianity, such as the antiquarian Moses Shapira, who attempted to sell ancient biblical fragments of questionable authenticity to the British Museum. But he reserved particular vitriol for Firkovich. One of his books, purportedly an account of his travels among the Karaites of Crimea, is in fact a pointed polemic against his old mentor.

26. In the second edition of 1894, this recommendation had been removed.

27. London *Daily News,* January 24, 1874.

28. Built in 1864 by Aga Rashid Nashashibi, the mansion later became home to Dr. Abraham Albert Ticho, an ophthalmologist, and his wife, Anna Ticho, an artist. The first floor served as an eye clinic until Dr. Ticho's death in 1960.

29. Bertha Spafford Vester, *Our Jerusalem: An American Family in the Holy City, 1881–1949* (Jerusalem: American Colony, Ariel Publishing House, 1988), 138.

30. Yihye Kapah, *Milchamot Hashem* (Jerusalem: P. Anav, 1930) (Hebrew).

31. J. Leveen, introduction to the index volume of G. Margoliouth, *Catalogue of the Hebrew and Samaritan Manuscripts in the British Museum,* part iv (London, 1935; reprinted 1977), quoted in Fred N. Reiner, "C. D. Ginsburg and the Shapira Affair," *British Library Journal* 21, no. 1 (Spring 1995): 112.

32. Shapira to C. D. Ginsburg, *Athenaeum*, August 11, 1883, 179.

33. Shapira, Letter to Hermann Strack, May 9, 1883, quoted in Reiner, "C. D. Ginsburg and the Shapira Affair," 113.

34. Myriam Harry, *The Little Daughter of Jerusalem,* trans. from the French by Phoebe Allen (New York: Dutton, 1919), 261.

35. Hermann Strack, Letter to the *Times* (London), September 4, 1883; quoted in Reiner, "C. D. Ginsburg and the Shapira Affair," 114 and note 40.

36. *Autobiography of Sir Walter Besant* (London: Hutchinson, 1902), 162.

37. Charles Clermont-Ganneau, Letter to the *Times* (London), August 21, 1883.

38. Reiner, "C. D. Ginsburg and the Shapira Affair," 110.

39. Chanan Tigay, *The Lost Book of Moses: The Hunt for the World's Oldest Bible* (New York: HarperCollins, 2016), 310.

40. J. L. Teicher, "The Genuineness of the Shapira Manuscripts," *Times Literary Supplement*, March 22, 1957, 184.

41. W. F. Albright, "On the Date of the Scrolls from 'Ain Feshkha and the Nash Papyrus," *Bulletin of the American Schools of Oriental Research* 115 (1949): 13.

42. See, e.g., Shlomo Guil, "The Shapira Scroll Was an Authentic Dead Sea Scroll," *Palestine Exploration Quarterly* 149, no. 1 (2017): 6–27.

43. Item 32270, "Bible: The most original MS. of Deuteronomy, from the hand of Moses (? ben Amram)," Bernard Quaritch, *A General Catalogue of Books*, vol. 3 (London: G. Norman, 1887).

44. Tigay, *The Lost Book of Moses*.

Chapter Six. Dreamers and Visionaries

1. See Marcel Serr, "Understanding the Land of the Bible: Gustaf Dalman and the Emergence of the German Exploration of Palestine," *Near Eastern Archaeology* 79, no. 1 (2016): 27–35. See also H. Rohde, *Deutschland in Vorderasien* (Berlin: E. S. Mittler und Sohn, 1916), 134–36, and Gustaf Dalman, "The Search for the Temple Treasure at Jerusalem," *Palestine Exploration Fund Quarterly Statement* (January 1912), 38.

2. W. F. Albright, review of *Arbeit und Sitte in Palästina* by Gustav Dalman, *Journal of Biblical Literature* 57, no. 2 (1938): 235.

3. Dov Schidorsky, "Libraries in Late Ottoman Palestine Between the Orient and the Occident," *Libraries and Culture* 33, no. 3 (Summer 1998): 267.

4. Thomas Willi, "Mission Among the Jews, Holy Land and Aramaic Studies: The Case of Gustav Dolman," in *Let Us Go Up to Zion: Essays in Honour of H. G. M. Williamson on the Occasion of His Sixty-Fifth Birthday*, ed. Iain Provan and Mark Boda (Leiden: Brill, 2012), 22.

5. Simon Sebag Montefiore, *Jerusalem: The Biography* (New York: Vintage, 2012), 375.

6. Mark Twain, *The Innocents Abroad*, ed. Shelley Fisher Fishkin (Oxford: Oxford University Press, 1996), chap. 52.

7. Shlomo Avineri, "Theodor Herzl's Diaries as a Bildungsroman," *Jewish Social Studies* 5, no. 3 (June 1999): 40.

8. Theodor Herzl, *Old-New Land*, trans. Lotta Levensohn (New York: Bloch, 1941), 248.

9. Yana Tchekhanovets, "Early Georgian Pilgrimage to the Holy Land," *Liber Annuus* 61 (2011): 453–71.

10. Robert Curzon, *Visits to Monasteries in the Levant* (New York: Cosimo Classics, 2007), 193.

11. Else Lasker-Schüler, *Hebrew Ballads and Other Poems,* ed. Audri Durchslag and Jeanette Litman-Demeestère (New York: Jewish Publication Society, 1980), 51.

12. Amos Oz, *The Hill of Evil Counsel: Three Stories,* trans. Nicholas de Lange and Amos Oz (San Diego: Harcourt, 1976), 11–12.

13. Two other models are housed at the German Protestant Institute of Archaeology in the Holy Land, which is also home to part of Conrad Schick's book collection. Other models can be found in Europe (e.g., the Bijbelsmuseum, Amsterdam). At a Sotheby's auction in 2013, a Conrad Schick model fetched £242,500.

14. Quoted in E. W. G. Masterman, "Obituary: The Important Work of Dr. Conrad Schick," *Biblical World* 20, no. 2 (1902): 146–48.

15. See Rehav Rubin, "Stephan Illes and His 3D Model-Map of Jerusalem (1873)," *Cartographic Journal* 44, no. 1 (2007): 71–79.

16. Trained in Britain, Avi-Yonah served in the 1930s and 1940s as an archivist and librarian at the Department of Antiquities in Jerusalem. After the British departure and the establishment of Israel in 1948, he could no longer access the Old City or conduct archaeological excavations in Jordanian-occupied East Jerusalem. Rather than using a trowel and sifting screens, he consulted the texts of Josephus and his own imagination to build the model.

17. Lili Eylon, "Models of Jerusalem," December 20, 1999, at http://www.mfa.gov.il/mfa/aboutisrael/state/pages/models%20of%20jerusalem.aspx.

18. John Cummins, *The Voyage of Christopher Columbus* (New York: Saint Martin's, 1922), 157; Charles F. Richardson, *American Literature, 1607–1885,* vol. 1: *The Development of American Thought* (New York: Haskell House, 1970), 79.

19. Ernest Lee Tuveson, *Redeemer Nation: The Idea of America's Millennial Role* (Chicago: University of Chicago Press, 1968), 129.

20. Ample literature exists on the history of the American Colony including Mia Gröndahl, *The Dream of Jerusalem: Lewis Larsson and the American Colony Photographers* (Stockholm: Journal, 2005); Jane Fletcher Geniesse, *American Priestess: The Extraordinary Story of Anna Spafford and the American Colony in Jerusalem* (New York: Anchor, 2009); Odd Karsten Tveit, *Anna's House: The American Colony in Jerusalem* (Cyprus: Rimal Publications, 2011); Bertha Spafford Vester, *Our Jerusalem: An American Family in the Holy City, 1881–1949* (Jerusalem: American Colony, Ariel, 1988); Helga Dudman, *The American Colony: Scenes from a Jerusalem Saga* (Jerusalem: Rubin Mass, 1998).

21. See Gröndahl, *The Dream of Jerusalem;* Dov Gavish, "The American Colony and Its Photographers," in *Zev Vilnay's Jubilee Volume: Essays on the History, Archaeology, and Lore of the Holy Land,* ed. Ely Schiller (Jerusalem: Ariel Publishing House, 1987), 127–44 (Hebrew); and *1914 Catalogue of Photographs Made by the American Colony, Jerusalem, of Sites, Scenes, Ceremonies, Costumes, Characters, Paintings, Etc., of Bible Lands, Including Jerusalem, Galilee, Damascus, Baalbeck, Petra, Sinai, Etc.* (Jerusalem: American Colony, 1914).

22. Bernard Montagnes and Benedict T. Viviano, *The Story of Father Marie-Joseph Lagrange: Founder of Modern Catholic Bible Study* (Paulist Press, 2006), 28, 26.

23. Empress Eudocia came to Jerusalem circa 450. She permitted the Jews, banned from the city since the year 135, to return. As a convert herself, she expressed great devotion to Saint Stephen. The patriarch Juvenal had pointed out to her the traditional site of the saint's martyrdom. There she built a church and instructed that she be buried under the entrance. When Jerusalem fell to the Persians in 614, the conquerors destroyed many Christian churches, including the one Empress Eudocia had built to honor Saint Stephen.

24. Hershel Shanks, "The Religious Message of the Bible," *Biblical Archaeology Review* 12, no. 2 (1986), available at https://members.bib-arch.org/biblical-archaeology-review /12/2/4.

25. Montagnes and Viviano, *The Story of Father Marie-Joseph Lagrange*, jacket copy.

26. Mary Jean Dorcy, O.P., *St. Dominic's Family: Over 300 Famous Dominicans* (Charlotte, N.C.: TAN Books, 1990), n.p.

27. Other research libraries of late-nineteenth- and early-twentieth-century archaeology and geography of the Levant include the Kenyon Institute and the W. F. Albright Institute.

28. Eliezer Ben-Yehuda, *Hachalom Veshivro* (The Dream and Its Realization), in *Collected Works* (Jerusalem: Ben-Yehuda Publications, 1943), 2.

29. See Yoseph Lang, *Speak Hebrew! The Life of Eliezer Ben-Yehuda* (Jerusalem: Ben-Zvi, 2008) (Hebrew); Eli Schiller, "Eliezer Ben-Yehuda at the École Biblique Library," *Ariel* 188 (2009): 91–92 (Hebrew).

30. S. Y. Agnon, *Only Yesterday*, trans. Barbara Harshav (Princeton: Princeton University Press, 2002), 301.

31. Eliezer Ben-Yehuda, "Hatzilu!" *Ha'Or*, January 9, 1911.

32. Zalman Shazar, "Baron David Günzberg and His Academy," *Jewish Quarterly Review* 57 (1967): 12.

33. Ben-Yehuda, "Hatzilu!"

34. Mikhail Pokrovsky to Albert Einstein, May 26, 1926, Central Zionist Archives, Jerusalem, 91-402 (German), available at http://alberteinstein.info/vufind1/Record/ EAR000068369/Related#tabnav.

35. In October 2015, a federal district judge in Washington, D.C., entered a $43.7 million judgment against the Russian Federation for ignoring a U.S. court order to return thousands of Jewish religious texts. Over objections from the State Department, which feared that sanctions could disrupt diplomatic relations, District Judge Royce Lamberth ordered the sanction to pressure Russia to return the Schneerson Collection—more than twelve thousand books and manuscripts seized in Russia in the early twentieth century, and twenty-five thousand pages stolen from the Lubavitch community by the Nazis and then taken as war loot by the Soviet Red Army. This resulted in a Russian ban on any loans to museums in the United States.

36. Barry Davis, "Valuable Hebrew Manuscript Collection to Be Digitized," *Jerusalem Post*, November 7, 2017.

37. See Omer Bartov, *Erased: Vanishing Traces of Jewish Galicia in Present-Day Ukraine* (Princeton: Princeton University Press, 2007). The National Library holds the autograph manuscript of Agnon's posthumously published novel *Shira*, parts of which Agnon tore up and intended to burn (ARC 4° 1270 01 681).

38. See Oleg Grabar, *The Dome of the Rock* (Cambridge, Mass: Belknap Press, 2006), 66. During renovations of the al-Aqsa Mosque between 1938 and 1942, roof beams made of cedar of Lebanon were replaced. One of the old beams was discovered to have been engraved with a Greek inscription: "In the time of [our] most saintly archbishop and patriarch Petrus . . . this whole house of Saint Thomas was erected from the foundations." Since there was no known Byzantine Church of Saint Thomas in Jerusalem, the mystery remains, but the name of Patriarch Petrus narrows the dates to 524–554.

39. William Harvey, *Church of the Holy Sepulchre, Jerusalem: Structural Survey Final Report* (London: Oxford University Press, 1935), 121.

40. Gustavo Testa, *Il santo sepolcro di Gerusalemme: splendori, miserie, speranze* (Bergamo: Istituto italiano d'Arti Grafiche, 1949), 13.

41. Roberto Paribeni, preface to Luigi Marangoni, *La chiesa del Santo Sepolcro in Gerusalemme: Problemi della sua conservazione* (Venice: Custodia di Terra Santa, 1937), 16–17. See also Masha Halevi, "Reshaping a Sacred Landscape: Antonio Barluzzi and the Rebuilding of the Catholic Shrines in the Holy Land: Political, Geographical and Cultural Influences" (Ph.D. diss., Hebrew University of Jerusalem, 2009).

42. Robert Ousterhout, "A New 'New Jerusalem' for Jerusalem," in *New Jerusalems: Hierotopy and Iconography of Sacred Spaces*, ed. A. Lidov (Moscow: Indrik, 2009), 882–98.

43. Raymond Cohen, *Saving the Holy Sepulchre: How Rival Christians Came Together to Rescue Their Holiest Shrine* (Oxford: Oxford University Press, 2008), 71.

44. Ibid., 79.

45. Adina Hoffman, *Till We Have Built Jerusalem: Architects of a New City* (New York: Farrar, Straus and Giroux, 2016), 89.

46. Morton Smith, *The Secret Gospel: The Discovery and Interpretation of the Secret Gospel According to Mark* (London: Gollancz, 1974); see also Stephen C. Carlson, *Gospel Hoax: Morton Smith's Invention of Secret Mark* (Waco, Tex.: Baylor University Press, 2005). According to Noam Zadoff of Indiana University, "Smith's understanding of Jesus was influenced by the way [Gershom] Scholem portrayed Sabbatai Zvi: a charismatic figure performing magical deeds who breaks Jewish law and promotes libertinism among a small, esoteric circle." Noam Zadoff, "The Archive, the Students, and the Emotions of a German Israeli Intellectual," *Jewish Quarterly Review* 103, no. 3 (July 2013): 415–28.

47. Jacob Neusner, "Who Needs 'The Historical Jesus'?" *Bulletin for Biblical Research* 4 (1994): 115.

48. Guy Stroumsa, *Morton Smith and Gershom Scholem: Correspondence, 1945–1982* (Leiden: Brill, 2008), xx.

49. See Tony Burke, ed., *Ancient Gospel or Modern Forgery? The Secret Gospel of Mark in Debate* (Eugene, Ore.: Cascade, 2013).

Chapter Seven. Rescue and Return

1. Their shelfmarks at the Syriac library of Jerusalem were SMMJ 25 and SMMJ 28.

2. Hananel Mack, *Introduction to Jewish Prayers* (Tel Aviv: DOC, 2001) (Hebrew).

3. The Cornerstone Ceremony, New National Library of Israel, YouTube, posted April 24, 2017, https://www.youtube.com/watch?v=SwsEDumLXpY #11.

4. David Shavit, *Hunger for the Printed Word: Books and Libraries in the Jewish Ghettos of Nazi-Occupied Europe* (Jefferson, N.C.: McFarland, 1997), 12.

5. Schocken quoted in Stefanie Mahrer, "'Much More Than Just Another Private Collection': The Schocken Library and Its Rescue from Nazi Germany in 1935," *Naharaim: Zeitschrift für deutsch-jüdische Literatur und Kulturgeschichte* 9 (2015): 4; Adina Hoffman, *Till We Have Built Jerusalem: Architects of a New City* (New York: Farrar, Straus and Giroux, 2016), 61.

6. Mahrer, "'Much More Than Just Another Private Collection,'" 1–2; Wendy Moonan, "A Jewish Treasure Stays in Israel," *New York Times,* August 3, 2001 ("Leonardo da Vinci"). The world's oldest illustrated Passover manuscript, the so-called "Bird's Head Haggadah," now displayed at the Israel Museum in Jerusalem, is also subject to dispute. Descendants of German Jewish lawmaker Ludwig Marum claim the medieval Haggadah was confiscated after Marum was arrested by the Nazis (he died at Kislau concentration camp) and sold in 1946 without their consent. They have demanded compensation.

7. Shavit, *Hunger for the Printed Word,* 48. According to Shnayer (Sid) Leiman, a former professor of Jewish Studies at Brooklyn College, at least some of the yeshiva's library survived. A Talmudic tractate from that library, printed in 1925, turned up at the Kedem auction house in Jerusalem in 2017, for example, and sold for $7,380. See Barbara Finkelstein, "Mystery Behind the Lost Books of a Cherished Lublin Yeshiva," *Forward,* August 31, 2017.

8. Claims Conference/Conference on Jewish Material Claims Against Germany, *Descriptive Catalogue of Looted Judaica,* partially updated 2nd ed., New York, 2014, at http://art.claimscon.org/wp-content/uploads/2013/09/Descriptive-Catalogue-of-Looted-Judaica-FINAL-14-November-2014.pdf.

9. Elisabeth M. Yavnai, "Jewish Cultural Property and Its Postwar Recovery," in *Confiscation of Jewish Property in Europe, 1933–1945, New Sources and Perspectives: Symposium Proceedings* (Washington, D.C.: Center for Advanced Holocaust Studies, U.S. Holocaust Memorial Museum, 2003), 132–33.

10. Elisabeth Gallas, "Locating the Jewish Future: The Restoration of Looted Cultural Property in Early Postwar Europe," *Naharaim* 9 (2015): 25–47.

11. "Memorandum submitted by the Commission on European Jewish Cultural Reconstruction to Rabbi Philip S. Bernstein," May 17, 1946, in *Hannah Arendt and Gershom Scholem: Der Briefwechsel, 1939–1964,* ed. Marie Luise Knott (Frankfurt am Main: Jüdischer Verlag, 2010), 115–19.

12. Ibid., notes to letter 51.

13. One example of a book returned under this program: a copy of *Sefer Mitzvot Gadol* by Rabbi Moses of Coucy, printed in 1546, looted from the Schor-Frankel family collec-

tion in Poland during World War II. Recently discovered in the University of Potsdam Library, it was returned to descendants of the family in Israel.

14. Yitzhak Y. Melamed, "The Lost Textual Treasures of a Hasidic Community," *Jewish Review of Books* 9 (Spring 2012), available at https://jewishreviewofbooks.com/articles/251/the-lost-textual-treasures-of-a-hasidic-community/.

15. Anatole France, *On Life and Letters: Second Series,* ed. Frederick Chapman, trans. A. W. Evans (London: J. Lane, Bodley Head, 1914), 92.

16. Moses Mendelssohn, *Jerusalem; or, On Religious Power and Judaism* [1783], trans. Allan Arkus (Waltham, Mass.: Brandeis University Press, 1983).

17. Bertha Spafford Vester, *Our Jerusalem: An American Family in the Holy City, 1881–1949* (Jerusalem: American Colony, Ariel Publishing House, 1988), 134–35.

18. Ibid.; Bible (London: Samuel Bagster and Sons), Manuscript Division, Library of Congress (13), available at http://www.loc.gov/exhibits/americancolony/amcolony-holyland.html#obj13.

19. See Noah S. Gerber, *Ourselves or Our Holy Books? The Cultural Discovery of Yemenite Jewry* (Jerusalem: Ben-Zvi Institute and Hebrew University, 2013) (Hebrew).

20. See Gish Amit, *Ex-Libris: Chronicles of Theft, Preservation, and Appropriating at the Jewish National Library* (Jerusalem: Van Leer, 2014), 137–40 (Hebrew).

21. Yitzhak Ben-Zvi, "The Property of the Migrants," JDC Archives, Records of the New York Office of the American Jewish Joint Distribution Committee, 1944–1952, Jerusalem, JER. 250; Yitzhak Ben-Zvi, "Four Days with Yemen Immigrants," March 1, 1950, 3, JDC Archives, Records of the New York Office of the American Jewish Joint Distribution Committee, 1944–1952, JER. 250.

22. Yitzhak Ben-Zvi, *Shivtei Israel Bierushalayim* (The Tribes of Israel in Jerusalem), vol. 2 (Tel Aviv: Omanut, 1936), 3.

23. Yitzhak Ben Zvi, "Hamachon Lekheker Haedot Hayehudiot Bamizrah Hatichon [The Institute for the Study of the Jewish Communities in the Middle East]," *Davar,* April 7, 1949, 2. A decades-long controversy about the fate of many Yemenite infants was recently reopened when the Israel State Archives released more than two hundred thousand previously classified documents. See Judy Maltz, "$5,000 a Head," *Haaretz,* May 7, 2017.

24. "People of the (Stolen) Book: Did Israel's National Library Engage in Systematic Theft?" *Haaretz,* January 2, 2015.

25. Yosef Meyouhas, *Yaldei Arav* (Arab Children) (Tel Aviv: Dvir, 1928), ix–xi, translated by Menachem Klein in *Lives in Common: Arabs and Jews in Jerusalem, Jaffa and Hebron* (Oxford: Oxford University Press, 2014), 39.

26. Maureen Meehan, "Eviction of Silwan Family Sets the Scene for Accelerated Ethnic Cleansing of Jerusalem," *Washington Report on Middle East Affairs,* January–February 1999, 27, 98.

27. *Jerusalem: A Medical Diagnosis; The History of Jerusalem Reflected in Medicine and Beliefs,* ed. Nirit Shalev-Khalifa and Eilat Lieber (Jerusalem: Ben-Zvi Institute, 2014), 235.

28. See Klein, *Lives in Common.*

29. Matti Friedman, *The Aleppo Codex: A True Story of Obsession, Faith, and the Pursuit of an Ancient Bible* (Chapel Hill, N.C.: Algonquin, 2012).

30. Mohamed A. Hussein, *Origins of the Book: From Papyrus to Codex* (Greenwich, Conn.: New York Graphic Society, 1972). A second codex, known as the Damascus Keter, was written in Castile in 1260, then made its way to a synagogue in Damascus, from which it was stolen in 1942. Auctioned in London in 1962 it was purchased for the National Library in Israel (MS Hebrew 4° 790).

31. Maimonides writes: "Since I have seen great confusion about these matters in all the scrolls I have seen, and similarly, the masters of the tradition who have written down and composed [texts] to make it known [which passages] are *p'tuchot* and which are *s'tumot* [the differing enjambments of lines of text in traditional Torah scrolls] are divided with regard to the scrolls on which to rely, I saw fit to write down the entire list of all the passages in the Torah that are *s'tumot* and *p'tuchot,* and also the form of the songs. In this manner, all the scrolls can be corrected and checked against these [principles]. The scroll on which I relied for [clarification of] these matters was a scroll renowned in Egypt, which includes all the 24 books [of the Bible]. It was kept in Jerusalem for many years so that scrolls could be checked from it. Everyone relies upon it because it was corrected by Ben Asher, who spent many years writing it precisely, and [afterward] checked it many times. I relied [on this scroll] when I wrote a Torah scroll according to law" (*Mishneh Torah, Book 2: The Book of Love,* trans. Menachem Kellner [New Haven: Yale University Press, 2004], Hilchot Sefer Torah, 8:5).

32. Friedman, *The Aleppo Codex,* 277.

33. Quoted in Nina Burleigh, *Unholy Business: A True Tale of Faith, Greed and Forgery in the Holy Land* (New York: Smithsonian, 2008), 118–19.

34. Constantine Mavrides, "The Diaries of Constantine Mavrides (May 15–December 30, 1948)," in *Jerusalem 1948: The Arab Neighbourhoods and Their Fate in the War,* ed. Salim Tamari, trans. John N. Tleel (Washington, D.C.: Institute for Palestine Studies, 1999), 12.

35. Shulamith Hareven, "On Being a Levantine," in *The Vocabulary of Peace* (San Francisco: Mercury House, 1995), 81; Shulamith Hareven, *Many Days: An Autobiography* (Tel Aviv: Am Oved, 2002), 78–80 (Hebrew). Hareven would become the first woman inducted into the Academy of the Hebrew Language.

36. Hareven, *Many Days,* 87.

37. Amit, *Ex-Libris,* 87.

38. Quoted ibid., 88; Shlomo Shunami, *On Libraries and the Librarian* (Jerusalem: Rubin Mass, 1968), 63–64 [Hebrew]. See also Amit, *Ex Libris,* 95.

39. See Kamal Moed, "Educator in the Service of the Homeland: Khalil al-Sakakini's Conflicted Identities," *Jerusalem Quarterly* 59 (2014): 68–85; and Kamal Abdel-Malek, "A Stranger in the House: Khalil Sakakini and Alter Levine," in his *The Rhetoric of Violence: Arab-Jewish Encounters in Contemporary Palestinian Literature and Film* (New York: Palgrave Macmillan, 2005).

40. Khalil al-Sakakini, *Yawmiyat Khalil al-Sakakini: Yawmiyat, Rasa'il, Ta'ammulat* (The Diaries of Khalil al-Sakakini: Diaries, Letters, Reflections), ed. Akram Musallam

(Ramallah: Institute for Jerusalem Studies and the Khalil Sakakini Cultural Center, 2003–2010), vol. 2, entry for February 17, 1914; Moed, "Educator in the Service of the Homeland," 71.

41. Khalil al-Sakakini, *Yawmiyat Khalil al-Sakakini*, vol. 8, entry for April 30, 1948. See also Gideon Shiloh, *Such Am I, O World: The Life and Diaries of a Palestinian Educator in Jerusalem* (Jerusalem: Keter, 1990) (Hebrew).

42. Archbishop Cornelios, supreme judge at the ecclesiastical court, is also in charge of the court archives of the Greek Orthodox Patriarchate. In a ledger of marriage certificates spanning the years 1922–1925, we find Houris listed as Σπυρίδων Χούρίς, witness to the wedding of his colleague, a forty-five-year-old Jerusalem architect named Nikoforos Petasis.

43. Simon Goldhill, *Jerusalem: City of Longing* (Cambridge: Harvard University Press, 2009), 114. For more on David Ohannessian, see the essay by his granddaughter Sato Moughalian, "From Kutahya to al-Quds: The Birth of the Armenian Ceramics Trade in Jerusalem," *Stambouline* (December 8, 2015), and Hoffman, *Till We Have Built Jerusalem*, 279–88.

44. Wasif Jawhariyyeh, *Storyteller of Jerusalem: The Life and Times of Wasif Jawhariyyeh, 1904–1948*, ed. Salim Tamari and Issam Nassar, trans. Nada Elzeer (Northampton, Mass.: Olive Branch, 2014), 178.

45. Nasser Eddin Nashashibi, *Jerusalem's Other Voice: Ragheb Nashashibi and Moderation in Palestinian Politics, 1920–48* (Reading, UK: Ithaca Press, 1990), 8. The college, originally built as a Crusader church, was converted into a madrassa by Saladin, who named it after himself and left it an ample endowment. In the aftermath of the Crimean War it was given to the French government as a token of peace, then confiscated again during the First World War when Kemal Pasha aimed to turn it into the most distinguished college in the Ottoman Empire. See Salim Tamari and Ihsan Salih Turjman, *Year of the Locust: A Soldier's Diary and the Erasure of Palestine's Ottoman Past* (Berkeley: University of California Press, 2011), 40–42, and Rowaida Fadel Ahmad, "Al-Salahiyyah School in Jerusalem, 588–1336 A.H./1192–1918 A.D." (M.A. diss., al-Najah University, Nablus, 2015).

46. Rashid Khalidi, *Palestinian Identity: The Construction of Modern National Consciousness* (New York: Columbia University Press, 2009); Nashashibi, *Jerusalem's Other Voice*, 9.

47. Hoffman, *Till We Have Built Jerusalem*, 292. The volumes in the National Library include dictionaries and Arabic idiom collections compiled in the late 1890s of the kind consulted by Isaaf Nashashibi (AP 1, AP 57, AP 61, and AP 133).

48. See Basheer Barakat, *Catalog of Manuscripts of Is'af al-Nashashibi Library* (Jerusalem: Mu'assasat Daar al-Tifl al-'Arabi, 2002). In the meantime, not a single Palestinian public library had been established in Jerusalem since 1967, until 2015. Al-Quds University Public Library was established with funding from the Kingdom of Bahrain and expertise from the United Nations Development Programme in a restored three-story building on Aqbat Rasas Street just inside Damascus Gate.

49. Naomi Pfefferman, "'Dead Sea Scrolls' Exhibition—600 Artifacts and a Touch of Controversy," *Jewish Journal*, March 6, 2015.

50. Hamdan Taha, "Archaeological Heritage in Palestine: The Combat Against Looting," *This Week in Palestine* 184 (2013): 21; Toby Axelrod, "Dead Sea Scroll Travels to Berlin," *Jewish Telegraphic Agency*, May 23, 2005.

51. Patrick Martin, "Jordan Asks Canada to Seize Dead Sea Scrolls," *The Globe and Mail*, December 31, 2009 (updated online May 2, 2018).

52. Benjamin Weinthal, "Israel Pulls Out of Dead Sea Scrolls Exhibit in Germany," *Jerusalem Post*, December 3, 2017.

53. A reminiscence of Yeshivat Torat Chaim can be found in Samuel Mirsky's *Eretz ve-Yamim: Ishim, Demuyot u-Mekomot* (Jerusalem: Sura, 1953), 9–15.

54. Gabriel Tsifroni, "Ozar Sifrei Kodesh veSifrei Tora Nitgala Beveit Kneset Natush Ba'Ir Ha'tika [A Treasure Trove of Holy Books and Scrolls Was Discovered in an Abandoned Synagogue in the Old City]," *Ma'ariv*, June 19, 1967, 1, 8 (Hebrew). A few weeks later Herzog told a journalist that "as a token of gratitude we gave him food and allowed him to stay in his apartment." Raphael Bashan, "Haaluf Chaim Herzog [General Chaim Herzog]," *Ma'ariv*, July 7, 1967, 16 (Hebrew).

Epilogue. The Closed Gate

1. Nicholas L. Paul, "Porta Clausa: Trial and Triumph at the Gates of Jerusalem," in *Writing the Early Crusades: Text, Transmission and Memory*, ed. Marcus Graham Bull and Damien Kempf (Suffolk, UK: Boydell and Brewer, 2014), 89 ff. The story is related by the ninth-century Benedictine monk Rabanus Maurus Magnentius (or Hrabanus Maurus), in J.-P. Minge, *Patrologiae cursus completus, series Latina*, vol. 110 (Paris: Garnieri Fratres, 1864), 133–34, and is also depicted in a fourteenth-century fresco in the church of Santa Croce in Florence. The tradition of dismounting and entering Jerusalem on foot extends from Caliph 'Umar Ibn al-Khaṭṭāb in the seventh century to General Edmund Allenby, commander of the British Egyptian Expeditionary Force, who entered Jerusalem in December 1917.

2. Origen, *Contra Celsum* VI 23, in *Ante-Nicene Fathers*, vol. 4: *Tertullian, Part Fourth; Minucius Felix; Commodian; Origen, Part First and Second*, ed. A. Cleveland Coxe (New York: Christian Literature Publishing, 1885), 583.

3. Mark Sheridan, "Nitria," in *Christianity and Monasticism in Northern Egypt*, ed. Gawdat Gabra and Hany N. Takla (Cairo: American University in Cairo Press, 2017), 136.

4. Leo Strauss, "Thucydides: The Meaning of Political History," in *The Rebirth of Classical Political Rationalism: An Introduction to the Thought of Leo Strauss*, ed. Thomas L. Pangle (Chicago: University of Chicago Press, 1989), 72.

5. Emmanuel Levinas, *In the Time of the Nations*, trans. Michael B. Smith (London: Bloomsbury Academic, 2007), 32–33.

6. Emmanuel Levinas, *Beyond the Verse: Talmudic Readings and Lectures* (London: Athlone, 1994), 38; Sigmund Freud, *Totem and Taboo* (New York: Courier, 1998), 16.

7. Umberto Eco, *The Name of the Rose*, trans. William Weaver (New York: Houghton Mifflin Harcourt, 2014), 198; Salman H. Bashier, *Ibn al-'Arabi's Barzakh: The Concept of the*

Limit and the Relationship Between God and the World (New York: State University of New York Press, 2012), 61.

8. Eco, *The Name of the Rose,* 306.

9. David Blumberg and Raquel Ukeles, "The National Library of Israel Renewal: Opening Access, Democratizing Knowledge, Fostering Culture," *Alexandria* 24, no. 3 (2013): 7.

10. See Oliver Wardrop, "Professor Tsagareli's Catalogue of the Georgian Manuscripts in the Monastery of the Holy Cross at Jerusalem," *Journal of Biblical Literature* 12, no. 2 (1893): 168–79. For a general overview of how the Patriarchate functioned a century ago, see Theodore Edward Dowling, *The Orthodox Greek Patriarchate of Jerusalem* (London: Society for Promoting Christian Knowledge, 1913).

11. Iskra Hristova-Shomova, "The Greek Manuscripts of the Book of Job in Jerusalem and in the St. Catherine Monastery of Sinai and Their Relationship to the Slavic Translations of the Book of Job," *Byzance et les Slaves* 96 (2011): 181–92; Kathleen Maxwell, *Between Constantinople and Rome: An Illuminated Byzantine Gospel Book (Paris Gr. 54) and the Union of Churches* (London: Routledge, 2016).

12. An image of the stolen illumination, catalogued as NLR GR 382, is included in the monumental *Byzantinische Miniaturen: Schätze der Buchmalerei vom 4. bis zum 16. Jahrhundert* (Regensburg: Schnell & Steiner, 2002), fig. 154.

13. N. Poulakakis et al., "Ancient DNA and the Genetic Signature of Ancient Greek Manuscripts," *Journal of Archaeological Science* 34, no. 5 (May 2007): 675–80.

14. The webpage of a digitization project called Palamedes explains: "The legendary Greek Palamedes was famous for his extraordinary wisdom and ingenuity. Euripides dedicated to him the lost tragedy *Palamedes*. He is the namesake of the research project PALAMEDES (PALimpsestorum Aetatis Mediae EDitiones Et Studia)." Using new technology the project unveils layers of the ancient texts and allows scholars to collaborate and study them online. Palamedes home page, http://www.palamedes.uni-goettingen.de/ (accessed September 24, 2018).

15. T. E. Lawrence, *Seven Pillars of Wisdom* (Ware, UK: Wordsworth Editions, 1997), 323.

16. Walter Benjamin, "The Task of the Translator," in *Illuminations,* trans. Harry Zohn, ed. Hannah Arendt (New York: Harcourt Brace Jovanovich, 1968), 69–82.

ACKNOWLEDGMENTS

For their generous support of our research, we thank Ariel Weiss of Yad Hanadiv and David Blumberg of the National Library of Israel, two Jerusalemites endowed with expansive visions for the city and its literary heritage. We also owe a debt of gratitude to Stanley Cohen, director of the Scone Foundation, and to Tom Ogilvie-Graham of the Saint John's Eye Hospital in Jerusalem.

For graciously hosting us during the writing of this book, we are grateful to the Van Leer Institute of Jerusalem—in particular to Gabriel Motzkin, Sinai Rusinek, and librarians Bayla Pasikov and Pinchas Maurer.

We are most grateful to those who have generously shared with us their deep knowledge—and love—of Jerusalem: His Beatitude Theophilos III, Archbishop Aristarchos of Constantina, Archbishop Cornelius, the late Dr. John Tleel, and Agamemnon Tselikas of the Greek Orthodox community; His Beatitude Nourhan Manougian, Kevork (George) Hintlian, Father Pakrad Berjekian, Father Shrourq, Krikor Maksoudian, Verj Nersessian, and Father Koryoun of the Armenian community; Sheikh 'Azzam al-Khatib and Sheikh Najeh Bkeerat of the Islamic Waqf; Yona

Aker and Rabbi Schwartz of the Karliner community; Ariella Amar and Rabbis Ovadia Morad and Yosef al-Gamil of the Karaite community; Noam Ben-Yosef of the Israel Museum; Mustafa Abu Sway and Ali Qleibo of al-Quds University; Rachel Lev of the American Colony Archives; Yusuf Uzbeki of the al-Aqsa Library; Baruch Yonin of the Schocken Library; Khader Salameh, Haifa Khalidi, and Raja Khalidi of the Khalidi Library; Moti Ben-Ari of the Ben-Zvi Institute; Eilat Lieber of the Tower of David Museum; Natalia Ostrovsky of the Jerusalem Municipality; Shachar Beer and Ori Kraushar of the JDC Jerusalem Archives; the late Jill, Duchess of Hamilton; the late Cardinal Carlo-Maria Martini; Adnan Husseini; Fahmi al-Ansari; Nafez Nubani; Lenny Wolfe; Dina al-Basha; Abuna Shimon Can; Rabbi Baruch Shochat; Rabbi Shlomo Fruchthandler; Yishayahu and Rachel Winograd; Jonathan Ben-Dov; Qasem abu Harb; Yana Tchekhanovets; Derek Hopwood; Maria Mavroudi; Johannes Pahlitzsch; Felix Albrecht; Laura Schor; Nirit Shalev Khalifa; Father Sergey Loktionov; Father Pawel Trzopek; Father Mark Sheridan; Father Eugenio Alliata; Yoav Ashkenazy; Menahem Klein; Sima Zalcberg; Avriel Bar Levav; Moshe Hillel; Hanan Benayahu; Anthony Bale; Michele Campopiano; Lorenzo Perrone; Idan Pinchas; and Nathan Wasserman.

For opening the doors to the Jerusalem Ethiopian Orthodox manuscript library, we thank His Holiness Abba Methias, His Grace Abune Enbaqom, Abba Kaletsidk Mulugeta, and Getachaw Hailu.

Our special thanks to Barbara Boehm, Melanie Holcomb, and Christopher Noey of the Metropolitan Museum of Art in New York; to Haggai Ben-Shammai, Malachi Beit Arieh, Yael Okun, Benjamin Richler, Milka Rubin, Raquel Ukeles, and Reuven Gross of the National Library of Israel; and to Pnina Shor, Shai Halevi, Robert Kool, and Alegre Savariego of the Israel Antiquities Authority.

We are grateful to Gali Tibbon and Anna Gawn for their photographs; to Oren Myers for his photographic expertise; and to Michal Sopher, Timna Alper, and Jean-Michel de Tarragon for advice on preservation. We thank Uri Tal for his assistance with Arabic translations and Anastasia Keshman for translating for us Bishop Uspensky's diaries from the Russian. Thank you to Tony David, who took part in the project in its earliest stages, and to Sarah Stroumsa, for her enlightening comments on chapters of the book.

We also acknowledge our gratitude to the Institute of Historical Research in London, which hosted the Jerusalem Survey of Archives and Libraries in 2005–2007 (particularly to David Bates and Peter Jacobsen); and to Vincent Lemire and the European Union–funded "Open Jerusalem" project, for supporting a revision of that survey in 2014.

For receiving us at their libraries and archives, we thank Father Justin of Saint Catherine Monastery, Sinai; Kathleen Doyle, Collin Baker, and Ilana Tahan of the British Library; Felicity Cobbing of the Palestine Exploration Fund; Naomi Speakman of the British Museum; Tom Foakes and Charlotte Dickerson of the Museum and Archive of the Order of Saint John, London; and Hetty Berg of the Ets Haim Library in the Jewish Historical Museum in Amsterdam. In Saint Petersburg we were assisted (through correspondence) by Dr. Olga Vasiliev, Boris Zajkowski, Shimon Iakerson, Daria Vasyutinskaya, and Dan Shapira.

For her steadfast encouragement from the very beginning, we thank our literary agent Judy Heiblum. For shepherding this book into print with consummate skill and patience, we thank our editors at Yale University Press, Heather Gold and Susan Laity.

It also gives us pleasure to acknowledge the support and encouragement of friends in Jerusalem: the late Sister Abraham (Kirsten Stoffregen-Pedersen); Sister Daniela of Viri Galilaei; Mirvat Azzeh; Brigitte Boulad and Ralph Tarraf; Mazen and Yvette Qupti; David Geer and Paul Busschots; Yehudah and Tamar Mirsky; Karen Brunwasser; Matti Friedman; Alan McDonald; and George Tsourous.

Our final words of gratitude belong to our respective families: to Mark and Jonathan, who took part in many of the adventurous journeys throughout Jerusalem and beyond; to the late Miriam Mack and Gershon and Tzipi Mack; and to David Balint and Liz Azose; Judy Lash Balint and Don Uslan; Karina Korecky; and Romy Halfon.

INDEX

Page numbers in italics indicate illustrations.